THE BRASS RING
by *Senator William E. "Bill" Fears*

IO148005

© United States Copyright, 2001
Sunstar Publishing, Ltd.
204 South 20th Street
Fairfield, Iowa 52556

Design & Layout: *Sharon A. Dunn*

LCCN: 2001095049
ISBN: 1-887472-92-4
Printed in the USA.

THE BRASS RING

Senator William E. "Bill" Fears

Sunstar
PUBLISHING LTD.

Table of Contents

Chapter 1
ARKANSAS & FLORIDA

It all began September 28, 1920, when Earl Fears, Junior, was born on a 150-acre farm near Jonesboro, Arkansas. The farm belonged to Alfred B. Fears and Alice Virginia Fears, his grandparents. Earl Fears, Jr., knows little about his grandfather – who died, soon after his birth, of a carbuncle, which could have been cured nowadays. He has learned that Alice Virginia, his grandmother, had been married to a Dr. Margrave, a self-taught physician from Kentucky, and had one son named Carl Margrave who settled in Lodi, California, and married a schoolteacher named Ethel. Alfred B. Fears and Alice Virginia had seven children, and all the living ones worked on the farm, and all eked out a meager living. There was the eldest, Aunt Myrtle L.; the twins, Edward and Fred; Arthur Earl, Earl Jr.'s father; Uncle Alfred Beetle, the youngest; and perhaps a couple who died.

None of Alfred B. Fears' children, wives or relatives were formally educated except for a couple of years in a one-room schoolhouse, and a whole lot of "hard knocks" experience. Earl Jr. knows little of this except that he was born in a one-room log house built on the Fears' farm, but his family got enough to eat so that he wasn't brain damaged too early. Aunt Myrtle was a beautifully structured woman, and somehow got to New York City, took some kind of secretarial course, and found a secretarial job. She was intelligent, and learned to speak, read, and write proper English. She also learned the proper social amenities of the time. Somehow she met and married a United States Military Academy (USMA) graduate named Frederick E. Humphreys.

It was learned that the "E" was for Erastus, really! Uncle Frederick, then a Second Lieutenant in the army, graduated from West Point in 1906 at the top of his class and was a Cadet Captain in his senior year, and was assigned to the Corps of Engineers, as was the custom for high-rankers on graduating. In 1909, Lt. Humphreys was then assigned – with Lt. Frank P. Lahm, and Lt. Benjamin P. Foulois – to the U.S. Army Signal Corps to take flight instruction from Orville Wright himself, who with his brother Wilbur had just sold their airplane to the U.S. Army Signal Corps, to perhaps be used in observation missions. This flight instruction took place at College Park, Maryland, the site of a present-day airfield that has existed since 1909. Earl Jr.'s mother was named Kate, and Kate's mother and father were sharecroppers from proud Irish immigrant stock. Grandfather William Scarry actually emigrated from Ireland during the potato famine, and it wasn't much better economically for him in Arkansas. There were several children born, namely Dewey, Garfield, Winfield, Tom, Mary, Kate, and Ruby. They all lived in a company house with no running water, no indoor toilet facilities, and no screens on the windows. There was an outhouse and all bathed once a week (maybe) in a washtub heated on a wood-burning stove. All picked cotton to make a meager living but ate better than in Ireland, around an abundance of flies. Anyhow, Earl Jr. enjoyed visiting his cousins in the delta on the river bottoms where he could fish with a bamboo pole. He remembers the snakes on the banks were plentiful, and there were plenty of cottonmouth water moccasins, which he didn't know were poisonous. Anyway, he learned to avoid the ones which coiled as if to strike, and he petted the others. All the "young'uns" went barefooted and padded around in the dusty roads and fields in the summers.

Earl Jr. was about eight years old when he had his first experience with sex. Cousin Bonnie, who was two years older than Earl Jr., invited him into the outhouse and showed him her sexual organ, which Earl Jr. had never seen on any other girl. It was bare and looked like a "skinned rabbit." Earl Jr. didn't know what he was looking at, and simply ran out of the outhouse frightened. (In these days, there was truly no sex education in school, and the Monkey Trial had just been for the "faith" people and not the scientists. How could they hang the alleged "witches" in Salem as heretics, and rule with Darrow having to put up with that stupid provincial Judge on that Tennessee Court? At that time, people were so ignorant and uneducated in Arkansas and Tennessee except for the few college-educated. Many of them didn't buy the theory of evolution.) This vaginal exposure made a lasting impression on Earl Jr. and he dreamed about this thing for years, until he learned the purpose of this organ later.

Arkansas A&M College near Jonesboro was located in beautiful woodlands during the '30s, and Earl Jr. and the adventuresome neighborhood boys used to walk down the Frisco railroad tracks out to these lovely woods called "Billy Goat Hill." There was an abandoned brick kiln along the way. It had metal cars on rails, and the boys pushed each other on these small rail cars through the abandoned kiln. It was dangerous but fun. In the beautiful woods they climbed trees, hunted squirrels with BB guns, and had a wonderful time. Someone always brought a Boy Scout mess kit, and some stolen bacon and eggs from home, which were cooked over a wood fire. The boys were always careful not to shoot one another in the eyes with the BB guns, or to start a fire spreading into the woods. This open-air food was more palatable than *Chicken Cordon Bleu* prepared by any French chef, which Earl Jr. found to his taste in the later affluent times when he dined in the best restaurants in France. The boys also fried sugar pancakes for dessert, which were more delicious than *crepe suzettes*, with good old fresh maple tree syrup from the Arkansas farmers. These were carefree, happy days, and the old adage about "ignorance is bliss" is apropos.

Jonesboro, Arkansas, was divided geographically into quarters like the directions of the compass. The grammar schools were actually named the East, West, South, and North Schools. There was a centrally located Junior High School and a Senior High School. Earl Jr. attended grammar school at East School where the middle class children attended. The South School was attended by the poor children across the railroad tracks, and the North and West Schools were attended by the more socially affluent. There was segregation then, and the African-Americans attended the worst furnished schools, if they attended any. "Nigger Town," as it was then called, was separated by an eight-foot-high fence from the white part of town. In those days racial and sexual prejudices were well entrenched in the entire South, including Jonesboro.

The community built a professional ballpark in the East side of Jonesboro, and one had to go though "Nigger Town" to attend a baseball game. The stands were built of rough lumber, and no one had heard of Astro Turf at that time so the ball diamond was truly grass, when it would grow, and dirt otherwise. Earl Jr. didn't have any money for tickets to see the games, so as many boys did in those days, he helped pick up trash and clean the stands on the grounds in exchange for an admission ticket.

Great pitchers like Dizzy Dean and his brother Daffy Dean probably played with the St. Louis Cardinals when they were winning pennants. Earl Jr. never could understand why Dizzy lost his job as a sportscaster because of his colorful English. Until Earl Jr. attended a day school in New York City, he thought it really was "slud into third," and "he swang at the ball" but "ole Dizzy" simply aggravated the English teachers with his colorful expressions and got fired. Probably with as little education as Dizzy had, he really thought this was proper English. At this time, Jonesboro had its U.S. Senator, Hon. Hattie Caraway, and there was Bob Burns and his musical "bazooka," and a little later Sen. Fulbright, who was a Harvard and Cambridge scholar. He must have had some money, and probably had attended a preparatory school somewhere to matriculate to Harvard.

Arkansas has had many exciting people, and now it has even had a President, Hon. Bill Clinton. Guess he was the first Arkansas President! He is certainly colorful, and deserves more credit for his accomplishments than he received. Earl Jr. feels that he has done much for

Arkansas, and for the U.S. He certainly came from a very modest background, and had the motivation and the intelligence to be awarded degrees from Georgetown University and Yale Law School. This is a great accomplishment for a poor boy from Arkansas. They even awarded him a scholarship to Oxford University. Have no idea who his mentor was, but someone had to give him a helping hand, as Uncle Frederick and Aunt Myrtle helped Earl Jr. It is rumored that the Fulbrights helped Bill Clinton along the way to success. It's unimaginable that a poor boy from Arkansas, and especially from Hope, Arkansas, got to be President of the U.S. – and for a second term! It is quite understandable that he was elected Governor of Arkansas because all Arkansas governors have been interesting and colorful people.

Another lasting impression occurred in the "bottoms" near the living grandfather's house near Marked Tree, Arkansas. In those days, there was no public welfare as such, such as aid to dependent children, food stamps, meals on wheels, etc., which would have made Congressman Gingrich and Hon. Dick Armey happy. People either worked for their food and lodging, or starved, or died of hypothermia. There was plenty of dietary deficiency in many families. One poor man's wife died leaving him with several young children. They all had "pellagra" from lack of proper diet, and it's probably true that he couldn't handle his problems anymore. Earl Jr. was about nine years old, and visiting his cousins in Marked Tree. A crowd had gathered on a ditch bank and Earl Jr. approached the center of a crowd, but left in a state of shock. This poor man had cut his throat with a straight razor; then changed his mind, and tried to stuff grass into the wound to stop the bleeding. It didn't work and he died anyhow. What a horrible sight. Earl Jr. has believed in the "Welfare System," President Franklin D. Roosevelt, and the Democratic Party ever since. Earl Jr. is now 81 years old, been through combat, and still has nightmares about this terrible experience.

Jonesboro, Arkansas, is a nice friendly little town. It has the Arkansas State University which used to be called Arkansas A&M, until the '40s when it became Arkansas State College.

Earl Jr. got his break in life in the middle '30s, and early realized that a life of poverty wasn't the way to go. Aunt Myrtle had remarried Uncle Frederick after an early divorce, came to Sarasota in her 16-cylinder "Gene Tunney" Cadillac to visit Earl Sr. and his family. (For those too young to remember, Gene Tunney was a world champion boxer, and he had married a wealthy woman. He was handsome, well-dressed, and had a lot of class.) Aunt Myrtle discovered that Earl Jr. was educable and talked Earl Jr., Earl Sr., and Kate into allowing Earl Jr. to travel to New York City where he might get a better education. Earl Jr. wanted to escape from poverty anyway, and was glad to leave Sarasota for New York City. Earl Jr. packed his meager belongings, and left with Aunt Myrtle, riding in the big black Cadillac town sedan. This was about 1934.

Life's progress for a boy is much easier, and success comes to one born the "All-American" type with a great profile, and with blond hair and blue eyes like Paul Newman. Few Clark Gables with big ears really make it. Anyhow, Earl Jr. was a scrawny kid, weighing about 120 pounds, and was gifted with great big ears which stuck straight out, even worse than Gary Hart's. It's difficult to make an impression when one doesn't have the great physical features of a Robert Taylor. The big ears were hereditary, for Uncle Fred and Uncle Edward, the twin uncles, had enormous floppy ears, and large bulbous noses. This handicapped them, and the ears handicapped Earl Jr. These ears are equated to being a dummy. After all, according to the evolution theory, we all descended from apes anyhow. Some monkeys are pretty intelligent, sometimes more so than humans. Anyhow, arriving in New York City at about 16 years of age, Earl Jr. was taken to a dentist. He suffered from severe caries and had never had a tooth filled; also, a big molar was rotted to the gum line. The dentist was a West Point graduate with huge massive "Popeye Arms." This was a painful experience for Earl Jr. in pulling the large molar, and the deep drilling of other decayed teeth. However, after many times in a dental chair he still has all his teeth but two, and that isn't bad now that he is 81 years old and was neglected early. They are crowned, capped, filled, and repaired in many ways. He still has his teeth because he never smoked cigarettes in his lifetime. Earl Jr. is convinced that smoking destroys one's gums by constricting small blood vessels, which then causes tooth loss.

Uncle Frederick and Aunt Myrtle went to Palm Beach, Florida, for a vacation, but it probably was so that Uncle Frederick could "lick his wounds." While in Florida, Uncle Frederick had a heart attack at age 57 and died, but Earl Jr. really thinks he died of cirrhosis of the liver. William Earl Jr., who was a student in Yale at the time, attended the funeral at Arlington National Cemetery where Gen. Humphreys was buried with full military honors. What a waste that a man of brains, talent, and a part of great history was buried that cold day. Gen. Frank P. Lahm, Uncle Frederick's old flight training buddy, showed up in dress uniform, but not Gen. Foulois, another flying buddy, which seemed strange. Gen. Lahm was at this time Commandant of the West Point of the Air in San Antonio, Texas, where all the army aviators were trained at Randolph and Kelly Fields. (Earl Jr. hopes this history is moderately interesting to the readers of this book. Now we will get onto more interesting parts of this story, we hope.)

Aunt Myrtle and Uncle Frederick together tried to improve the knowledge, education, and the living conditions of Aunt Myrtle's environmentally deprived relatives, especially Aunt Myrtle's brothers, but nothing succeeded. Uncle Edward was a private in the Infantry in WWII serving in combat in France. When Edward returned, he worked at one menial job after another. He was a nomad moving about in Illinois, Arkansas, Maryland, Missouri, and any place he could find a job as a house painter. He married a lady from Illinois and sired two children, Alice and Eddie. Cousin Eddie served in the Marine Corps in WWII and sent his paychecks home to his father, Uncle Edward, for safekeeping. This was for Eddie's education, but Uncle Edward spent all Eddie's planned savings. Uncle Edward also used all Earl Jr.'s clothing and personal belongings. When Earl Jr. came home from WWII, he found his storage trunk broken open at the house in

Maryland, and found no clothing, which was hard to take. Uncle Edward, on being asked about the clothing said, "I didn't think you would come back." Earl Jr. felt like killing him, but refrained from such violence. Cousin Alice has been married about three times, and lives in East Alton, Illinois with her third husband. She has no children, and that would probably be a blessing for the childrens' sakes.

In the late '30s, Uncle Frederick bought the "Gene Tunney" 1930 Cadillac Town Sedan, which was a monster with a V-16 cylinder engine. This car was very impressive and burned about a gallon of gas every 5 miles. It was black with plenty of brass and chrome accessories. When William Earl was in high school in Maryland, he loved driving this car for it was so impressive to all the poor boys in the neighborhood. This was at a time when Florida required no operator's license, and in Maryland where everyone spent the summer, if one was more than 16 years of age, one could get a driver's license for 50¢ by mail, with a 3¢ stamp. Uncle Frederick had a huge "Army Engineer's" insignia on the front emblazoned with the name Gen. F.E. Humphreys. This saved him from a ticket once when he was driving on a one-way street in New York City. Earl Jr. was in the Cadillac, and believes nowadays the General would have been cited for drunk driving. The policeman blew his whistle, and Uncle Frederick stopped and told the policeman he was only going one way anyhow. Back then, there was "big shot" influence, and when the officer saw this massive Cadillac with this tall impressive driver, and the huge brass plate on the front grill he simply told the General to go ahead. In the late 1920s, Uncle Frederick bought a 200-acre farm on the Sinepuxent Bay near Ocean City, Maryland, where all the relatives spent the summers. Uncle Frederick had a son by Aunt Myrtle, but this baby died while still an infant; then Aunt Myrtle tried to improve the lives of her brothers, and her relatives, including William Earl. She enrolled the twin brothers, Uncle Edward and Uncle Fred, in some kind of military school, but they couldn't succeed intellectually so she gave up. Uncle Alfred, the baby brother, ended up in Texas, and with some older friends was convicted of armed robbery as an accessory, and served five years on a prison road gang at hard labor. This was really hard labor too, working on the road gangs where several prisoners died of rattlesnake bites. Uncle Carl Margrave was a half-brother with great character, and was a very industrious worker who had a lifelong job as an agent with the Southern Pacific Railroad. His wife, Aunt Ethel, was a schoolteacher and taught Uncle Carl good English, and the social amenities. Uncle Carl visited Earl Jr. as a boy in Jonesboro and built him a punching bag rack including a punching bag. He taught Earl Jr. how to box and punch this bag, which saved Earl Jr. from a beating later in life in a military school, which we will relate later.

Earl Jr. decided that he would infringe on his brother Carl E.'s territory, if he went back to Tennessee from Florida, and the poverty was a little more bearable in the East; so he stuck it out hoping his lot would improve, which it did. Uncle Frederick and Aunt Myrtle spent the summers on the Humphreys' farm on Sinepuxent Bay, near Ocean City, Maryland, and Earl Jr. lived on the farm each summer. He was very useful for he was a great "gofer" and a chauffeur to all. By this time, he was a gangling teenager. He didn't know it, but he endeared himself to Uncle Frederick, the early aviator, by flying an old Piper J-3 floatplane from Ocean City, Maryland, where the pilot was carrying brave passengers for rides from Ocean City. Earl Jr. met one Lee Savage from Chincoteague, Virginia, who owned the plane. Lee later, because of his early flight training, got to be a 1st Lt. in the Army Air Corps as a Service Pilot, and Earl Jr. also got to be a 1st Lt. in the Army Air Corps. When Earl Jr. moved to Virginia, where Lee Savage lived, and started a law practice they bought a used four-place Cessna 170 together, which each flew many places for several years. Earl Jr. and Lee flew the plane to Cuba in 1958, just before Castro took over.

Anyhow, Uncle Frederick was thrilled by Earl Jr. landing the plane in the Sinepuxent Bay in front of the Humphreys' farm. He entered the cockpit and his eyes lit up. After that, the relationship between Earl Jr. and Gen. Humphreys improved.

On settling down in the Humphreys' mansion in New York City with Aunt Myrtle and Uncle Frederick, and Uncle Alfred, Earl Jr. (with a private bathroom and a large private bedroom for the first time in his life) walked around the corner about five blocks away and entered the 9th grade in DeWitt Clinton High School Annex. It was still the Great Depression; the classes were crowded; the teachers weren't getting paid well, and they simply didn't give a damn. In two classrooms, Earl Jr. sat on a radiator instead of sitting at a desk. In those days, attendance wasn't mandatory, and a student could get an education himself if one had the perseverance. Earl Jr. was disgusted, and did nothing except take the New York Regents' tests, whereupon he failed some subjects. This is a branch of the same high school which Gen. Colin Powell attended. They did have a great ROTC unit to which Earl Jr. belonged. Like Powell, Fears did well in Military Science. However, the only way to get a free education in the City College of New York was to be in the upper 10% in grades from high school, and have top scores in the Regents' Tests. (When Powell attended City College there was open enrollment. Powell barely graduated and was no outstanding liberal arts student, but he got high grades in Military Science and was the top cadet.) Anyhow, Earl Jr. then went to Maryland, and lived a couple of years with Uncle Fred and Aunt Sarah, and cousins Frederick and William A. He attended Maryland High Schools in the 9th and 10th grades, and at least passed the subjects; that is, the subjects which were offered.

Education in a rural Maryland High School consisted of a minimum of subjects; no foreign languages, and no science laboratories; and perhaps a year of algebra. This was still the time of the Great Depression and the teachers were paid $800 per year, when they got paid at all. Earl Jr. was right back in poverty again with few clothes and eating scrapple for breakfast, but so were most other boys there. There were CCC Camps to keep young men off the streets, where they got meals and a dollar per day for planting trees, digging ditches, and the like. Earl Jr. became friendly with some of the CCC Camp boys, and learned to box some more, or better than before. The American Legion sponsored boxing matches between the CCC Camp boys and the local boys, through the American Legion Post, and charged admission. Earl Jr. participated in these fights and made the fantastic sum of $10 for three rounds each time he boxed, except he was finally defeated by a CCC Camp boxer in his weight class. Aunt Myrtle found out about this easy but dangerous money, and that ended that. As was the case in most rural areas, there were some affluent families whose sons attended private preparatory schools like Mercersburg Academy, Christ Church School, Severn Academy, and some other private schools in order to matriculate to higher educational institutions.

Earl Jr. was right back in poverty again in Maryland living with Uncle Fred and sleeping in the same bed with cousin Freddie, but it wasn't as bad as Sarasota or Arkansas. Earl Sr., Kate, and Carl E. had moved to a place called Moscow, Tennessee, and Earl Sr. got a job with a Chevrolet dealership as a body and fender repairman, and brother Carl E. was a big football hero in Moscow High School and later Somerville, Tennessee. Earl Jr. visited the family in Somerville, where they now lived in a modest rented house. Earl Jr. did meet the Somers family members, for whom the town was named. They had some inherited wealth and plenty of clout in this little town. One of the Somers boys entered West Point, and then entered the Army Air Corps. Don't know his first name but he was called "Zeke" Somers. He flew B-29s in the Pacific Theater, and later retired a General in the Air Force. Another younger brother attended law school, got to be a lawyer, and finally retired as an Appellate Judge in Tennessee, but not until after he had also entered the Army Air Corps and won his wings. William Earl met this brother in Somerville sometime in 1991 while visiting brother Carl in Moscow, where Carl now lives "like he likes it," in seclusion on a farm he bought near his wife's relatives. This retired Judge stayed in the Air Force reserves, and he too retired a General. Earl Jr. is convinced it helps to advance to be born in an influential family, and both these Somers men, after the door was opened, grabbed the "Brass Ring." They both deserve lots of credit. Gen. "Zeke" Somers got this nickname because of the Tennessee accent, which he never lost, any more than Ross Perot will lose his Texas drawl.

Uncle Frederick realized that Earl Jr. had educational potential, so in the fall of 1938, Earl Jr. returned to New York City and was entered in a Quaker School named Friends Seminary, which was in the middle of "Hell's Kitchen." He had to ride the subway daily from 76th Street Westside to 14th Street Eastside and change trains twice. He was given tests and admitted to the 11th Grade. This was a great social and educational shock. Half of the students were of Jewish descent, all already speaking French and German, for they had been students there since kindergarten and had very high IQs. Earl Jr. tried to "hit the ground running" for this was his last chance. Uncle Frederick tried to get him prepared to enter the USMA at West Point. Earl Jr. learned early that there were no Jewish or Greek descendants on welfare. The Jewish and Greek families are very supportive of each other, and the children were motivated. Somehow they take care of one another. The Greeks have an organization called the AHEPA, which is a society to help other Greeks when they immigrate to this country. Earl Jr. developed great friendships with Greek descendants such as State Senator Peter K. Babalas – a Virginia State Senator, who served with Sen. Fears in the '70s and '80s in the Virginia General Assembly – and one John Parker, Esq., who was a lawyer and later in life, a governmental relations expert with the Mobil Oil Co. It appears that a friend of Parker's grew up with him in Brooklyn. This friend was William Tavelereas, then CEO for Mobil Oil Co. Parker wasn't without talent though. He speaks four languages fluently, including Greek and French spoken in the home, for his mother was French, and had a degree in medicine. These friends initiated Fears into the AHEPA, and if the Greeks like a person they can be a great help in life.

Earl Jr. finished the 11th grade at Friends Seminary and was still too far behind to enter a good college. He had tried to take both French and German the same year, but had to drop German in order to keep up with his other subjects. In Friends there were great teachers, all with majors in the subjects they taught. For example, the French teacher was raised in Paris and graduated from the Sorbonne. Likewise, the German teacher had been born in Germany. Several of the teachers rented a campsite at Bantam Lake, Connecticut, to help the wayward types advance. Earl Jr. attended the study camp and took courses in Plane Geometry, English, and Ancient History. After the camp finished the summer courses, Earl Jr. took standardized tests in all the subjects and passed them all. He was admitted to the 12th Grade, and took the advanced courses in math, such as Solid Geometry and Trigonometry, in which he got "A" grades. He also finished the second year in French. He feels that the great Friends Seminary English teacher Rowse B. Wilcox taught him more about Shakespeare than he learned in college. Fortunately, the math teacher, Roland Reade, took a liking to Earl Jr. and really helped him with his college matriculation. It was a good feeling, for the "big-eared ugly duckling" had never had much help before from teachers.

Eddie's son, Jeff, one of Earl Jr.'s cousins, left the Naval Academy in his junior year, but did enter Oral Roberts University, and it is believed got some kind of degree in religion. It appears he became a reborn Christian and was a missionary somewhere in Poland. Eddie's other son, Douglas, graduated from the Coast Guard Academy as No. 1 in his class, has found his "Brass Ring," and is now serving on an Admiral's staff.

During the '20s and '30s, Arkansas was a sparsely settled state of about 1.5 million people. If it hadn't been for the TVA, and the caring President Franklin D. Roosevelt, most poor souls would have had even worse economic times. Farming corporations owned most of the land, and single owners owned the corporations, the land, and the cotton gins. The rest worked for them for 50¢ a day. An affluent "Arkansawyer" had two old Fords up on blocks in the front yard. Eggs and scrapple were considered a "scrumptious" meal.

Aunt Myrtle had sold the Fears' farm in Arkansas for her mother, Alice Virginia, after grandfather Fears' death and bought a small bungalow in Jonesboro on Creath Avenue. On this farm site is now located Arkansas State University. The Fears' property there is now worth millions. Aunt Myrtle placed Alice Virginia, Earl Sr., his wife, Kate, and Earl Jr. in this house for a long while.

Earl Jr. remembers little of this, but does recall there were two unusual trees in the front yard. In the summer, these trees housed some weird colored worms. They were black with yellow stripes and were squished all over the concrete walk. As nasty as these worms were, they made wonderful fish bait for catching catfish and carp from the Arkansas rivers. Of course, no one could afford a rod and reel, so one rigged a bamboo pole with string, a bolt for weight, and a wire hook. A cork stopper was added to the line, which would float and bob under water when a fish bit the worm. People did eat the mud cats. They used the carp for hog feed. Now there are catfish farms supporting many people. The youngsters even caught crayfish from the ditch banks, but no one had sense enough to eat them. William Earl paid a fortune for some crayfish in New Orleans after he got educated. Also, Earl Jr. visited Switzerland in the '60s and paid $30 for a bowl of *bouillabaisse* which contained crayfish rather than shrimp. Just think how an industry was lost to Earl Jr. in Arkansas because of his ignorance and lack of education.

The college in Jonesboro is now named Arkansas State University. In the '30s, it was called Arkansas A&M (Agricultural and Mechanical). To Fears, it was just a glorified trade school to train farmers and mechanics to make a living. Earl Jr. then had little respect for the alleged college until he learned that one of his neighbors had attended the school and got to be a Major General in the Air Force.

In 1970, Earl Jr. served a month on reserve duty as a Major with the Army at Ft. Meade, Maryland, and while on duty met a young Captain from Jonesboro. Fears' Uncle Tom had left the "sharecropper's farm" in the '20s after serving in WWI in Europe, and had settled in Jonesboro to sell automobiles. Uncle Tom had been "gassed" in combat, and had lung damage, so he was receiving disability benefits. This gave him his little nest egg to start in business. Anyhow, Uncle Tom died in the '60s, and this Captain's father, who had worked for the same auto agency, bought Uncle Tom's interest in the agency. Uncle Tom had purchased real estate in foreclosures during the Great Depression, and became a millionaire in the '70s. This opened the door for Fears to talk about Jonesboro with the Captain. One Bill Weaver was Uncle Tom's partner and lived a millionaire's life until he died at 99 years old, according to the Captain.

Earl Jr. questioned the Captain about one Ray Cole, a neighbor from Jonesboro, and learned that Ray Cole was a Major General in the Air Force stationed at Scott Air Force Base near Chicago. Fears called Scott Air Force Base on the military "WATS" line, and after being shunted through several aides reached the General. Gen. Cole asked, "Who the hell are you?" Earl Jr. identified himself as a boy from Jonesboro, and Gen. Cole became more receptive. He told Fears that he had gone to Arkansas State for a couple of years, entered the Army Air Corps for Aviation Cadet training, and later after commissioning had flown B-29s in the Pacific Theater in WWII. He got to be a Lieutenant Colonel and served as a Squadron Commander in combat. When the war in the Pacific ended in victory, Gen. Cole, via the Air Force, received an Aeronautical Engineering degree, and then got an MBA from Harvard. He was gradually promoted to Major General. He must have had a great combat record, for usually one doesn't get the "brass ring" as a General Officer unless one hears the "sound of guns" in combat. After learning of this success story starting with Arkansas State, Earl Jr. now has the highest regard for Arkansas State University, and for Gen. Cole, a successful boy from Jonesboro, Arkansas.

Cousin Eddie married a lovely girl from Salisbury, Maryland. He got to be president of a small bank in Bishopville, Maryland, after working for a bank in Cambridge, Maryland. But in the usual Fears' manner, he "blew this," was fired, and tried his hand at being a stockbroker, a store clerk, and a manager of a seafood plant. He was great in talking himself into a job, but couldn't please any of his employers. His lovely wife divorced him and married a very wealthy man who had inherited his wealth. Eddie and Carolyn had two wonderful boys. One son graduated number one from the Coast Guard Academy and is now a Lieutenant, and was an aide to an Admiral. The other son, a tall and very handsome man, was a cadet in the United States Naval Academy (USNA), but was "boarded out" in his junior year for lack of motivation. Earl Jr. had never heard of a third year midshipman studying aerospace engineering, and wanting to be an aircraft pilot, being dismissed from the academy. Earl Jr., now a State Senator with some "clout," learned that Jeff, the USNA boy, was in love with a girl cadet, a beautiful gymnast, and Jeff was "love moping" and neglected his duties. Upon learning the problem Earl Jr. telephoned the Commandant trying to get Jeff reentered into the academy. The Admiral called the Senator after reviewing Jeff's record. Earl Jr. told the Admiral Jeff was "love moping" over a lady cadet. The Admiral said, "If he loves this cadet more than the Navy, we don't want him anyhow." That was that!

The last year at Friends Seminary it was Physics and advanced math courses, and a real "cram course" in 2nd-year French with Madame Carmine, a lovely French lady from the Sorbonne. It was a great year for Earl Jr., and all courses went well. An attempt was made for admission to West Point, but unlike now with 5,000 cadets in the corps, there were only 1,000 or so then. West Point gave their own exams and they were very difficult. Anyhow, a second year student from Villanova College got the principal appointment; Earl Jr. was accepted at University of Tennessee, Case School of Applied Science, and Tulane University. He took a shot at MIT, and Rensselaer but it was "no go." Fears had taken an aptitude test and scored high in science and engineering. He entered Pennsylvania Military College in the course of Industrial Engineering, and did make the Dean's List. Like Uncle Frederick, he did play on a polo team for activities, and had hoped to enter West Point the coming year by exam waiver. That didn't work out so he transferred to Yale University School of Engineering. Competition was great, and the courses difficult, but Earl Jr. made it through the sophomore year with perseverance, and lots of luck. One of the West Point disappointments was with a hard-nosed screening Sergeant at the Army Recruiting Station in New York City. He just didn't think the "floppy-eared, scrawny kid" was officer material. Please believe that physical features have a lot to do with worldly success, especially in the military, as well as the business world.

The West Point preliminary medical examination didn't go well for Earl Jr. either. The medical examiner told Earl Jr. that he would have to be circumcised because he had an adhered prepice. Earl Jr. believes the doctor was Yiddish, but Earl Jr. went through that painful operation experience at the age of 17 years at Columbia University Hospital. This was done under a local anesthetic. Anyhow, while overnight in the hospital, because the stitches caused pain and swelling, Earl Jr. got an uncontrollable erection. It was so painful that he rang for the nurse to call the doctor. She didn't do that but brought in an ice pack, and wrapped the inflamed erection in ice. What a relief that this big mannish nurse knew exactly what to do. The swelling subsided immediately but Earl Jr. had a "red face."

Earl Jr. couldn't get the appointment to West Point on the first attempt, but a recruiter from PMC came to convince Uncle Frederick and Aunt Myrtle that they wanted Earl Jr. in PMC. This was the school which Uncle Frederick had attended before he entered West Point so they were both "sold" on it right away. Earl Jr. entered the "rat year" in PMC in 1940. A cadet named O'Brien in this class from New York City had an appointment to West Point for 1941, but on a football game trip away from PMC this cadet drank too much whiskey and was expelled from PMC. Of course, he lost the appointment to West Point, but secretly Earl Jr. was pleased, for this cadet was a big arrogant Irishman and the son of a New York City detective. Besides that, Fears found out the overbearing Irishman had poured ink into Fears' shoes, and he called Earl Jr. "Cadet Ears." This was poetic justice for Cadet Fears.

Earl Jr. learned that PMC was not highly accredited, and that was probably the main reason Earl Jr. made the Dean's List with his high grades. Anyhow, since Earl Jr. couldn't get into West Point, he had decided to try to enter a prestigious college, but he had no money for tuition. At this time, there were free schools in New York City. Earl Jr. talked to the admission officers of Coopers Union Institute of Technology, City College of New York, Webb School of Naval Architecture, and Stevens Institute of Technology. But since they were free or had low tuitions, the requirements were upper 10% of high school class grades, at least a 120 IQ, and high grades in their own entrance examinations. (At that time all of these were closed enrollment schools. Now with affirmative action, admission to these schools is by open enrollment, but they simply "flunk out" those who can't meet the standards.) From experience William Earl found the graduates of these colleges are usually bright, and all have good jobs. Earl Jr. learned that he could earn his room and board at Yale University on a bursar's job. He applied to Yale for a transfer, and was admitted to the sophomore class with full transfer credits on the condition that he take a summer course in calculus, which he did – taught by a friend and math major from Norwich University. The tutor did a good job, for Yale accepted Earl Jr. without any conditions because of the high grades from PMC, and the certificate from the tutor indicating that he did well in calculus. However, this was a "two-edged sword," for instead of placing Fears in the math class with engineers, he was placed in an advanced math class with math majors. They were most competitive, but Earl Jr. did finally get a "C" in the course.

Now those "big ears" got Earl Jr. in trouble in PMC with a Cadet Captain by the name of Coggeshall, who just didn't like the "ugly duckling's" looks. The Captain was a handsome blond who thought he was God's gift to women. Coggeshall "gigged" Cadet Fears at every "Guard Mount." It was Cadet Captain Coggeshall's job to inspect the guard at every "Guard Mount" and Cadet Fears had to "pull" guard about every two weeks like all "rats." There was no way to avoid Captain Coggeshall. Every time Fears got "gigged" for uniform, rifle, beard, or long hair, he had to walk tours on the drill field with rifle and pack. Fears, as a "Brother Rat," got no relief. Fears then learned to play all bugle calls on the bugle and became one of the Corps' buglers. Coggeshall continued to "gig" Cadet Fears for such infractions as dirty bugle and improper bugle call, or other infractions. It did no good to complain to a regular Military Tactical Officer, for an upperclassman can do no wrong. "Brother Rat" can only reply with, "No excuse, Sir." PMC was strictly military, like VMI and the Citadel. Why women want to enter VMI or the Citadel and take this punishment, Earl Jr. will never know.

When we all really got busy to try to defeat the enemy in WWII, all the old air mail pilots got to be Generals, or Colonels, but poor Uncle Frederick missed it all by dying too young. Gen. Curtis LeMay was still a Lieutenant at that time, but in 1945 was the C.O. of the greatest air armada in European theater of combat, the 8th Air Force in England, called the "Hollywood Air Force" because of Col. Jimmy Stewart and Major Clark Cable. So the esteemed Uncle Frederick didn't get the "brass ring," for providence took care of that. In the '30s however, Uncle Frederick did become a millionaire, mostly through inheritance, for his forefathers founded the Humphreys Homeopathic Medicine Co., which prospered in the '30s, before the Food and Drug Administration got into the act. This company did a thriving business when no one could afford a physician. The company did especially well in South America. Earl Jr. recalls Uncle Frederick and Aunt Myrtle flying down to Rio in an old Pan American Airways flying boat to "hawk the pills" and returned with Aunt Myrtle's fingers covered with topaz and aquamarine rings. Uncle Frederick was doing all he could with what influence he had to get Earl Jr. an appointment to his old alma mater, the U.S. Military Academy, but Earl Jr. missed that "brass ring" too.

The Humphreys Homeopathic Medicine Co. was a very interesting company in the '20s and '30s. It made most of its profits in South and Central America, all with small bottles of pills such as Humphreys 66 and Humphreys Witch Hazel, which was great to use as an aftershave lotion. These medicines didn't cure nor kill one. They were great placebos which kept patients coming back, and continued to make the company money, as well as Uncle Frederick. Uncle Frederick and Aunt

Myrtle purchased a great gray stone house at 41 Riverside Drive in New York City in the '20s and lavishly furnished it with a gas log fireplace in every room, Italian marble mantlepieces, and huge French provincial pieces of furniture in each large decorated room. They even had a grand piano with a player built in. This place had an immense dining room for entertaining guests such as the Vanderbilts, the Rockefellers, and even Charles Schwab, the CEO of Bethelem Steel Company. Schwab owned a palatial mansion occupying an entire block on Riverside Drive. Of course, this was when there was a small income tax and the rich were very rich, and believe it but the poor were really poor. The blacks had no rights whatever, and there were no labor unions. Henry Ford paid workers the great salary of $5 per day so they could buy his Model T Fords in one color, black!

If Uncle Frederick had not died in 1941 with the rank of a Brigadier General in the N.Y. National Guard, he having been the first solo military pilot in the army would probably have been a Four Star General in WWII. He had just received an inquiry from the War Department. There was no Pentagon then. Gen. Frank P. Lahm was already a Major General, Benjamin Foulois was a Major General. Incidentally, Gen. Foulois died a bachelor in some kind of retirement quarters at Andrews Air Force base in Maryland, and had been Chief of the Army Air Corps, probably in 1936. One of the conference rooms at Andrews is named the Foulois room. A street at Ft. Belvoir, the army engineer-training base, is named Humphreys Boulevard. Uncle Frederick also has a picture and memorabilia in the Corps of Engineer's Museum there. Earl Jr. remembers when Gen. Doolittle was a First Lieutenant in the Reserves, "barnstorming" about the country, and remembers when Gen. Spaatz was flying the mail in an old biplane while he was a 20-year in-service First Lieutenant. The Army Air Corps did not start to grow until after 1941. The country really geared up for combat after Pearl Harbour. Earl Jr. was really proud to have lived a little bit of this history, and is proud to have served as a First Lieutenant in the U.S. Army Air Corps from August 1943 until September 1946.

There were few "cry babies" in the service then, and all these guys went through a living hell, but 99% did their duties even though they were scared to death.

There seemed to have been some resentment and jealousy between Gen. Foulois and Uncle Frederick. There was none between Gen. Lahm and Uncle Frederick. Gen. Lahm and Uncle Frederick were "ring knockers" from West Point, and somehow Gen. Foulois was promoted through the enlisted ranks to Second Lieutenant, which was unheard of then. I think it was because Gen. Foulois was one of the first observation balloon pilots. Capt. Rickenbacker was a staff car driver for Gen. Pershing in WWI, and convinced the General he wanted to fly. He learned to fly with the French and, of course, we all know the rest. When Earl Jr. was a Vice President of Avemco Insurance Co., he met Gen. Foulois at a banquet at the Aviation Club in DC, and made the mistake of introducing himself as the nephew of Gen. Frederick E. Humphreys, right after Gen. Foulois had just told the audience he was the first military solo pilot. Gen. Foulois turned a little pale, and simply turned and walked away. When Uncle Frederick was buried with full military honors, Gen. Lahm attended the funeral in 1941, but Gen. Foulois did not. Even Earl Jr. noticed this. He thought Gen. Foulois would have been glad to talk to a relative of his old "flying buddy," but something was wrong.

Uncle Carl and Aunt Ethel died within a couple years of each other, and left their beloved nephew, Earl Jr., a Japanese Tea Set that the Executor of the estate never mailed to him. Too bad it wasn't Royal Copenhagen or Wedgwood for Earl Jr. would have pursued the claim.

After Uncle Alfred finished his prison term, he went to live in New York City in the Humphreys' mansion as the "lackey" of Aunt Myrtle, and lived off the Humphreys' income for years. It was during the Great Depression, and a felon couldn't get a job, or anything else for that matter. Uncle Frederick got fed up with Aunt Myrtle's dedication in trying to improve the lot of her mother, brothers, and other relatives, and ran off with another woman; so Aunt Myrtle divorced him. But that new marriage didn't last; so Uncle Frederick divorced this new wife and remarried Aunt Myrtle. Aunt Myrtle had developed a lot of class and she put up with Uncle Frederick's many eccentricities, and Earl Jr. had heard the "family gossip" that Aunt Myrtle was good in bed.

Uncle Alfred still lived in the Riverside Drive mansion after Uncle Frederick moved back in, and "sponged" off the second-time-around newlyweds. It was the Great Depression Era still. Uncle Alfred tried his hand at several jobs, but never really made a living. After Earl Jr. moved into the mansion to attend Friends Seminary, Aunt Myrtle rented a room to an engineering graduate from Stevens Institute of Technology. His name was Howard Brevoort, and he was a real "whiz" in mathematics. He helped Earl Jr. catch up with mathematics so that Earl Jr. could take the advanced fourth year mathematics courses in his senior year at Friends Seminary, and ultimately matriculate to an engineering type college, which he did successfully.

Uncle Frederick got to be President of Humphreys Medicine Co., and hired Uncle Alfred as a glorified mail clerk and "gofer." Then, as the Food and Drug Administration came onto the scene with more and more supposedly protective laws and regulations, the patent medicine companies lost customers and were forced out of business, after which the Humphreys Co. Board of Directors fired Uncle Frederick in 1941. It wasn't only because of "waning business," but also because Uncle Frederick became an alcoholic, and took too many naps on his office couch.

Chapter 2

NEW YORK CITY, PMC, & RELATED EVENTS

Arthur Earl and Kate Fears had another child eight years younger than Earl Jr. They named this boy after Carl Margrave, Arthur Earl's half-brother in California. Without really boring our readers, in a word, Aunt Myrtle interfered with the lives of all her brothers. She convinced her brother Earl Sr. to leave depressed Arkansas and move to Sarasota, Florida, perhaps to better his life, but this move was a disaster. Arthur Earl, with at most a fifth grade education, had attended a trade school in Memphis, and learned to be an auto mechanic, and a body and fender repairman. In Arkansas, Kate's brother, Tom, employed Earl Sr. Tom had a garage and auto dealership. That relationship didn't last long, so Earl Sr. opened his own body and fender repair shop in Jonesboro, and he did "eke out" a family living for his wife and two sons in Jonesboro during the Great Depression. Uncle Tom and one Bill Weaver finally got the Chevrolet dealership in the area, and were very financially successful. Had Arthur Earl remained with them, all would have gone well, for this business grew and the partnership employed many employees.

The Fears family moved to Sarasota, Florida, rented a house with a metal roof because of hurricanes, and Earl Sr. opened an auto repair shop with one Earl Long, who did radiator repairs. This partnership again turned into a financial disaster. The family then moved into an old trailer court, and Earl Jr. attended Junior High School there and Carl E. attended grammar school.

Earl Jr. made friends with sons and daughters of the more affluent society in Sarasota. One boy was the son of a physician, and he later joined the Royal Canadian Air Force and was killed in combat in WWII. A couple of girls came from prosperous families. One boy, whose father was a newspaper printer, later married a girl whose father was a lawyer. This son of the printer was one Davis Parker, Esq., who after the war finished law school, and very soon was a senior partner in his father-in-law's firm. In the '60s, Earl Jr. and wife Belle visited Sarasota, and had dinner with Davis and Charlotte, his wife. They treated the Fears' to a night tour with the new partner of Williams and Parker, and by now a wealthy person from investing in the booming real estate market after WWII. Parker died at the age of sixty-two without living a longer and happier life. His "nose to the grindstone" approach caused him to have a massive heart attack. Earl Jr. is convinced that the best way to be financially successful is to inherit wealth or say "I do!"

William Earl, after wasting time in poorly programmed high schools in the Eastern Shore of Maryland in the middle '30s, finally convinced Uncle Frederick (the West Point graduate) and Aunt Myrtle that he was ready for New York City. There he enrolled in a Quaker School, Friends Seminary, in the 11th grade. They allowed him to enter although he was not up to speed academically with the other students who had attended Friends Seminary since their early grades. Fears knew this was the last chance there was for him to do something in life other than "chop cotton" in Arkansas. These Quaker teachers, and the students with the Quaker philosophy, were most kind and tolerant, and best of all, were helpful in helping Fears catch up with his studies. There was an occasional remark about the "big-eared lad" but no one really overdid comments.

Somehow, with hard work and much study, student Fears graduated with fairly good grades, and with all the necessary credits to qualify for some good college. Student Fears was a member of the basketball team, and the bowling team at Friends and actually won his letter "F" in athletics, and this isn't a pun of sorts.

"Rat Year" at PMC was pure hell for Cadet Fears, because of his ugly duckling appearance. If he had been a big handsome football player, life would have been much easier. Cadet Fears often wondered in later years how Clark Gable fared in the Officer's Candidate School in Miami, or Gen. Singlab when he went through West Point. Both these men were marked with big ears, but they didn't protrude as much as Cadet Fears' did.

On one occasion, Cadet Fears' mettle was really put to the test. At each dining table were seated ten cadets. A Cadet Captain named Mike Benson, who had flunked out of Yale, and was a 26-year-old senior, sat at the head of the table. On each side was a Cadet Sergeant, a couple or so Cadet Corporals, senior privates, and finally three "brother rats" (freshmen), with Fears at the very end. The rats had to eat a square meal (hand to mouth at right angles); had to pass food to the upperclassmen before they could eat; had to stand on a chair and mock an ape, and had to do all kinds of demeaning things. One of the Corporals sitting next to Fears always took Fears' dessert. This day, when he reached for Fears' dessert, Cadet Fears struck him across the hand with a dull case knife. What a sacrilege, and Captain Benson beat Fears' hand with a large spoon. Cadet Fears was in a "heap of trouble." This sophomore Cadet corporal continued to take Fears' dessert until Fears hit him across the hand with the knife. Cadet Fears thought the "hand spanking" by Cadet Capt. Benson was all of it, but he got a new surprise!

This cadet was of Chinese descent from New York City. He was a resident of Chinatown, and his father was an undertaker there. Anyhow, the Chinese Cadet, Ralph Kimlau, challenged Fears to the gym that afternoon to give Cadet Kimlau satisfaction in the boxing ring. At this point, Cadet Fears was wishing he hadn't triggered this problem. Anyhow, Fears showed up in the gym, and there was Kimlau in the ring with boxing shorts, boxing shoes, tank shirt, and with hands and wrists all taped. Fears had no boxing regalia; so he kicked off his street shoes to stocking feet; took his shirt off down to a T-shirt; and kept his cadet trousers on. Surprise! There stood Capt. Mike Benson in Fears' corner as his second. On one side of the ring were some "brother rats" and on the other side of the ring were upper classmen, but no one seemed to be cheering for Cadet Fears. Fears asked about rounds and rests, but – behold – there were none; no gloves either, for this was a "grudge" fight – fight until someone was down and out. Mike Benson whispered in Fears' ear that if he didn't beat the "Chinaman," he would beat Fears later. Cadet Fears was scared to death for Kimlau looked like a pro.

Now if you recall, Cadet Fears had done some boxing in the American Legion, and Uncle Carl had weaned him on a punching bag. Nevertheless, Cadet Fears felt like he was "out of his league." Fears had his fists and wrists taped so they wouldn't get broken. Capt. Benson told the two to go to it. Fears stood in the middle of the ring looking like a rank amateur. When Cadet Kimlau advanced, Fears suddenly lunged forward with a right feint, struck Kimlau as hard as he could hit him right smack in the nose with his left fist. The blood flew from Kimlau's nose, but he still advanced again. Fears hit him in the nose again with a hard right. Things got so bloody Fears told Capt. Benson to throw in his towel, and he would concede the fight to Kimlau. The Cadet Corporal just wouldn't quit, even if Fears had killed him. All was quiet in the gym and all left quietly. Fears went to the shower, and Kimlau went to the hospital with a broken nose and two black eyes. Next morning for breakfast there was no Cadet Corporal Kimlau. Fears thought he would get expelled, but no one did anything. This was the name of the game, a fair fight.

After a couple of days, Cadet Kimlau showed up at the mess table with a taped nose and black eyes. Nothing was said by anyone, but no one ever took Cadet Fears' dessert again. Fears always admired Kimlau for his great perserverance. Kimlau joined the Army Air Corps, in WWII, became a B-24 pilot, and was shot down and killed in the Pacific Theater as a WWII hero. They named a public square "Kimlau Square" in Chinatown in New York City in honor of him. Mike Benson beat out Cadet Capt. Coggeshall for a Second Leutienent's Commission in the Marine Corps, and became a Colonel. He was wounded badly in the

Pacific Theater, and finished his career as an instructor with NATO in Norfolk, Virginia. PMC must be a good military school, for one graduate in the class of '65 is now a retired Four Star General, having served on the Joint Chiefs of Staff. His name is Gen. John H. Telleli, Jr.

Fears has met several Generals who aren't "ring knockers" from the "West Point Protective Association." There was Gen. Curtis LeMay, SAC Commander; Gen. Russell Daugherty; and Gen. Maxwell Thurman, who was Southern Army Commander in the taking of Noriega from Panama. Thurman was a Kansas State graduate, and Gen. LeMay was an Ohio State graduate. When Lt. Fears was in the Army Air Corps, one usually had to be a West Point graduate to get quick promotions; however then Gen. George C. Marshall was a VMI graduate.

Chapter 3

YALE UNIVERSITY

William Earl tried again to enter the USMA. Although the entrance exams would be waived because Fears was an honor student in engineering at PMC, he couldn't get the Congressional appointment, which was given to a Villanova College first-year student living in Ocean City, Maryland. It's a good thing that Fears didn't enter the Academy because most of the members of Class of '43 were killed or died in POW camps in WWII. Most of them died in the South Pacific after they had been stationed in the Philippines where all West Pointers were assigned. Now the "big-eared handicap" was a two-edged sword later at Yale University.

Fears wanted a better education than PMC could offer, so he applied for a transfer to Yale School of Engineering and was accepted, provided he studied differential calculus during the summer under a mathematics tutor, and proved he could keep up with the sophomore class in calculus at Yale. Bill Miller, his calculus instructor, died as a hero in an airplane crash in the Korean War, but Fears can never thank him enough for his help in the summer of 1940. In fact, Fears was placed in a calculus class with mathematics majors, and not in the engineer's class, which proved much harder. The sophomore class at Yale was very difficult for the "ole Arkansas boy," but he managed to get two "B"s and three "C"s in this very difficult curriculum with heavy competition and great professors who had written the textbooks. So our student entered the junior year with even more difficult subjects such as Physical Chemistry and Electrical Engineering. Fears got a "B" in Electrical Engineering, which was the nemesis of most junior year engineering students, but a "D" in Physical Chemistry, which he never really understood. To him a "mole" was some kind of Arkansas animal which bores through the ground. This year is when the big-eared appearance was a two-edged sword.

A Professor Milligan in metallurgy liked the "ugly duckling," and helped him work hard for an "A." The Physical Chemistry professor had a lisp, and felt sorry for Fears. Somehow, with a little extra tutoring, Fears passed his classes. At Yale, classes are small and the teachers personally grade the exams. One poor fellow studying Chemical Engineering flunked out because he failed both Organic Chemistry and Physical Chemistry. Somehow he entered the University of Alabama and graduated with honors, it is believed.

One who graduates from a prestigious school such as MIT, Yale, Harvard, and the like, can find a door open for employment in good positions all over the country, if one is also in the financial and social elite group. But in all fairness to the elitist society, once the door is opened, the novice has to "hit the ground running" and has got to "cut the mustard" to advance to management level. There are hard working, smart, but financially poor students who climb the ladder of success, and get the "brass ring." I recall one Bob Von Mehren who graduated with honors from Yale, and then honors in law from Harvard. He entered the law firm of Plimpton and McLean in New York City as a law clerk, and through hard work and ability is now a senior partner and heads the litigation section of this prestigious law firm. Another Yale undergraduate named Arthur Strong Whiteman was a member of the Yale basketball team for two years, but he gave up basketball to concentrate on his studies. He was an honor graduate in mathematical physics, and in his senior year was taking graduate subjects. He went on to Yale or Harvard, and got his PhD with honors. The last one heard of him was that he was a Fellow in the School of Advanced Science at Princeton; and it is believed he worked on the "Manhattan Project" in WWII with Dr. Oppenheimer, the father of the atom bomb. These brilliant scholars can enter the gristmill of work with success and can always make it anywhere, but occasionally an average student with average intellegence can get the "brass ring," but that's with some luck and some help from a mentor or two. Earl Jr. so admired the brilliant and self-sufficient ones, and it was a great experience to have at least rubbed elbows with the famous ones. Either your family owns the company like Steve Forbes, Henry Kellogg, or George Pillsbury, or one must be loaded with native intelligence and ability or "born to success" or says "I do" to a rich wife whose father has a part ownership in a profession or a business.

William Earl waited on tables in the graduate dining hall at Yale for his board. In this job, Fears had to rush from the graduate dining hall, where he waited on a table seating the future President Ford, and future Supreme Court Justices White and Stewart. His bicycle was a handy means of transportation. Fears feels if he hadn't had to work in the dining hall he might have made higher grades. Incidentally, there was a very secret and snobbish fraternity on campus and the real "big shots" were the only ones initiated into this one. After WWII, President George Bush, the Navy pilot war hero and a holder of the Navy Cross, got to be the captain of the Yale baseball team, and was initiated into this secret fraternity called the "Skull and Bones." I don't know if any of these iniaees are on any welfare program or food stamps. Of course, President Bush was born wealthy, but he went out to Texas and parlayed his inherited wealth into another fortune by forming an energy company called *Zapata*. This means "shoe" in Spanish. He did well in making money, and in politics. Now all that money has propelled his sons into success and politics. Other rich boys like George Pillsbury, Henry Kellog, Jack Stroube and Earl Slick have parlayed their inherited fortunes into more wealth. The old adage that "money gets money" is certainly true. Wally Ford married Henry II's daughter and was one of the Fords. All Fords went to Yale, and one married Harvey Firestone's daughter. Surely none of these had to beg for a job.

In case the reader is interested in the individuals named, I'll start with George Pillsbury. He was the heir to the Pillsbury Baking Co. business. You know Pillsbury pancakes, and the like? He just sold the company to some English firm and doubled his fortune. Not bad, but what happens to the employees? ... Jack Stroube's family owned the Stroube Oil Co. in Oklahoma and Jack ended up buying and selling oil leases in Dallas, and parlayed his family money into a fortune. ... Earl Slick's family owned Slick Oil Co. in Oklahoma. Earl Slick was a navy pilot during WWII and with his "nest egg" formed Slick Airways, which carried freight all over the world. He sold his company to another airfreight company, took his fortune, went to North Carolina and made a second fortune in real estate.

Yale has a worse caste system than India, and money is the wedge to open the social door. African-Americans aren't the only ones discriminated against. One must have financial or high social status to enter the elitist fraternities at Yale. The captain of the football team or the baseball team would qualify also. One would suppose it is the same thing at Harvard, Dartmouth, or Cornell. Not so at MIT, for one has to be a genius to enter there, and there is no football team. To get through that school one must work his or her "butt off." This latent financial and social elitist group guards the gateway to success in life. How President Bill Clinton got elected to office, with his social and financial background, are mysteries to Earl Jr., also from Arkansas. Every community has this latent society to take care of its members, so Earl Jr. continued with his inferiority complex until late when he got a little taste of sweet success on his own by defeating one Honorable E. Almer Ames for the Virginia State Senate. Ames and Fears both reside in Accomac, Virginia. In the 1967 election Fears received over 400 votes and Ames got less than 170 in the Accomac precinct. Ames was one of the members of an old Eastern Shore of Virginia family and part of the elitist society, and the "ole Arkansas boy" is a "come here." Ames never forgave Fears for defeating him and, being President of the local First Virginia Bankshares Bank, made a long speech to keep Fears off the board of the local bank when Fears was nominated. Ames made sure that Fears advanced in none of his other local endeavors either.

In a job in Baltimore with ASARCO, roommates Lynch and Fears worked in the summer of 1941 for $35 per week as metallurgists, living together in a boarding house where they got a room and board each for $10 per week. In this way, Fears helped pay part of his expenses at Yale. At that time, tuition was $800 per year, and with a bursar's job, Fears could pay his room and board at Yale. Now tuition and expenses at Yale amount to more than $36,000 per year. Everything is relative: that is, only the wealthy can attend Yale – or one must be a genius with a scholarship stipend.

The Asians are good students, study hard, and get good grades. Maybe this is the reason Asians have all the financial scholarships in the Ivy League Schools, and the reason a cadet of Korean descent was the number one scholar in one of the graduating classes at the Air Force Academy. American Anglo-Saxon students just aren't willing to work hard enough to matriculate to prestigious educational institutions.

Fears also had other summer jobs, such as working as a house man in a hotel, a soda jerk, mowing lawns, and working in an illegal gambling joint in Ocean City, Maryland, to make and save enough money to buy clothes and attend Yale. This was during the Great Depression and people were glad to get jobs paying $1 per day. Certainly young people didn't get married, and no one had children out of wedlock. There was no public welfare and if a girl got pregnant, the girl and the boy responsible were expelled from school.

Earl Jr.'s bursar's job at Yale was waiting on large round tables in Woolsey Hall, the graduate dining hall. At Fears' assigned table sat Byron "Whizzer" White and Potter Stewart, freshmen law students who later were both appointed to the U.S. Supreme Court. Also at the same table sat Gerald Ford, later President of the U.S. Fears was a junior undergraduate at this time.

At one political function in Williamsburg, Governor Mills Godwin – who had switched from the Democratic Party to the Republican

Party – called Sen. Fears over to meet President Ford. Everyone was dressed in formal dinner jackets, and Earl Jr. looked every part the State Senator. He told Gov. Godwin and the President that he had met the President in 1941. Fears said, "I was the President's waiter at Yale when the President was a student in law school." The President replied, "The hell you say," and a photographer took a picture of the President, Gov. Godwin, and Sen. Fears together, which Sen. Fears has and cherishes as a part of his memorabilia. He uses it to prove to his grandchildren that he isn't lying, but then they don't even know who Gerald Ford really is!

Yale University's School of Engineering was a great experience for an "ole Arkansas farm boy." In 1940, there were few blacks, few Jews, and no women in the undergraduate colleges. For William Earl, with such a poor background, all courses were difficult because of the competition, the great teaching staff, and curve grading, but William Earl passed the most difficult ones such as Physical Chemistry and Electrical Engineering. In fact, to Fears' surprise, he got a "B" in Electrical Engineering in his Junior year. He lived in a dormitory called "The Cloisters" with another engineering student named Don Lynch, and one Bill Keogh, a history major who quit school in his junior year to enter the Army Air Corps as an Aviation Cadet.

Keogh earned his commission and his pilot's wings, and flew troop carrier planes during WWII. He achieved the rank of First Lieutenant and after the war got a job with the U.S. Information Agency, served in the Far East, and retired as some kind of executive in that agency. In 1963, William Earl had lunch with Keogh in DC. Keogh was still a bachelor, and Fears guesses Keogh decided they had nothing in common, for they never met again.

Don Lynch was a genius, never studied, got "A"s and "B"s in all subjects, and graduated "Tau Beta Phi," which in engineering is equivalent to "Phi Beta Kappa" in liberal arts. Don Lynch never entered the Armed Forces, but worked for General Electric Co. somewhere in Connecticut. He rose to Division Manager, but was killed in an auto accident in 1961, leaving a wife and four children. Incidentally, Don's father was Dennis Tilden Lynch, one of the old-time great editorial writers for the New York Herald Tribune.

Bill Keogh was also brilliant, but a bit strange. He used to stick a pencil up his nose and tickle it to promote a great sneeze, which seemed his greatest pleasure. Don Lynch played poker with the "rich boys" to make his spending money. Lynch was deferred with a so-called 2-B deferment in war industry, but so was William Earl.

The only "A" William Earl got in Yale was in a metallurgical course taught by a Dr. Milligan. He liked the "big-eared" William Earl, for he probably related to him. Milligan wasn't very handsome himself. He helped William Earl get a summer job with American Smelting and Refining Co. in Baltimore along with Don Lynch. Don worked in the assaying department, assaying for gold and silver in the electrolytic tank sediments, and Fears ran quality controls on the acid tanks, the copper "mattes," and the rare metals such as tellurium, selenium, and the like.

While in his senior year at Yale, Fears tried to apply for a direct commission in the Navy, for they were accepting Engineering Graduates for technical jobs in the CBs (construction battalions) and in various fields of aeronautics. One applicant made it and was killed in an aircraft accident. Another made it in the CBs and was killed somewhere in the Pacific by a Japanese sniper. Again, Providence saved our aspiring warrior. Finally Professor Milligan convinced our fledgling engineering graduate he would be more useful to the war effort by working in some war industry.

Fears' roommate, Don Lynch, had already accepted a job with General Electric. Keogh was proficient in a couple of Asiatic languages. Anyhow, Keogh didn't get to be a fighter pilot hero, and our honor graduate Lynch had a very promising management career "nipped in the bud." What a tragedy for the country! Our average student Fears has yet to relate his WWII experiences, but Providence somehow protected him from his own ambitions in wanting to be a veteran of combat, or the like.

Again Providence saved our student's life, for in his senior year the U.S. was all geared up for war and "smack in the middle" of it. William Earl tried to join the Yale flying group which went together to Pensacola, Florida, for Aviation Cadet Naval flight training, but never got past the interview with the "big ears and other minor problems." About 40 in the Class of '43, which had accelerated in the summer and graduated in Dec. '42, trained at Pensacola. A couple were killed in training and one, René Chouteau, a magnificent swimmer at Yale, got to be a flight instructor. He was hit in the head by a cadet in a taxiing accident in which the student cadet taxied out and struck Lt. J.G. Chouteau with a propeller. Most of the others in this class who won their wings and commissions were carrier pilots in the Pacific, and were killed in combat at Midway and Coral Sea. One in the class won his wings early as an Aviation Cadet in the Army Air Corps and went to combat in the Pacific as a fighter pilot. He too was killed in action.

Fortunately, during the last year at Yale, there was a mandatory exercise program started for the future warriors. Rather than waste his time doing push-ups and running up and down stairs in the Payne Whitney gymnasium, Fears took the Red Cross Life Saving Courses. Although he was still the big-eared scrawny 130-pound kid, he managed to pass all the written and practical tests for the Instructor's Badge, and wore it proudly on the beach in Ocean City so the girls might notice him. No luck: for they all looked at the unattractive frame and migrated to the muscular guards on the beach. Anyhow, this badge got Fears a job as a lifeguard at a public swimming pool in Cincinnati, after he quit his job with Wright Aero Corp., visited the draft board and volunteered for induction.

It took the board three months to call him up. He was assigned to Ft. Thomas, Kentucky, as a draftee for classification and was assigned to the Corps of Engineers, and was to be sent to Camp Claiborne, Louisiana. This was the place he would be assigned to a survey team, practice swimming rivers, and building pontoon bridges, while fighting off water moccasins and coral snakes.

Somehow, a Major in the Army Air Corps found the 201 file on Fears and summoned him to the orderly room. He explained to Fears that he had read Fears' 201 file and found he had an engineering degree from Yale, had built aircraft engines, had a score of 140 in the AGCT tests, and had a good physical profile. He wanted Fears to sign up in the Army Air Corps as a pre-aviation cadet, for the air corps really needed air crews since so many were being lost in the war in combat. This is just what Fears wanted to do in the first place, and since it was a volunteer assignment, our hero signed up with the Army Air Corps, and was shipped off to Kessler Field, Mississippi, where he learned to salute and all that.

There they had a "hog-calling" contest for cadet officers and because of his prior military training, Fears was the best "hog caller" of the lot and was named the Cadet Wing Commander. This allowed him to wear three white adhesive tapes on his left arm, or maybe it was four. This entailed lots of responsibility, and a great opportunity to make all the other cadets mad, which it did! However, the Tactical Officer, an Air Corps Captain, did place a letter in our cadet's file as a leader of men. The next assignment was to Canisius College in Buffalo, New York, where the cadets were to learn things a pilot was supposed to use such as navigation, meteorology, and how to march. But this time Fears hid in the rear ranks so he wouldn't be noticed, and he didn't enter the "hog-calling contest" there to pick Cadet Officers. If he couldn't be the real thing – as a Second Lieutenant, U.S. Army Air Corps – he didn't want to play officer and be noticed too much.

Our graduating student, in December 1942, with his degree in engineering from Yale, had decided he would take Professor Milligan's advice and work in a war industry rather than try to be a war hero. He accepted a job with Wright Aero Corporation near Cincinnati, and when he reported for work at 85¢ per hour he was assigned to a foundry casting aluminum cylinder heads, and magnesium housings for R2600 aircraft engines. These were used in other aircraft, but the B-25 was the predominant aircraft. Before our graduate could get to Cincinnati, he had to work on a mail truck in the wet snow delivering Christmas packages, and earned $75 and damned near died of pneumonia. With bus money, he arrived at Cincinnati and went to work. The war manpower commission had given him a 2B deferment as essential to the war effort, and he wasn't subject to the draft. He paid a family near his work site $10 per week for an attic room with breakfast.

The foundry was filled with smoke, fine sand particles, and carcinogenic compounds for making sand casting molds. Most of the people working in this environment died of lung cancer or other lung ailments. This was before OSHA, but everyone was so glad to get a job after the Great Depression. They took the risk, and Fears didn't know better!

Fears got interested in Patents and Patent Law, and after being assigned to the 4:00 PM to 12:00 midnight shift, he was able to enter law school at the University of Cincinnati for morning classes. Our fledgling engineer was able to finish a semester of law before his next plan, which was to enter the armed forces with a direct commission if possible.

Chapter 4

JOBS

This job as a metallurgical engineer paid the fantastic wage of 85¢ per hour. The only way to save money was with overtime pay. What a "hell of a job." It was in a foundry casting aluminum cylinder heads and magnesium housings for aircraft engines. This job lasted Fears seven months. The foundry had no safety fans nor other safety precautions, for OSHA wasn't in existence at this time. The foundry was polluted with smoke, carcinogenous compounds, and small sand particles. If Fears had stayed on this job he would have died from lung disease, as many of the other workers did, in a couple of years. There wasn't any worker's compensation at that time. Fortunately, he entered the Army Air Corps as an Aviation Cadet and was paid $75 per month. This probably saved his life, but then after Commissioning as a Second Lieutenant flying was quite risky, especially in combat in the European Theater. It took ten months of hard training just to get commissioned after hours of difficult training, and terrible living conditions during WWII.

While working in Cincinnati, Fears joined four other fledgling engineers, and rented a very nice luxury apartment in a small modern apartment building a couple of blocks from law school. Another engineer sharing the apartment entered the law school class with Fears, but he took no further interest in law after one semester. Fears learned that this fellow, Vernon Swan, later worked for Presto Corp. as a metallurgist. Fears got bored with his work and felt somewhat guilty for not being in the armed services. He applied to the Naval Officer Procurement Board and the Army Officer Procurement Board for a direct commission in either service. The Army indicated maybe they could commission him in the Ordnance Corps, but his company superintendent would have to release him from the war manpower commission. Fears discussed this with the tough superintendent of his plant, and the employer simply said no. "If I let you out every young engineer in the company will want to do the same thing. You can work or fight the hard way," meaning Fears could quit his job and be drafted.

One time riding on a streetcar, Fears didn't offer his seat quickly enough to some "little elderly lady" and she said, "Young man, why aren't you in the service?" Fears replied, "I'm 4-F for you see, lady, I tested positive for gonorrhea." There was laughter in the streetcar among the other passengers. Fears knew he shouldn't have made the remark, but this helped him decide he would quit work, and get drafted so he could do what his liberal arts friends were doing.

There was a heavy "wash out" rate throughout the cadet programs, because by now the Army had more officer trainees for all its programs than it needed; so orders were to get rid of as many as they could, and of course send them to the ground forces as privates starting all over again. Two weeks before graduation, Fears was assigned to a group of six cadets to take a course in installations. This course lasted a week. Fears always had a sixth sense about people, and from the start of this course with a Second Lieutenant instructor, an Irish Catholic from Boston, Fears immediately felt he was in trouble. The tactical officer, 1st Lt. Barringer, had told the teachers in all sections to send him one cadet from each section for "wash out." The big-eared kid from Arkansas with the southern accent was picked by Lt. O'Conner to appear before Lt. Barringer for an oral technical examination. Fears answered the examiner's questions correctly, and was sent back to his duties, and didn't go before the "wash out" board. A few moments later, Lt. O'Conner was called before the Captain and he didn't look too happy when he returned. Fears did pass the course that week with a low grade, learned that no one but him had survived the intentional elimination, and still wonders if there was not a protective letter in his

201 file. Fears is convinced that it was his appearance and southern mannerism which caused the problem, not his knowledge or ability. Anyhow, two weeks later, our cadet graduated with his class and his commission. He happened to bump into O'Conner on the street, and they saluted each other, and it was all our new Second Lieutenant could do to restrain himself from punching O'Conner in the nose. President Carter said the thought and intent to commit a wrong was pretty bad, so perhaps there would be another day of reckoning.

It appeared our trainee was going to be stuck at Canisuis College in Buffalo, New York, for the duration of the war, so he wrote a letter to his acquantance, Maj. Gen. Frank P. Lahm, one of his Uncle Frederick's co-trainees on the Wright Airplane. Gen. Lahm had been the C.O. of the training command which started at Randolph Field, Texas. He wrote the General that he was stuck in the program, since there was a great pool of preflight trainees being held all over the U.S., and our hero wanted to get on with the training and see combat. Gen. Lahm never answered, but in about a week Fears was moved from the classes, placed in the office to help the Captain, and was told he already had an engineering degree and didn't need to attend classes. In another week, he was shipped to Seymour Johnson Field, North Carolina, for further training as a cadet. He then went on to Engineering Officer's School and further training in all phases of maintenance and flying until he was commissioned in June of 1944 as a Second Lieutenant U.S. Army Air Corps. All through the training programs he had close calls with tactical officers because he was still the same big-eared scrawny fellow and didn't really look like officer material. The training command was washing cadets out of the program because they didn't need any more. He roomed at the final base with another engineering graduate from Drexel Institute of Technology, who had a bad ankle, but this guy couldn't be touched. He didn't do PT or close order drill, for he spent much of his time in his room at a drawing board designing autogyro blades. His name is forgotten but as soon as this guy was commissioned he was sent immediately to Wright Patterson Field as a design engineer for the Army Air Corps. There must have been some kind of protective letter in the "ugly duckling's" file too, for our hero made it through and was assigned to Kelly Field, San Antonio, Texas, for further training. Then he went on to Dallas to an executive base where passenger aircraft were being used to fly "big shots" around the country.

Chapter 5

Out of New York

The new Fears family rented a $50 per month house in Accomac and settled down with $5,000 in the bank from William Earl's war service savings. William Earl and Belle slept on a sofa bed again, with Barbara and now Brad sleeping in the bedroom in separate beds.

William Earl, now "Bill," opened a one-room law office, and Dr. Belle built a small medical office from which she practiced family medicine. Bill paid $15 per month for the one-room law office, and paid a one-armed functionally handicapped secretary $15 per week as salary. Finally, a house was built on a 3% G.I. loan for $15,000 on a piece of farm property donated by Belle's father, a great country doctor. Bill did much of the work himself since he was an engineering graduate. Now the house is assessed at $100,000 or more for tax and insurance purposes.

It was a long hard struggle just to make a living, but a lot cleaner, safer, and better living conditions than living in Pittsburgh or New York City. Bill was the first out-of-state lawyer to start a practice in this "clannish" rural community. Most of the lawyers went into a relative's office, and they were all local boys. But Bill enjoyed hunting and fishing, and Bill worked hard to earn a living in spite of the local prejudice, and of the local lawyers' resentment, he survived!

This rural area has only the usual economic and social classes: the "haves" and the "have nots." The living haves either inherited wealth, or it was given to them. One successful lawyer married a Smith-Douglas Fertilizer Co. heiress worth millions; another while still in high school was "clipping bond coupons." His mother is a Zimmerman and owns half of Baltimore. Anyhow, Bill continued to learn that the two best ways of having anything, especially in a rural area, is to inherit it or marry it. The very rich boy joined another rich boy and built a great "Taj Mahal" law office, and now they have all the rich, retired "come heres" as clients while the poor boys are still struggling. Believe it: money draws money. The proof of this is to simply look at the majority of CEOs or members of Congress. One will find that most CEOs and officials had good family contacts. To start from scratch one must already have wealth, or be a genius like Bill Gates of Microsoft.

A friend of lawyer Fears was traveling by subway one early morning in New York City, after partying late, and was shot. He did get to a hospital but died the next day from shock and peritonitis. Before he died, he said a bunch of Spanish-looking youngsters "stuck him up" with a pistol and wanted his wallet. He was a WWII veteran and he was not about to capitulate; so he was shot resisting the robbery. This should teach everyone not to resist, but give the robbers your wallet and your valuables. These marauders probably would have shot him anyway, but this convinced Fears that New York City was no place for a country wife and two young children, so he started to plan to move someplace to a rural area.

In the meantime, he had passed the U.S. Patent Office Examination, which is very difficult. Fears thought with all this background an employer would beg for his services, and pay a high salary. Not so, for qualified Patent Attorneys are a "dime a dozen," and several hundred were stuck in the U.S. Patent Office as "cubby hole" examiners with no place to go. Fears used his G.I. educational benefits and enrolled in the International Correspondence School Accounting Courses. It took two years studying at least two hours every night to complete the courses required for the CPA certificate, but this gave Fears a new or supplemental career as a bookkeeper and income tax return preparer.

Fears couldn't decide whether to move to the Eastern Shore of Maryland, or to the Eastern Shore of Virginia, but having already passed the Ohio Bar Exam, he thought the Virginia Bar and the Maryland Bar would admit him on motion, but no such luck! Each state had a requirement that one must have practiced five years or more before the Bar of Admission before one could be admitted on motion; so Fears took the New York and Maryland Bar Examinations at about the same time. Virginia required a six-month residency before one could even take that Bar Examination. He did pass the Maryland Bar Exam, and half of the New York Examination but decided to move to Virginia. The one big event that finally convinced Fears to get out of New York was the second year in the City.

Fears was riding the crowded subway to work, and behind him someone coughed on the back of his neck. He felt the back of his neck and it was wet, and when he looked at his hand it was bloody. He turned around and there was a very thin Asian, probably Chinese. Fears guessed the poor fellow had tuberculosis, but this was the "back breaking of the camel." From then on he knew he was going to move on to cleaner pastures.

He moved his wife and children to Accomac, his wife's hometown where her father practiced country medicine, and rented a small house to declare a residence in Virginia to meet the six-month residency requirement. That requirement has since been ruled unconstitutional by the Federal Courts, but too late for Fears. He took the Virginia Bar Exam, passed it, resigned from his job in New York City, and set up shop in Accomac. He first practiced with an older lawyer for the huge salary of $35 per week, but this relationship only lasted six months.

One reason for the six-month residency requirement in Virginia is to protect the turf of Virginia lawyers. In Florida and California, it's even worse. There is no motion admission. One must take the examination in Florida and California. (The exam is graded with a red pencil too!) A graduate of the University of Florida Law School doesn't have to take the examination. Talk about protecting one's turf!

The Fears family finally set up two shops in Accomack County. Dr. Belle built a small medical office on a lot taken from her father's farmland, but on a main street in the Town of Accomac. Lawyer Bill opened a one-room law office on the second floor of Dr. Edmond's building right across from the Court House. He paid $15 per month rent, and hired a secretary for $15 per week who had secretarial training and had to type with one hand. She had a deformed hand from birth, and could only use her other hand, but she could type very well on a mechanical typewriter. Later Fears was elected Prosecuting Attorney, and could pay this secretary, named Sue Mason, a decent salary for he then made $6,000 per year as county prosecutor which in 1955 was enough to survive.

During this time, our lawyer managed to build a two-story house next to Dr. Belle's office on a loan guaranteed by the V.A. under his G.I. benefits, at the then-low rate of 3% interest. The house cost about $15,000, for lawyer Fears did most of the planning, supervision, and some of the physical work himself. Since he was an engineering graduate, he laid off the footings, and did some of the other work. Now the house is assessed and insured for $100,000 or more. What inflation there is from 1952 to the present!

Now our struggling couple, with the two young children, started making a little money. Bill practiced law, and Belle practiced family medicine. Dr. Belle never had a nurse. There were no malpractice actions at that time, and people were glad to have a country physician; and then it was a reasonably pleasant time. Both children were "A" students in grammar school, and Bill and Belle were at least making a living.

Anyhow, since this chapter also has to do with the plastic surgery problem, we must get back to this. Poor little Barbara was a lovely girl, but William Earl had "marked her." Her ears were relatively small compared to her father's but they stuck off from her head. In other words, she was born with floppy ears. Both parents, knowing she would have grief from this appearance, decided early on that they would employ a plastic surgeon to pin her ears back. Lawyer Fears owned a one-third interest in a Cessna aircraft and flew Barbara to and from the Medical College of Virginia in Richmond, 30 minutes each way, for the operation. After the operation he quickly flew her back home, with Dr. Fears acting as the flight nurse. The operation was much more successful aesthetically than William Earl's, and Barbara has matured into a very attractive lady. She had one other problem. When she was about 11 years old, she had one large tooth in front and no others had erupted. Barbara was seen by an orthodontist, and then by an oral surgeon in Salisbury, Maryland, and was operated on for her teeth. The oral surgeon cut the gums over each tooth, and cemented a plastic cap on each tooth. Thank Heavens the poor child's teeth finally came through. She has a full set of teeth now, and is an attractive woman at 52 years old.

Brad Fears was a handsome little boy with blond curly hair, and was a happy baby. He had a bad habit of going to sleep early and waking at 5:00 AM with a big smile on his face, wanting his bottle and wanting to play. These were interesting and happy years.

Belle found an angel by the name of Sarah Ayres who lived with the Fears family and simply took care of the two children. She was like a mother hen; she was a good influence on the children, and raised them well. In later years when she retired Dr. Belle bought her a trailer, equipped it, and Sarah lived next door to her sister whom she loved very much. Dr. Belle supplemented Sarah's necessities including a knee replacement, cataract operations, and other things until Sarah died at an age of probably 76. The children and grandchildren loved her very much, as did the entire community. She never married, but finally succumbed to cancer. Bill and Belle are certain this great lady is in Heaven.

No one should try to go through life with a noticeable facial defect, for after William Earl had his operation his success in life did improve, and certainly Barbara's appearance and quality of life were assured for her future.

Our new country lawyer wanted to take the CPA examination in Virginia, but the ICS certificate wouldn't qualify, and a new turf group got the CPA Board to require that one work at slave labor wages for two years for a CPA before one could get certified. The Land Surveyors even went a little further. They required one to work as an apprentice for six years for a licensed surveyor before the fledgling surveyor could even take the examination; even though one had taken surveying courses for an engineering degree. This is the best profession economically for a young person to enter, for a college degree isn't necessary.

Now in Virginia one doesn't have to get a law degree to pass the Bar Examination. For years all one had to do was study law in a law office for three years, and then one could take the Bar Examination. The law school Deans got into the act, and tried to get the General Assembly to require a degree from an accredited law school to qualify. Sen. Fears supported this legislation, but the newspaper editors ridiculed the General Assembly by contending they were undemocratic, and among other rationale the media pointed out that Abraham Lincoln never attended law school. The politicians got scared of the voters, for at that time the "political drumbeat" was "there are too many lawyers in the legislature," and voted against the legislation. Sen. Fears had an opponent once, a farmer who ran against him on that platform, and he almost won the election. Now the U.S. Supreme Court allows lawyers to advertise as they couldn't do before 1984. The respect for lawyers in the public arena is just one notch above "pimp," and perhaps used car salesmen, not to mention "evangelistic self-ordained preachers." Sen. Fears was proud to be a lawyer when he was first admitted to the Bar, and now wishes he had continued his career in engineering of some sort. There are too many lawyers, and perhaps some of the more recently licensed law schools should be closed.

Everyone now wants to carry a briefcase and look important. None of the smart youngsters desire to get their hands dirty with medicine or dentistry, or for that matter in a trade where they are needed. There is a lot to be said for the "Inns of Court" in England where every Tom, Dick, and Harry cannot be licensed to practice law.

A Federal Judge named Hon. Richard Kellam studied law in his brother's office, was a Circuit Judge for Virginia, a good Democrat, and lately a U.S. District Court Judge by presidential appointment. He probably was a good Judge, but he was a better politician. He is now deceased.

The Accomack-Northampton Bar in Virginia now has a new lawyer who is white, and married to an African-American obstetrician. She is from Boston, and has settled in this rural area, studied for three years in a African-American woman lawyer's office who has a J.D. degree from the University of Pennsylvania. Now the non-law-school graduate is practicing law. She did have a Master's Degree in something, studied some courses at the University of Cincinnati in law, and was smart enough to pass the old democratic Virginia Bar Examination. She drives most lawyers in the area up the wall, for she doesn't know well the rules of evidence law, and "shotguns" all facts at trials.

In all fairness to New Yorkers, those born and raised in New York City love the place and have no desire to live anywhere else. They think everyone living in the rural south or the country west are "hicks," for they, the New Yorkers, own the commercial centers, the largest church congregations, the art centers, and may attend some of the best and most inexpensive higher educational institutions, some even free. They are willing to tolerate the high taxes, the high crime rate, and the traffic congestions to live in New York City.

Belle and Bill Fears attended the 200th anniversary of Friends Seminary, Bill's high school alma mater, located in "Hell's Kitchen" near 15th Street and 2nd Avenue in New York City. From the Class of '39, about 10 people attended a dinner sponsored by one Barbara Valentine Hertz, a very bright lady who had graduated from Barnard College, and had served as Editor of Parents Magazine for years. One of the classmates named Ruth Osgood, a Wellesley College graduate, appeared in an old jumpsuit with tennis shoes for the dinner. She and her husband lived on Long Island. She told the group this was the only way to travel at night in the city in the subway as a woman. If a woman wore expensive clothes on the subway, she was just asking to be mugged. The Fears family didn't want to live in this kind of environment, so they moved to the country and raised their children and grandchildren. It isn't very lucrative in the country, but it's a lot more conducive to a long happy life. The New Yorkers can have their paradise, if they have plenty of money to ride taxicabs or limousines, and live way out in the wealthy suburbs.

NEW YORK CITY VERSUS ACCOMAC, VA

An apartment was found on Long Island for the Fears family, now consisting of Bill, Belle, Barbara, and little Brad. It was a nice apartment in a new project and the rent was reasonable. It took our budding patent lawyer an hour-and-a-half on the bus and subway, with a change in the subway, to reach his office on Wall Street one way; so to avoid the subway rush he left home an hour early and left the office an hour late. This impressed the boss, Mr. Deller, for he thought his new employee was conscientious. Fears shared the office with a fine gentleman named Millword, who smoked one cigar after another; so in self defense Fears lit up a couple of cigars each day, but it took years to kick the tobacco habit. Deller's success in editing the four-volume "Walker on Patents" was because he had a very bright woman lawyer named Fannie Mann, Esq., who on a full-time basis did the research, and actually edited the books. Deller simply paid her and took the credit.

There were six lawyers in the office with Deller, and a staff of about six secretaries. These lawyers were really well educated with science or engineering degrees, as well as law degrees, except one really brilliant fellow named "Gene" Kalil. He was a patent agent – no law degree. We were all simply editors for Deller, and were nothing but office legmen. We wrote the Patent Applications, and Deller signed each one as the attorney of record when it was finished and shipped it off to the U.S. Patent Office. Fears left the office after two years for a rural practice. One good guy by the name of Charlie Catlin simply turned into a "beach bum" at Fire Island, New York. Millword was old and probably has died. He really had nothing good to say about Deller. Two men stayed for several years. When Deller died, Maurice Penel, Esq., Deller's second in command, got to be head of the Patent Department. He was a "nitpicker" and the poor fellow died of cancer, leaving a very fine scientist and lawyer named Ewan McQueen, Esq., who also retired as head of the Patent Department for International Nickel Co. One Herbert Goodman, Esq., quit when Fears did, returned to college, and got additional credits in Organic Chemistry. He became the head of a patent department for a small chemical company. Eugene Kalil, Esq., quit the office, returned to law school, got his J.D. degree, passed the New York Bar Exam, and became a senior partner in a medium-sized patent law firm in New York City. He had a wife, no children, and lived in a nice apartment on Madison Avenue near his work. His firm ended up doing most of the litigation patent law work for International Nickel Co. Fears visited New York City on business about 20 years later, visited Kalil's office, and had lunch with him. There were really only two highly successful people in Deller's office; one was Deller himself, and the other was Kalil, and Kalil is now privately handling International Nickel Co.'s work in the patent law litigation field. This is more than just poetic justice, it's a victory for all the very bright people who simply go through life without ever getting to grab a "brass ring." Fears couldn't find an apartment of any quality in the center of Manhattan close to his work as Kalil did, because at that time no landlord wanted to rent to a family with young children. It has gotten better now, for the very wealthy have nice apartments, but the average middle class family with young children live in a crime-ridden low-cost high-rises. Little wonder the Fears family moved to a rural area where they could relax and breathe decent air in a good environment free of drugs and crime.

Chapter 6

CINCINNATI LAW SCHOOL

First Lieutenant William E. Fears finally came home from Europe and the Great World War II, and found his wife in Accomac, Virginia, in September 1946. They bought a new automobile for $1,200 and wife Belle kept it at her family home in Accomac, from whence the depressed Lieutenant went forth to get an apartment in Cincinnati where he was reentering law school. He was depressed because he had no civilian clothes, no apartment in Cincinnati, and had returned to the difficult civilian world. He caught a train in Wilmington and headed for Cincinnati, which was an all-night trip. After the train ride our Lieutenant finally was detrained at the Cincinnati railroad station.

Somehow he made it from the railroad station to a hotel, checked in, sent his uniform to a one-hour cleaner, had the dry heaves all day, and felt like hell. There is nothing which feels better than being on one's knees after a sickening drunk and feeling the cold porcelain of the commode on one's cheek. He finally promised the Lord that he would never take another drink. (Fears didn't take another alcoholic drink for many years afterward.) The Lieutenant found it difficult to find an apartment, but remembered the maid's apartment on University Court where he had once shared a larger apartment with three other engineers. The new owner had children in college, and luckily the small maid's apartment was vacant. The nice landlord rented the apartment to Fears for $45 per month, and with the G.I. bill's stipend this was wonderful, for the apartment was only 3 blocks from Law School. Lt. Fears came back to Accomac, picked up the car and a small trailer and the delayed newlyweds headed for Cincinnati so our Lieutenant could finish his legal training. He entered classes and the second semester was completed with "A"s and "B"s. Dr. Fears got a salaried position in a Catholic Hospital on a daytime job for $40 per week, so the young struggling couple made it through the first year very well. The other two-bedroom luxury apartments were occupied by successful young middle-aged couples.

While Fears was in law school, he and his wife had many happy times. The elderly owners lived in one of the apartments to help their tax situation. The other tenants sort of adopted the Fears and at least four of the couples played bridge and "Penny Ante" poker together. One guy was president of the Golden Pheasant wine company and kept all his friends supplied with refreshments. One Frank Getman and his wife, Dottie, were special mentors. Frank rose to be chairman and chief executive officer of the Vick Chemical Co., and after retirement Frank and Dottie moved to Florida. They are both dead now and their only son has a terminal disease. Everyone kept in touch through divorces, deaths, and all that. Then the big shock: Belle got pregnant, and our law student was informed by the landlord that the Fearses would have to vacate the nice little apartment if they were going to have a child.

William Earl scurried around to find a larger apartment which a student could afford on $120 per month. He found one and took his bride to view it. The first drawer she opened disturbed a whole nest of cockroaches and water bugs. The bride, being a doctor, said "No way," for she claimed the bugs would get into everything and there was no way to get rid of them. Our law student, after much anguish, finally found an apartment in a low-cost housing project for poor folks, with two bedrooms and no bugs for it had been fumigated with cyanide gas several times. Fortunately this was prior to the drug culture and before all the public housing projects became infested with crime and drugs, which seem to go with this culture.

So the Fears' moved into these comfortable quarters. Dr. Belle delivered her baby, Barbara Anderson Fears, in a wonderful Cincinnati Hospital, but with birth difficulties and necessary blood transfusions furnished by the great people in the housing project, law school friends, and Belle's friends from the hospital. Baby Barbara was all bruised in the eyes and head from a forceps delivery, which was bad enough. She was also a screamer – all night, every night. All at least had separate beds, and William Earl and Dr. Belle had graduated from a folding studio sofa to a double bed.

In spite of all this, law student Fears completed his second year in law school with fairly reasonable grades, but not the highest. Belle had to stop work so she could take care of the baby, and the couple remained in the housing project until law school could be completed. While Dr. Belle was working in a Catholic hospital, our law student met a plastic surgeon with privileges in this hospital. This surgeon had been in the Army as a plastic surgeon, and was a Colonel when he was released from duty. He claimed to have plenty of battlefield experience. Our law student was tired of being called "ears" and felt his lot would improve if he could get rid of the floppy ears so the Colonel agreed to pin the law student's ears back. It was an operation done under a local anesthetic, very painful with many so-called mattress stitches. This means many stitches through the ears, through rubber pads to prevent the stitches from pulling through the ears. The operation wasn't perfect, but the "damned" ears were back. In those days, which was 1947, the costs were relatively inexpensive so our student could pay the bill. It took weeks for the ears to heal and the stitches were removed. Our law student had a difficult time avoiding questions in law school. He simply told his audience that he had a brain operation to improve his intelligence, for his head was swathed in bandages.

Belle had an older friend from Accomac, now in Cincinnati. His name was Bill Sturgis, a member of one of the first families in Virginia, and he had married a very wealthy woman named Schmedlapp. This dear lady had a huge mansion in the best section of Cincinnati, and had a couple of sons. Belle telephoned Bill Sturgis to say "Hello," and the family invited the young couple to the mansion for tea and a very cordial introduction. Later that year, Mrs. Schmedlapp-Sturgis invited them to a very formal dance on New Year's Eve to the elite Cincinnati Country Club. All the friends in the other apartments above the Fears' scurried around collecting jewelry and accessories to dress the young couple for the grand visit to the New Years' gala. Fortunately, law student Fears had his old "tails" from his days at Yale, and with the furnishing of white tie, vest, shirt, studs, and cuff links of 18K gold by their friends they were prepared for the grand visit to the club with their new friends. Mrs. Sturgis even sent her stretch Cadillac limousine with chauffeur to pick them up.

Mrs. Schmedlapp-Sturgis had a son by the name of Horace who somehow was a movie producer or agent of some sort. He was married to a movie actress by the name of Carole Landis who sat at the Sturgis' table for dinner. All were introduced, and our law student danced with the actress. He asked her if she knew a Lt. Col. Hutchinson, whom Lt. Fears had met in the Officer's Club in France. Col. Hutchinson was a rich fellow from Texas, and his father had bought him an AT6 airplane, which the Colonel had learned to fly at the ripe old age of 16 years. This propelled Hutchinson into the Army Air Corps at the right time where he became a great B-17 combat pilot, and rose to the rank of Lieutenant Colonel at 25 years of age. He also had a chest full of medals for combat valor.

Carole Landis was a very beautiful woman and had a fantastic figure. Fears can understand why the wealthy Horace Schmedlapp was attracted to her. She had lovely auburn hair, but in all her films she wore a blond wig. Col. Hutchinson was bragging, as most men do, about dating Carole Landis and, of course, all his listeners at the officer's club were mesmerized. When the law student mentioned Hutchinson to Landis she reacted badly by ignoring Fears the rest of the evening. Unfortunately, Landis committed suicide by gassing herself in an oven, and Hutchinson ended up as a General in the Air Force.

Another General in the Air Force later told Fears, when Fears was a State Senator, that Gen. Hutchinson's nickname was "lion." At first Fears thought he had said "lying" but the other General explained that it was "lion" because Hutchinson was always on the prowl. Hutchinson probably never married. He was apparently able at his job, but unlucky in love. The other General was the Commanding Officer of the Strategic Air Command, and apparently a very capable officer to reach the rank of Four Star General without much actual combat. Anyhow, he knew Hutchinson when he was serving as Gen. Russell Daugherty some-where. Daugherty also knew Lt. Gen. "Moose" Harden, and Lt. Gen. James W. Wilson under whom Fears served his short time in the 92nd Bomb Group. It all makes for a very interesting life, but with this knowledge and 90¢ one can get a cup of coffee.

Most of the people living in the housing project were very poor people. The interior rooms were all painted battleship gray and the floors were concrete, but after painting the bathroom a vivid green, and putting a second hand rug on the floor in the living room the place came to life. Kids were plentiful in the project, and the additional noise didn't bother the Fears as they were young and eager. The people there were kind, and very considerate of each other. Of course this was 1947, before the drug culture had developed fully. There are a few considerate wealthy people, but the poor at that time seemed more humane than the wealthy. William Earl really learned how to envy the rich. Anyhow, with a family to support he was interviewed by the director of the Alcoa Corp. Patent Department in the modest apartment in Cincinnati, and the boss, liking what he saw, hired Fears for the Alcoa Patent Department in New Kensington, Pennsylvania.

While William Earl was growing up in Arkansas and in Sarasota, Florida, he became a natural object of ridicule and torment by teachers and fellow students. This was during the Great Depression, and it seemed at that time people were meaner to each other and especially young people seemed to be less tolerant of each other than they are now. William Earl was really scrawny and had inherited large ears from the Fears clan, which stuck off from his head. Uncle Fred and Uncle Edward, the twins, had great big ears and bulbous noses and William Earl is convinced that these physical impediments and appearances contributed to their failures in life. While in grammar school, the other big kids and non-tolerant teachers seemed to pick on this "big-eared kid." His grades were poor because he was not encouraged. The big kids called Earl Jr. "Ears," "Dumbo," and like names. One fellow student in grammar school in Jonesboro, Arkansas, (unknown to William Earl) ran up behind Fears on his way home one day and broke a rotten egg over student Fears' head. William Earl had no idea who the other student was because the other student ran away very quickly. This treatment made a lasting impression on Fears, and really left a scar on his entire personality. Fears' life was a complete failure in his grammar school days and part of his high school years. Fears attended a public high school on the Eastern Shore of Maryland while living with his grandmother trying to make a better life for both of them. He got the same treatment from the older boys even there. In fact, one evening when Fears was playing with several boys around Ocean City, Maryland, three or four grabbed Fears, held him down under the boardwalk, took out his penis and rubbed sand on it. Fears' own cousin Freddie was in the group and Freddie even thought it was fun. The only one who didn't enjoy the alleged fun was Fears himself.

LAW SCHOOL TO PITTSBURGH

Our law student was now in his last year of law school, although he had one semester in 1943 before he entered the Armed Forces, and he had attended classes in the summer to rush his graduation, for to him, time was wasting since he had lost three years of his married life, and he wanted to get on with it. By now he had the 180 hours required for graduation, had a "B" average, and had finished all the required courses. The Dean said he would have to attend another semester for the residency requirement, but Fears talked the committee into allowing him to graduate, and so he did in June 1948. Also, he took

Judge Gundlefinger's course for the Bar Review, and took the Ohio Bar Examination, which he passed.

The ears were still not healed completely, but our new graduate had written several corporations asking for a position as a beginning Patent Attorney. Several employers responded with application forms and job descriptions, but a personal telephone call came from Andrew Smeltz, Esq. – Director of the Patent Department of the Aluminum Company of America Research Department. This man was a most congenial person, and he drove all the way to Cincinnati to have dinner with Bill and Belle in their low-cost housing apartment. Anyhow, Andy and William Earl "hit it off," and William Earl was hired on the spot to come out to New Kensington, Pennsylvania, for the position with a starting salary of $5,000 per year, which was a good salary in those days. Smeltz warned Fears that the Pittsburgh area was dirty, that most young families didn't want to work and live in Pittsburgh, but William Earl told Andy, "I think we can handle it." Fears doesn't think he would have gotten the job if he hadn't had the ear operation, and had the big floppy ears put back against his head. In fact, this operation changed his whole appearance, and his luck in life immediately improved.

The young couple packed up what they could carry in their car, sold the rest to a furniture dealer, and Belle was left with the baby and her parents in Accomac, Virginia, until our fledgling Patent Attorney reported to his job in New Kensington and found a suitable apartment in the area. He did find a nice large apartment in Tarentum, Pennsylvania, in an old mansion. The owner owned a furniture store in Tarentum, and had converted the place into three apartments. The owner lived on the first floor, the Fears family the second, and the owner's daughter and her new husband on the third floor.

The second-floor apartment in which the Fears family lived was spacious and quite nice, and the lower floor neighbors (the landlords) were very congenial at first. The landlord's daughter named Polly lived in the third-floor apartment of this old mansion, and she was also congenial. After a couple of months, Belle learned to clean walls with a sort of putty called "wall paper cleaner" in this sooty atmosphere near Pittsburgh. The landlady then began to complain that Belle didn't do her part by scrubbing the laundry room floor in the basement on her hands and knees, and began to annoy Belle, who had enough trouble cooking, cleaning, and taking care of baby Barbara. The community was filthy, for everyone burned soft coal to heat their furnaces because it was cheap, and all the metal smelting plants in the area spewed contaminates into the air. Barbara would play in the yard for a few minutes and return to the apartment absolutely dirty black. Our budding Patent Lawyer complained about all the dirt to an old Alcoa employee about 65 years old. The guy said he loved Pittsburgh and that during the Great Depression it was the cleanest city in the U.S. and that if our young lawyer didn't like it he should move somewhere else. This is exactly what our young friend did. He moved to New York City with his wife and child – with another on the way – and this old guy died of lung cancer a couple years later.

In one town called Donora, Pennsylvania, a lead smelting plant spewed lead particles into the atmosphere, and 15 people died. No wonder Andy Smeltz, Esq., had told our young lawyer that no immigrants liked the Pittsburgh area. This was in 1948 and 1949, before the EPA got involved and started to force counties and industries to "clean up their acts."

In all fairness to Pittsburgh, they did clean up the place, switched to oil and electrical heat and literally ran the polluting industries out of the counties, which may be good or bad economically, but now Pittsburgh is listed as one of the best and cleanest cities in which to live. Our young lawyer tried out his new looks with his ears pinned back and applied for a position with the International Nickel Co. in its Patent Department in its New York City corporate offices. He thought he was bettering himself and his new family. The great one in Patent Law, Anthony William Deller, Esq., had edited the patent law bible, called "Walker on Patents," a huge four-volume edition which had really nothing important in the volumes except the history of Patent

Laws. Deller interviewed our young lawyer, apparently liked his agenda, and hired him on the spot for $6,000 per year. Still this was a good salary at the time.

Chapter 7

AVIATION

William Earl always dreamed of flying an airplane, like most young boys did back in the Depression Era. He remembers living in Sarasota, Florida, in the early '30s, and there was a grass-surfaced airfield near Sarasota. An Army Air Corps pursuit squadron was stationed there. They had beautiful orange and blue colored open cockpit biplanes, and were practicing landings and take-offs with their white flying scarves – Eddie Rickenbacker style – flowing behind them from their leather helmets with goggles. When Earl Jr. was a teenager, he saw his first three-engined transport. This was a Ford Trimotor made of corrugated aluminum skin, with three engines of the pull type. They were early Wright radial engines. The crew during the Depression Era was carrying passengers up for short rides for 50¢ per person. William Earl had no money, so he talked the crew into allowing him to sweep out the aircraft if he could go for a ride, which he did. What a great thrill it was for an "ole country boy." Later in life while living in Berlin, Maryland, William Earl got his first opportunity to handle the controls of a Piper J-3 fabric-covered airplane with floats attached. The airplane was owned by one Lee Savage from Chincoteague, Virginia, and flown by a pilot at that time named Tom something-or-other. Tom, at the request of William Earl, flew the aircraft down Sinepuxent Bay to the farmhouse where Aunt Myrtle and Uncle Frederick spent their summers. The fledgling student pilot circled the house and the pair in the aircraft landed the floatplane in the Bay and taxied up to the shore in front of the Humphreys' property. Aunt Myrtle and Uncle Frederick came down the dock path to greet them. Uncle Frederick was the first Army Solo Pilot in 1909, flying the Wright Airplane under the tutelage of Orville Wright; so he was thrilled to see us. I think he decided then and there to try to get William Earl into the U.S. Military Academy.

The records show that Uncle Frederick was the first Army officer to solo the Wright Airplane, and perhaps the first to win his wings in the new Air Service. Col. Lahm and Brig. Gen. Foulois about 1940, when the U.S. was gearing up for war, were spot promoted to Major Generals in the U.S. Army Air Corps, and the rest of the information about Uncle Frederick has been dealt with.

Uncle Frederick, during WWI, wanted to go to France like Capt. Eddie Rickenbacker and try to become a combat flying hero. But being very bright, he was sent by the Army to MIT where he was to teach aeronautics to the brilliant air minded Army Officers. Of course, at this time little was known about aerodynamics. Uncle Frederick, just before WWI, was assigned to Mexico to help capture Pancho Villa. Lt. Foulois tried to use the airplane in that revolution, but it was a failure. Aunt Myrtle went to Mexico with Uncle Frederick, and lived a rugged existence with him in a tent. After the Mexican campaign and WWI, Maj. Humphreys wanted to make the Air Service a career, but the Army and Navy brass decided airplanes were useless to the armed forces. Gen. Billy Mitchell, chief of the air service, tried to prove their folly by sinking a battle ship with a single bomb before their very eyes. This infuriated the "brass" and Gen. Mitchell was court-martialed for insubordination and stripped of all his "goodies." There was no more air service for the military until the 1930's; so uncle Frederick resigned his regular commission, took a job with a family medical company, and accepted a commission in the New York National Guard in the Corps of Engineers. He became the Regimental Commander of the 102nd Engineer's Regiment, and then retired in 1940 as a Brigadier General at age fifty-seven.

If Uncle Frederick had not died in 1941 in Miami, he could have probably reached the rank of Four Star General. Both Lahm and

Foulois were spot-promoted from Colonel and Brigadier General, respectively, to Major Generals. Lahm took over the West Point of the Air in San Antonio, Texas, and Foulois assumed command of the 1st U.S. Army Air Corps at Andrews Air Force Base in Maryland. Foulois just died about 35 years ago at age eighty-five in quarters at Andrews Air Base. He had never married. They have named a convention room of Officer's Club at Andrews Air Base the "Foulois Room."

Later in life, when William Earl was in his first year in Pennsylvania Military College, he met a cadet whose uncle owned the Luscombe aircraft factory nearby. One weekend the two cadets went to the factory, and flew in a new Luscombe. It was a beautiful monoplane with one engine, but only side-by-side seats. This aircraft was very advanced at that time, for it was all metal, and stressed for several Gs. William Earl had a wonderful ride, and his love of aviation was renewed. There are some Luscombe Silvaires still in operation, but the company is no longer in existence. About this time, the P-40 pursuit plane was being built by Curtiss aircraft company, and the B-18 bomber was being built by Boeing Aircraft Company in preparation for the coming inevitable WWII. William Earl had just entered Yale University to study engineering, starting in his sophomore year. During his study of courses he took an elective course in aerodynamics. He remembers the professor demonstrating with mathematics that a body could never pass the speed of sound or it would disintegrate. It's fortunate that Dr. Werner von Braun and Gen. "Chuck" Yeager weren't students in that class, or they would have been completely discouraged.

During the course of study at Yale, William Earl continued to fly in some kind of airplane whenever he could get a chance. By the year 1941, just before the attack on Pearl Harbor, Lockheed Aircraft Corporation had started building a twin-engined fighter aircraft called the P-38 Lightning, and Boeing Aircraft Corporation started building the B-17 "Flying Fortress." During the bombing of Pearl Harbor, most of the P-40 pursuit planes were destroyed on the ground, and so were the "Fortresses." The Navy and Army commands had simply lined all the aircraft on the taxiways in neat rows, and it was simple for the Japanese to wipe them out in one or two passes. The Commanding General of the Army, and the Commanding Admiral of the Navy were both reclassified and returned to the U.S. in disgrace. The Admiral's name was Kincaid, and the General's name was Short. Then President Roosevelt with Congress declared war on the Axis powers, and the aircraft industry blossomed. The best heavy bomber remained the B-17 "Fortress," and the two best fighters were the P-47 Thunderbolt (built by Republic Aviation) and the P-51 (built by North American Aviation). William Earl tried to enter the Naval Aviation Cadet program but couldn't pass the difficult eye examination required by the Navy. The Army Aviation Cadet program was full, and was accepting no new trainees into the army in 1943, except through the existing ranks of the Army. The fledgling aviator did the next best thing to get into aviation: he took a job with Wright Aircraft Corp. in Cincinnati in a foundry casting cylinder heads, and housings for the Wright R-2600 radial aircraft engine. These engines were finally assembled at this plant, and shipped to the aircraft plants for installation in the B-25 Mitchell medium bomber, and other aircraft. William Earl was still trying to get into aviation in the armed forces; so quit his job with a 2-B deferment, volunteered for induction, entered as a private, and finally arranged an assignment to the Army Air Corps as an Aviation Cadet hoping to enter pilot training. Because he had an engineering degree from Yale and had experience in building aircraft engines, they assigned him to the cadet engineering training program for training in that field; so instead of being a pilot war hero with a B-17 crew in combat he was commissioned a Second Lieutenant with an engineering officer's MOS designation. Anyhow, he was now an officer in the Army Air Corps and somewhat of a war veteran back home.

It is interesting to point out that Lee Savage, because of his prior aircraft pilot experience, got a commission in the Army Air Corps as a First Lieutenant Service Pilot. These were wings with an "S" in the shield. He flew all kinds of aircraft as a ferry pilot all over the U.S. Most of the students from Yale who entered the Army and Navy aviation ended up getting killed in training or killed in combat. Had William Earl entered his flying career early in combat he probably would have been killed, wounded, or ended up as a prisoner of war. It's most interesting how fate deals out life in different ways to different people. One reason William Earl wanted to attend the USMA was that it had its own flight training facility known as Stewart Field, and in '42 one could graduate from the academy with his pilot's wings. One Col. George Buck from Mississippi graduated in the class of '42 from the Military Academy, married a lady from Accomac, Virginia, named Jane Ross. They made a handsome couple, and raised four girls. George served in WWII, and was an authentic war hero. He ended up in a P-51 Group in Italy and became a fighter ace and was wounded, but became a Squadron Commander and was promoted to Major. He returned to the U.S. and the U.S. Air Force then put him through the University of Michigan where he received his Master's Degree in Aeronautical Engineering, and later became the Commanding Officer of Holliman Air Force Base as a Colonel. He had a heart attack and was discharged with a disability. He is now deceased. Another West Pointer graduated from the Academy with his pilot's wings, and flew B-17s in the 92nd Bomb Group in England where William Earl served in the combat theater. This fellow's name was Victor Cherbak. He had flaming red hair, and got to be the Operations Officer of the 407th Bomb Squadron. They promoted him to Major just before the war ended. Col. Wilson, the Group Commander was a West Pointer, and saw that Cherbak was promoted fast. The non-West Pointers used to tease about the WPPA, standing for the "West Point Protective Association." Both these men were very good combat pilots and leaders, as they were trained at West Point. There is a 92nd Bomb Group Association to which William Earl belongs, and it is believed that Col. Cherbak is now deceased. Guess he remained in the U.S. Air Force, and continued his career there until he was promoted to Colonel.

After the new Fears family had settled in Accomac, built a house and built a medical office, and William Earl had bought a small law office in the Courtyard (by now Barbara and Brad had become seven or eight years old), William Earl visited a place called Kellam Field with a small airport with grass runways. He found an instructor pilot named George Colona who was the pilot for the Virginia Marine Resources Commission and operated the fixed based in Weirwood, Virginia. He was also licensed as an aircraft mechanic with the FAA. George had a J-3 Piper Cub in great condition for instructional purposes; so William Earl got George to check him out in the J-3, which he did. After a couple of hours, Fears was soloing the J-3. Then Fears, one Bill Parker, and Lee Savage bought a used Cessna 170 from one "Chuck" Fulton of Pocomoke, Maryland, and built a hanger for it at a single runway grass field called McMath field near Onley, Virginia, and hangered the Cessna there. This was an all-metal 4-place aircraft with a powerful 6-cylinder Continental engine. Fears checked out in this aircraft and was issued his pilot's license by the FAA about 1954. Savage already had an active license, and then Parker got his. The aircraft was flown a lot by all three owners, and without any mishap for several hundred hours. Now this Lee Savage was the same pilot from Chincoteague who had owned and operated the floatplane back in the '30s when Fears first flew in it. Savage was no longer active as a pilot, for he was over ninety years old, and has recently died. Fears is now eighty-one years old, and no longer has a qualified pilot's license. In 1958, Savage and Fears flew this aircraft from Onley, Virginia, to Cuba, before Castro took over Cuba and expelled Batista. On the way to Florida, they planned to land at Homestead at a small civilian airport shown on the map, to visit some Virginia folks running a business in Homestead, Florida. But in flying over the private airport, they saw that it was being "bulldozed," and was no longer active. Over in the distance was a huge airport with long runways. The map indicated that this was an Air Force Base. Fears noticed a small white Piper aircraft, obviously not military, take off; so Fears and Savage assumed this was being used jointly for civilian aircraft, as was Myrtle Beach, where they had previously landed and refueled.

Fears was piloting the Cessna 170. After seeing the small civilian airport was closed in Homestead, he flew over the Air Force base after seeing the white Piper take off, "buzzed" the tower rocking his wings hoping they would flash a signal light from the tower, either red or green, but there was none. This Cessna had antiquated radio and navigational equipment, and the flyers had no military radio frequency in the aircraft radio; so they had to depend on a green light signal. Since nothing came from the tower, Fears entered the normal traffic pattern and landed on the runway, which must have been 10,000 feet long. He taxied off the runway immediately, and started up the taxiway to the operations office when all "hell broke loose." Here came a command car full of soldiers with automatic rifles pointed at the flyers. Fears shut down the aircraft engine, and he and Savage deplaned with their hands in the air. They were both taken into custody and carried to the operations office, strip searched and interrogated for an hour. Both Fears and Savage fortunately had military ID cards, since both had remained in the reserves. A Major in the security section did the interviewing, and after viewing the IDs of both pilots teletyped personnel in the Pentagon and learned both Savage and Fears were authentic, and were not spies. He then suggested both reserve officers could remain overnight in the BOQ, and have dinner at the Officer's Club. Both men refused, and only had an interest in taking off and heading for Key West, which they immediately did. It appears the entire ruckus was that this Air Force Base was a Strategic Air Command based under the command of Gen. Curtis LeMay, known as "Old Iron Ass." Therefore, the base was restricted, and the Major thought perhaps the visitors were "plants" sent in by Gen. LeMay to test the security of the base. Our errant pilots learned that the General had done this before. The white civilian Piper aircraft that had taken off just before the Fears landing belonged to a flying club on the base for use by base personnel. All this was very interesting and it's exciting to know that our SAC bases were safe from the likes of Fears and Savage, but it was also scary as hell to both men looking down the barrels of those submachine guns.

After leaving the SAC base in Homestead, our Cessna 170 pilots headed for Key West, Florida, and landed there without incident, refueled, checked in and out with U.S. Customs, and headed across 100 miles of open water across the Gulf of Mexico toward Cuba. Fears was flying, climbing to 10,000 feet, hoping if the single engine quit they might be able to glide to one side or the other. Strange how a single engine makes funny noises at a time like this. Lindbergh was a very brave or foolish soul to cross the Atlantic on one engine. The sharks are plentiful and hungry in the warm gulf waters, and it makes one apprehensive when thinking of being eaten by a big fish. Fears recalls an earlier crash of a transport flying from Puerto Rico to New York, in which sharks attacked passengers in the water before they could be picked up by a U.S. Navy ship. Riflemen on the ship fired at the sharks, but a couple of passengers were mauled so badly by the sharks that they died.

In Cuba, the only radio navigational system was the old-time low frequency signal transmitted from Havana. This is the old "A&N signal," and the pilot simply flies on the "null" to the beacon in Cuba. However, our travelers, on seeing the landmass, flew off the beam and headed to a coastal town named Veradero, Cuba. This is a lovely summer resort on the water, where all the rich Cubans and Americans used to stay on vacation. The hotels were luxurious, the food was tasty, and there was a gambling casino operated by the Mafioso known as the International House. The landing strip was a Cuban Air Force Base, and is the place where the big air carriers used to land during the highjacking days because the runway was long enough for takeoff with a full load of fuel and passengers. Our travelers parked the Cessna, tied it down, and entered the town without incident and found the people very friendly.

Our tourists got a great room on the ocean front with two beds with all the accoutrements, including three delicious meals a day for $10 per day each. On donning bathing suits and going to the beach, a shark was seen stranded between the breakwaters and a small island of sand with a channel in which the shark was marooned. Fears stepped into the shallow water, grabbed the shark by the tail, and tried to throw the shark up onto the beach. It didn't work, for this 10-foot-long shark was too powerful for Fears to wrestle. The Cubans watching certainly thought Fears was *tanto* (meaning "nuts" in Spanish). Years later while watching the movie "Jaws," Fears was convinced that he was crazy to have tried this stupid stunt.

Reserve Lieutenants Savage and Fears had a very fine time in Cuba. Savage rented a jeep and motored the two travelers out into the countryside to the sugar cane fields. There they found twelve- and thirteen-year-old girls cutting sugar cane in the fields for 10¢ an hour. This is a hard, filthy job. It appears they first burn the cane before it's cut. No wonder the poor people of Cuba accepted Castro as their hero. The rich vacationers in Veradero were living very well, but the other 90% of the population were miserable. Anyhow, after a week, our Cessna travelers flew home on a very sunny, uneventful flight, and parked the Cessna in its hanger at Onley. This aircraft was silver colored from the natural aluminum skin; so Parker and Fears decided they would paint it bright yellow. This is quite a chore. First, the aluminum is coated with vinegar so the paint will stick, and then a special noncorrosive paint is applied with an air spray gun. The molding around the windshield was taped to keep the paint off the windshield. The aircraft was painted, new numbers were applied, and Fears took the first flight after the paint had dried.

It was a cold day for the takeoff, and on climbing out there was a terrible "pop." It scared the hell out of the pilot Fears and – after discovering what had happened – he turned around and returned to the landing strip. In taping and painting the molding around the Plexiglas windshield, the groove in which the windshield expands and contracts had been painted. On the takeoff, when the cold air contracted the windshield, it had no place to go, so it cracked on both sides with loud pops. This scared our pilot, and all learned a new lesson about aircraft. In the Army Air Corps there was a famous expression: "Flying consists of hours and hours of boredom, and seconds of stark terror." This is the truth. Fears flew the aircraft to a repair shop at a Norfolk, Virginia, airport and paid a heavy price to have a new windshield installed, and had the expansion groove freed so the new windshield wouldn't crack as the other had.

William Earl enjoyed his week in Cuba so much that he invited another traveling companion, also an active Army Reserve Captain, named Jimmy Belote, to fly in the same Cessna with him to Cuba in 1959. They refueled in Myrtle Beach, and there met a 70-year-old pilot and his wife flying a beautiful Navion, which was no longer in production, but was the Cadillac of single-engined aircraft flown by civilians. It had been used for the pilot training programs in the Navy. After Fears got through envying this beautiful airplane, our travelers left for Key West to check out with customs. On the way down the Florida peninsula, they ran into a ferocious thunderstorm with torrential rain. No small plane pilot wants to tangle with a Florida thunderstorm, so Fears sought out an airfield. Off to the East, he spotted a concrete runway, and quickly headed for a landing. In the rain he saw some silver wires flash below him on landing. These were high-tension electrical transmission wires, and unmarked because the airfield was no longer in use. This was an old navy auxiliary field used during WWII training. Another few feet lower and our flyers would have been fried. Talk about stark terror! That wasn't all of it, for when the aircraft touched down, the wheels bumped over some "cow flops" on the runway. This was now a cow pasture, but fortunately there were no cows on the runway. When the storm passed, our travelers "shooed" the two or three cows now in the runway off and took off for their next destination. They landed on a small dirt strip right at a motel in Key West. This was used for fly-in guests, and our new guests landed, tied down the aircraft, checked into a double room, and headed for the motel bar for their first *"Cuba Libre"* after the exciting experience just a couple of hours before. After a good dinner and a night's rest our flyers taxied over to the main Key West terminal, refueled and checked in and out with U.S. Customs for the 100-mile flight across the Gulf of Mexico. Fears again climbed to 10,000 feet for safety, and they headed for Havana this time. They landed at the municipal airport in Havana, taxied over to the terminal, tied down the aircraft, checked through Cuban customs without incident and took a cab to the National Hotel in Havana. After checking in they headed for the nearest bar for another alcoholic tranquilizer, which helped calm them some.

Capt. Belote and William Earl then hired a taxicab to take them to the Tropicana restaurant and bar in the center of the city. This was the year Mr. Castro ran the Batista regime out of Cuba. On the way to the Tropicana in the cab, gunfire erupted between Batista's militia and the Castro insurgents. Our travelers jumped out of the cab and jumped over a concrete wall with steps leading to the basement of a building and laid down behind the wall. The taxi driver beat them both over the wall with the comment of *muy peligrosa* (meaning very dangerous) and our travelers never doubted their *chofer*. When the gunfire was over, and all was quiet again, the driver and the travelers resumed their trip to the Tropicana.

That evening the Capt. and William Earl hired another cab to take them to the Tropicana for a great dinner, and the notoriously famous show. The food was great, the rum punch had kick, and the girls were beautiful. The Cuban musicians have a musical beat unlike any other in the world. It's a rhythm crossed between a "samba" and an African beat – really wonderful music, as now evidenced by the Cuban bands and singers now living in the U.S. and making fortunes.

The next day, which was Sunday, our travelers checked out of the hotel, fired up the Cessna, and headed for the lovely resort town called Veradero, which is about a half-hour's trip north of Havana on the coast. Fears landed the aircraft on the Cuban Army Air Base, tied the aircraft down, and headed for the terminal office exit. There, a fat Cuban in a white ensemble wanted to check the papers and wanted

$20 in cash. Fears wanted to know why, since they had paid all fees and perfected clearance papers in Key West. The guy in white said it was Sunday, and this was a special fee for landing. Fears called him a *ladrono* (meaning thief), whereupon the guard at the door slammed a shell into the chamber of his 45-caliber automatic pistol. Capt. Jimmy told Fears, "Pay the $20!" and Jimmy handed the fat Cuban the money. Then off our travelers went to the middle of the town looking for the same hotel Fears and Savage had stayed in before. Fears met the same manager who recognized him, and the same meals and rooms were furnished for $10 per day each. Because of the revolution, the place was relatively deserted.

The week spent in Veradero by our 1959 travelers was delightful with *huevos rancheros* for breakfast and broiled *langostinos* for lunch and dinner. Our travelers even went to the International House to try their luck at the blackjack table. An attractive blonde from Florida joined them. She claimed she had an unseen lucky bird on her shoulder and the bird told her when to bet. Our travelers listened to her bird, put up the money, and won a bit at the table. The bird woman shared in the profits. Before she came along, our tenderfoots were losing. Now the lady found out the travelers were flying back to Key West at the end of the week, and she wanted to ride along as a passenger, and the pilot Fears agreed. However, in the middle of the week the bird passenger showed up for dinner, and our two hosts treated her to a lobster dinner. She hung around and wanted to go swimming at night. William Earl, being young and full of vinegar, accommodated her. When they got down to the water's edge, with no one else on the beach, our blonde protégé took off her suit, and suggested that Fears remove his so the pair could go "buck bathing" with the sharks. Fears got suspicious that more was going to happen, and although he wasn't a prude decided something was too easy and too suspicious. He did not remove his trunks, passed up the invitation, and returned to the room with the lady in the presence of Capt. Belote for protection. Needless to say, the travelers took off for Key West at the end of the week without the bird woman. After landing in Key West and talking to the cute little barmaid at the motel with the landing strip, they learned that the bird woman had yelled rape on some poor sucker on the same beach in Veradero, the sucker had been arrested, and had to pay the bird woman and the Cuban authorities a bundle to get out of jail. Thank Heavens William Earl had the presence of mind to avoid this trap in Cuba. There is an old expression among servicemen, "An erected penis has no conscience," which is usually correct. Our travelers stayed out of Cuban trouble for the rest of the week, and returned to Key West without incident.

Before leaving Veradero and the wonderful hotel, our travelers made friends with the Cuban manager. At that time William Earl was smoking cigars, especially the magnificent Cuban-made cigars. The manager sent a box of the best Cuban cigars to William Earl each Christmas and, of course, William Earl sent him a money order for the same. After Castro took over and screwed up his relationship with the U.S., the U.S. authorities placed an embargo on Cuba, and no more cigars were received. One box was confiscated by the U.S. postal authorities. I guess some bureaucrat in the post office enjoyed Fears' wonderful Cuban cigars. Anyhow, letters were exchanged in Spanish between Fears and the hotel manager for a couple of years, but thereafter Fears' letters were returned and the manager never wrote to Fears again. No more cigars arrived.

It can only be guessed that Castro had the manager imprisoned or killed. However, one thing made William Earl happy. He and Jimmy were watching TV one evening when Castro was using the arena in Havana with his firing squads to get rid of political enemies. Our friends thought they saw the fat Cuban, who had "fleeced" them of the $20, shot by a firing squad in Havana arena. Occasionally, in a macabre way, one is glad to see a little poetic justice triumph. Our travelers returned home to the airport in Onley, hangered the aircraft, and related their experiences to the crowd of bar hangers at the Elk's Club, and the morning coffee crowd at Margarete's restaurant. Of course, no one believed the stories they told.

It's strange that at first the average U.S. citizen, and the U.S. authorities, were sympathetic with Castro until he and his crowd visited the U.S. and had the chicken feather plucking contest at the Plaza Hotel in New York City, and showed their rear ends as Marxist Communists. William Earl studied Spanish, and tried to convince President Kennedy that he should be appointed Ambassador to Cuba, and everything would get straightened out and friendly again. You see, Cuba is such a beautiful country and the people are very friendly, or before the rift they were. William Earl wanted to continue visiting Cuba, and enjoying those delightful Cuban cigars, but then Communism has messed all that up. William Earl even stopped smoking cigars, and never did smoke cigarettes for they are supposed to be bad for one's health. Oh well!

Parker, Savage and Fears continued to fly the Cessna 170 until around 1960. The engine had accumulated lots of time, and was starting to lose power. Fears answered an advertisement from an aircraft engine rebuilding company near Philadelphia, and flew the airplane to this place. The engine was overhauled and Fears went up to fly it back to Onley. The rebuilt engine had so much new power that the Cessna literally leaped off the runway on takeoff. The cost for rebuilding was about $1,200, and the other owners were very happy. A buyer was glad to buy the airplane, for by then too many lawyers had sued the aircraft companies for aircraft crashes in single-engine aircraft. Cessna and Piper were the only small aircraft builders left in the market, and the number of new plentiful "hungry lawyers" started to sue these companies. They stopped building the single-engined aircraft and restricted their production to multi-engined aircraft. The Cessna 170 was re-sold for what the three owners had invested in the aircraft.

Fears had flown the aircraft to many places. One time he flew it to Durham, North Carolina, but when he tried to return to Onley the weather was "socked in." Finally, the light on the control tower indicated a 1,000-foot ceiling, so William Earl decided to take off. The omni navigational instrument was old and in error most of the time, so Fears got under the cloud base at about 800 feet and started home. The terrain in the area is nothing but forest; not even any roads to follow, so Fears thought if he kept flying East he would pass over the Chesapeake Bay and be able to pick up some landmarks. In the haze he noticed a nest of radio towers blinking red near him with the tops of the towers with red blinking lights above him. Then stark terror set in. He expected any moment to collide with a tower or "guy wire" and meet sudden death, so he started to climb like a homesick angel until he reached 2,500 feet in the clouds.

Anyhow, he hadn't hit the towers near Portsmouth, Virginia, and it is still a mystery how the cross winds were so bad it blew the aircraft so much off course. Then Fears called on the emergency channel on the aircraft radio, and asked for help from any station. The tower at Patrick Henry airport in Newport News answered and picked up the aircraft on a radio beacon, and probably radar. They had asked Fears over the radio if he could make a 90 degree turns without spinning in so they could identify him, which he said he could, and he did. They gave him a proper heading to the airport, and asked him to let down 500 feet per minute. In about ten minutes, and at about 600 feet altitude, Fears saw the runway. He landed and taxied to the parking apron, kissed the ground, took a quick emergency "pee," and nervously drank a cup of coffee in the terminal. He reported to the tower on their summons, and no one "raised hell" for he had confessed and made a safe landing without hurting anyone or himself. This is about the time he decided to sell the aircraft, for it wasn't equipped for any kind of bad weather navigation. If one can't afford an expensive aircraft with reliable up to date instruments, with back-up installations, then one should only fly about his own airport, and just for fun, not transportation.

After the sale of the Cessna 170, William Earl continued to fly aircraft, but simply rented one when desired from the local fixed-base operator. He checked out in a Mooney M21, Piper Cherokee 140, and 160, and – without the burden of ownership – flew where he wished to go with better-equipped aircraft. An instructor pilot checking out Fears told other pilots that Fears could hit the end numbers on a runway and "grease one in" without a bump. Anyhow, his law partner (who was a student pilot) and pilot Fears rented a Piper Cherokee 140 to fly to Florence, South Carolina, to take a deposition. Judge Northam was flying from the left seat, and Fears in the right seat. The pair took a passenger to Newport News, and landed without incident. Then on departing for Florence the weather had deteriorated to the point that the cloud formation was low, and visibility bad. Fears suggested that Northam, the student pilot, head for a wide hole up in the blue and get on top of the cloud formation for better visibility. Northam started through the hole, but it closed around them. The aircraft was in a steep climb on full power when the "red stall warning light" came on. Fears took the yoke away from the student pilot before the aircraft fell off into a spin or spiral, after which the gyros would have been dumped, and Fears probably couldn't have recovered, Fears shoved the yoke forward, and built up airspeed to level off the aircraft in flight. Then he slowly climbed up through the crap until he was on top of the clouds with good visibility. He then called Air Traffic Control and got a heading toward Florence. The pair flew onward passing over the omni ranges until they reached Florence. On the flight to Florence, Fears turned the aircraft back to Northam. In Florence the airport was a short field. Northam was all puffed up because he didn't realize the danger of a spin, and was irritated at Fears. Anyway, Northam attempted a landing but came in too high and fast, so had to go around the pattern again. To an aviator there are two useless things and these are "runway behind one" and "blue sky above one." Fears convinced Northam to let Fears land from the right seat, which is a little difficult. Fears came onto the end of the runway at reduced speed, and greased the aircraft on the runway right on the directional numbers. Fears got a ride back to Norfolk on a commercial aircraft from Florence, and suggested that Northam get his cross-country time alone so that Fears didn't make him nervous.

Fears got home by commercial flight and apparently Northam flew the aircraft home without incident. Fears and Northam were law partners for several years. Fears, in the Virginia State Senate where the General Assembly elected Judges rather than by popular election, fought the "court yard provincial powers" to put Northam on the District Court Bench, and did replace an interim-appointed temporary Judge by the name of Honorable George Willis. This was an interesting political fight, but Fears won – not without political damage from the news media, however. They accused Fears of a conflict of interest for putting his law partner on the bench. This was ridiculous, for many General Assembly members had elected their law partners. Besides, Northam bent over backwards on the bench in Fears' cases, and if there was any doubt would rule against Fears to avoid any criticism. Judge Northam retired from the bench after ten years, and is reputed to be one of the best Judges the County has ever had. Judge Northam never took his tests for his pilot's license, and stopped flying. He bought a nice sailboat and spent his time thereafter navigating boats. It's interesting to Fears that Northam never invited Fears to go sailing with him, and Northam then bought a twin-engined power boat of yacht size, and again never invited Fears on this large motor boat either. Fears suspects Northam was still smarting over the aircraft incident. Now Northam has retired on a pension of about $75,000 per year. Fears has been defeated after twenty-four years in the Senate, partly because of Northam's election to the bench, and Fears is now retired from law practice. Also, Northam has stopped boating and has sold his powerboat; but his sons (a medical doctor and a lawyer) have bought another powerboat which Judge Northam uses.

While with the FAA for about a month in Washington, DC, Fears had the opportunity of checking out in the FAA's Piper Comanche 260, which is a safe aircraft with retractable gear and controllable pitch propeller. With everything tucked in, the aircraft will cruise at 160 mph. It was fully equipped for instrument flying. Just one trip, but the FAA instructor pilot didn't release Fears for solo. This aircraft was used by all the FAA employees who had pilot's licenses. At this time, Najeeb Halaby was Administrator, and Nathaniel Goodrich, Esq., was the General Counsel. Fears didn't find it exciting to be a government "drone." To him, each agency was doing some "empire building" and the FAA certainly had more employees in some departments than they needed to do the job. Fears took two months to resign, for one couldn't retire without a hearing to discover the reason. The truth wasn't good enough – that he was "simply bored with the job."

Anyhow, Fears ended up with Avemco Insurance Co., and one Bob Scott in the same rules department quit, and went to work for Page Aviation as its in-house counsel, and a guy by the name of Riley, who had been a prosecutor in New York City, also quit. Riley ended up as an Administrative Law Judge with the Department of Transportation, and we all wonder what happened to the safe ones who were satisfied to spend their thirty years in a no-dismissal job, followed by retirement. The ones who were ambitious and needed more action, and better opportunities, simply quit their jobs for "greener pastures." Even Najeeb became the CEO of Pan American Airlines for at least a year, and it went broke. Najeeb's daughter married the King of Jordan, so she returned to her roots in an Arabic country as a Queen. It is guessed that Najeeb found his fame and fortune someplace else. Najeeb had been a U.S. Navy pilot, and had reached the rank of Lieutenant. He got to know President Kennedy well enough to get appointed Administrator of the FAA, and so did Nathaniel Goodrich, Esq., "feather his nest" by being close to the President. The adage about "being at the right place at the right time" is certainly true.

William Earl was most fortunate to find a job after quitting the FAA. But, in spite of being forty years old, he did find a job with the Avemco Insurance Co. of Silver Spring, Maryland, after an interview with one Samuel Solomon, a wonderful man who was sixty-five years old and had been the CEO of Northeast Airlines, then defunct. Sam had just recently formed this general aviation insurance and financing company, and had good people running the company such as Arnold Johnson who had been with American Mercury Insurance Co. Fears was hired as an in-house legal advisor and claims manager of the company. The company was established and associated with the Aircraft Owners and Pilots Association as some kind of underwriter for them. The company did well, and is still doing well, but Sam was retired by the Board of Directors when Fears was with it, and Fears was promoted to Vice President. While with Avemco, Fears took his instrument pilot's examination, being a written examination given by the FAA, and passed it. He took some hours of flight work in a "Link Trainer" at the A.O.P.A. building, and took some flight instruction from an instrument instructor in a fully equipped Cessna 150 aircraft, and was about ready to take his flight instrument examination when he left Avemco. Avemco owned a Piper Comanche 260, and a Cessna 310 (a fully equipped twin-engined plane that was flown to Florida and to Dallas to Avemco's offices there). Fears got some stick time in these with the hired corporate pilot. Avemco had insured several aircraft that were involved in accidents. On one occasion, a Piper Apache had crashed on takeoff from West Point, Virginia, killing the four people on board. A student pilot was in the left seat, an instructor in the right seat, and two passengers in the rear seats. The aircraft took off – with one engine intentionally cut out by the instructor – did a wing over and crashed near the end of the runway. Of course, Avemco was sued by the dead passengers' families, and had to pay for the hull loss of the aircraft. Fears couldn't find the reason for the crash, so rented a Piper Apache with an instructor, and flew down to Melfa, Virginia, to a usually deserted runway and tried to emulate what had caused the crash. The left engine was cut out on takeoff, trim tab was adjusted, and the rudder was corrected for torque. The pilots had no problem controlling the aircraft. Fears concluded that the student pilot had rolled the trim tab handle the wrong way and when power was applied to the live engine on climb out the torque was too great for the pilot to hold the aircraft level on one engine, and they did a wing over into the stalled wing. This is one of those times when the "pucker factor" is rather high in trying something like this. Later the FAA, after several months of recon-struction studies, decided the instructor pilot was in error and to blame; so Avemco insurance company had to pay for the financial loss.

Sam Solomon let some "sharpie" named Jerry Worthington (who later got killed flying a Piper Comanche 260 in bad weather) talk him into buying an accident and health insurance company, and brought this man in to run that division of the company. But that part of the company lost a fortune in one year. For example, a farmer from Arkansas struck his mule in the mouth with his fist, and broke his fist so badly he claimed total disability under his policy. The company refused to pay, but a jury in Arkansas gave an excessive verdict for the farmer. There were other similar cases, which Fears had nothing to do with. After all the losses the Board of Directors retired Sam and brought in a "real jackass" named Sandy Hardy. Hardy died in his sleep a year later after Fears had left Avemco.

This new CEO had been a vice president of National Airlines and Fears can say nothing nice about this inept fellow. That year, after four years with the company, Fears resigned his job and went back to his law office in Accomac, Virginia. A year after he left the jackass died, and a very capable person named Arnold Johnson was elected by the Board as CEO.

Johnson really knew his business, and the company progressed. Had Fears waited another year he might have got the job as President of the company. One of the underwriters replaced Johnson after he retired; so it could have been Fears. Fears learned later that Hardy was a jackass with National Airlines, and that "Bud" Maytag, the owner of National, relieved this person as a Vice President of National.

After he quit Avemco, Fears did some work as a trial lawyer with a firm in Norfolk in which his friend State Senator Peter Babalas was a partner. One Savory Amato, Esq. (the senior partner of the firm of Amato, Babalas, Briet, Cohen, Rutter and Friedman in Norfolk), had a severe heart attack, retired and moved to Charlottesville to take up farming. Babalas asked Fears to come into the firm and take over Amato's cases primarily for trial.

After a year of this, Fears decided to return full time to his office in Accomac, for his old political enemy Judge Jeff F. Walter had died and a new Judge was on the bench. That year (1967) Fears ran for the State Senate against one E. Almer Ames, Esq., the sitting senator. At the same time, Babalas also ran for the State Senate. Both won seats in the Virginia Senate. They both were considered young "Turks" by the old "Byrd machine bunch" in the Senate, but each lasted over twenty years, and got to be leaders of the Senate with committee chairmanships, and remained close friends.

Then while he was a State Senator, and a retired Lieutenant Colonel, he talked the Wing Commander, Col. Dick Myers, of the First Fighter Wing, stationed at Langley Air Force Base, into letting him fly in an F-15 supersonic fighter. (Richard Myers is now a Four Star General and has been named by President Bush as Armed Forces Chief of Staff.) After about a month, he got a call from the Colonel's office to visit the Flight Surgeon at Langley to take a flight physical. The Flight Surgeon looked into both ends and no one saw anyone else, so after this Fears was cleared to fly. At 7:00 AM he was awakened and carried in a staff car by a lovely woman Captain to the flight operations of the Fighter Squadron, which was Eddie Rickenbacker's old squadron in WWI. An old "Spad," supposedly flown by Rickenbacker, is parked on the apron in front of the operation's office. There he met the new wing commander named Col. "Boomer" McBroon, who had replaced the other wing commander, Col. Myers who was promoted to Brigadier General. McBroon was an Air Force Academy graduate, and he is probably also now a Brigadier General, after taking the First Fighter Wing to Desert Storm and flying combat there.

Lt. Col. Fears was escorted to the operations building at Langley Field, and there fitted with flight suit, G-suit, parachute harness and oxygen mask. They even fitted him with flight boots which actually fit. Then he was placed in a "cockpit mockup," and had to memorize all the buttons and dails in the cockpit, such as how to operate the ejection mechanism; how to buckle up the three belts that are attached to the ejection suit; how to operate and plug into the forced oxygen system; how to operate the radar scope and the radio, and especially the intercom with the pilot in the front seat. The aircraft, which was a two-seated version, was complete with instruments, control columns, and throttles in both cockpits. This is used for training purposes to check out new pilots, unlike the combat version, which is a one-seater. Anyhow, it took about four hours of institution before Fears was released to fly by the instructor Sergeant in charge of the mock-up training.

Fears didn't have to go through the pressure chamber or the centrifuge because of his prior experiences in B-17s during WWII or otherwise. About 1:30 PM Fears and his pilot, a small bald headed Captain with senior pilot's rating (that is, with wings with a star above the wings integrally affixed) reported to the aircraft. The pilot's name was Capt. Van Etten, and Fears understands that the Captain flew combat missions later in Desert Storm. The Captain and Fears climbed up some platform steps for old men, got buckled into the cockpits, and all hoses and electrical cords were connected and checked in working order. The "crew chief" removed the safety pins from the wheels and control surfaces, and the engines were started by the auxiliary starter engine which is an external jet engine to start the main two engines. After everything was checked "OK," the Captain called the tower and was cleared to taxi out to the runway.

There at the end of the runway Cpt. Van Etten called Fears on the intercom and instructed Lt. Col. Fears to push his ejection handle forward to actuate the ejection mechanism. Van Etten told Fears that if they got a fire or engine failure they would have to eject. He said he would release the single canopy and Fears would have to eject first, for if Van Etten ejected first he would burn Fears with his jets; so Fears would have to go first. Mind you, there is a plastic facemask on one's helmet to protect one from a shattered windscreen in case of a bird strike shattering a windshield. Also, the facemask protects one's face from the windblast in ejecting into a 500-knot slipstream. Fears replied that in case of trouble for the Captain to give Fears just a few seconds, and go ahead for Fears said he would "probably die of a heart attack anyhow and wouldn't be able to eject."

All went well on takeoff with their wingman, some Air Force Academy Major, flying wing. His name is forgotten. They fly in pairs as a safety check on each other, and for the purpose of mock combat in the air. Both pilots flew out over the Atlantic Ocean near Nags Head, North Carolina, over a cleared operational area. Then the wingman went off into the "wild blue yonder" with Van Etten chasing the other aircraft on radar. Fears watched on his scope while Van Etten found his target and pressed the simulator button to release a simulated missile at the target centered in the circle in the radar gun sight. This was exciting, and then they climbed to 30,000 feet and went through the sound barrier with the afterburner. There was little noise up front, and Fears noticed little but the airspeed indicator on Mach scale indicating Mach 1.2. All the noise from these aircraft is behind the aircraft, and all one hears from the cockpits is the noise of the wind.

After playing around in the operations cleared area where the Navy and Air Force pilots practice maneuvers, Fears asked Van Etten if they could fly up the Eastern Shore Peninsula to his home area near Accomac. These aircraft cruise at 500 knots and a wide turn puts about three Gs on the passenger. Van Etten called the Air Traffic controllers at Oceana Naval Air Station and they wouldn't grant permission for a low-level flight up the Peninsula. Van Etten told the controller that the passenger was a retired Lt. Col. and a State Senator who wanted to fly over his home; so they were cleared to do it at 2,500 feet. Van Etten asked Fears to watch carefully for other low-flying aircraft, such as crop dusters, for the closure rate is so fast that pilots have to be especially careful at low altitudes. Anyhow, Fears showed Van Etten Accomac, and twice they flew over the Courthouse. On the second trip, people came out of the Courthouse to wave. Some noise must have been made to attract attention, but none up front in the cockpits. Supersonic aircraft can break windows without the pilot even realizing it, but none were broken that day because the afterburners were not fully activated. Then, they headed back to Langley for a very "slick" (perfect) landing.

The Air Force photographers were there, and took pictures of Fears in the cockpit, leaving the aircraft, and a couple more. The Colonel had one picture framed, and gave Sen. Fears a photo plaque with the signature of Col. McBroon, the Commander of First Fighter Wing, and the signature of LTC David J. Morrow, the CO of the 73rd Fighter Squadron from whence came the aircraft and the pilots.

Thereafter, the newspaper headlines read "Senator Fearless Fears Flies in F-15," and then a story. Some disgruntled taxpayer wrote a letter to the Editor of the Daily Press – unsigned of course – complaining that this was a waste of taxpayers' money and that a citizen such as him couldn't get a ride. Fears published a one para-graph reply that if the person would let him know his name and address he would get him such a ride, and would go with him to keep him company, but the disgruntled person never replied. Fears left that flight wishing he was twenty-one again, and could become an astronaut, but that was just being "Walter Mitty" at sixty-eight years old. Fears doesn't know what he would have done had the disgruntled constituent replied.

William Earl, now a retired Lieutenant Colonel from the U.S. Army Reserves, and a Virginia State Senator with a little clout, met a retired Four Star General who had been the Commanding General of the Strategic Air Command. This is the B-52 outfit that flew constant 24-hour missions in the Cold War with Russia carrying nuclear missiles as a deterrent, and protection for the U.S. and its allies. Gen. Russell Daugherty was a lawyer before he entered the service, but was not an Air Force Academy or USMA graduate. There is little known by Fears about his combat history, but he must have had a "lot on the ball" to succeed Gen. Curtis LeMay and Gen. Train, for he got to be the General in charge of the entire SAC. After Gen. Daugherty's retirement, he joined the firm of McGuire, Woods, and Battle in the Northern Virginia Office as a partner. Every year, Gen. Daugherty arranged to have a "SAC-KC-10" pick up some of his political and business contacts, and for public relations SAC would fly them out of Dulles Airport for a visit to SAC in Omaha, Nebraska. On one of these occasions, Fears arranged for his Accomac friend M/Sgt. Billy Bell to go on one of the trips with him out of Dulles. A KC-10 is a huge three-engined aircraft used for midair refueling. It also has about 40 passenger seats in the upper front compartment. Fears boarded with the General and Billy Bell along with the other passengers. The General knew that Fears had aircraft experience, and sent him up to the pilot's cockpit area to sit in the "jump seat" for the take off. This monstrous aircraft is the same as a civilian DC-10, but is a flying petroleum tank. The pilot and co-pilot of this aircraft were both young captains, and the refueling boom operator was a noncommissioned officer. On takeoff, Fears was watching all the gadgets in the cockpit, and suddenly at takeoff velocity there was a "bang bang" on the windshield. The aircraft had struck a couple of sea gulls, and they really splattered on the windshield. Didn't seem to bother the Gen. or the crew, but it scared the hell out of Fears for he was afraid a flock might be ingested into one of the engines. Fears recalled that seagulls had caused the F-80 flown by Maj. Bong (the Pacific war hero who had been relieved of combat duty in WWII after he had shot down forty Japanese planes in his P-38, and had received the Congressional Medal of Honor) to crash. All the instruments in the KC-10 didn't indicate any trouble, so all headed for the Missile Silos in the Dakotas.

On the way out to the Dakotas in the KC-10, it was fascinating to watch the crew of the KC-10 refuel a B-52 in the air. This is done by a crewmember who manipulates a controllable flying boom from the stern of the KC-10, and the B-52 maneuvers into position to accept the boom nozzle, and then the jet fuel is transferred into the bomber. Fears thought what might happen if there were a spark or a midair collision. After the B-52 was refueled, the aircraft landed in the Dakotas somewhere, and the passengers were given a tour through the underground missile silos, and the underground command center. The officers and men wore red scarves and had red backgrounds for their wings. Most of the officers were U.S. Air Force Academy Graduates, and probably were all from the top of their graduating classes. This was very exciting and educational, to say the least.

From here the aircraft took them all to Palmdale, California, and all toured through the B-2 factory where they were building this aircraft through an aircraft consortium of companies. This is the stealth flying wing configuration which is constructed of laminated carbon paper so that radar can't detect the aircraft in combat flight. Also, they told the passengers that this laminated construction is really stronger than aluminum skin. Fears doubts this aircraft will ever be employed in numbers for it is too expensive, and Congress is on a budget-cutting spree.

From Palmdale the KC-10 was flown to Omaha, Nebraska, to SAC Headquarters and the passengers were checked into the VOQ into very fine quarters. That evening all were entertained at the Officer's Club with drinks and dinner, and all was "top drawer." Sen. Fears sat with the CO and his wife, Gen. Daugherty, and a couple of other staff officers.

Fears had a quiet conversation with Four Star General Lee Butler, who was the SAC commanding general then. He was in charge of SAC and all the defense silos which they had just visited. Gen. Lee Butler is an Air Force Academy graduate with a Masters Degree in business of some sort. He was about 50 years old, but appeared only 25. The General was very personable and had good TV features. Fears learned that Gen. Butler has flown nearly every aircraft in the Air Force arsenal.

The next day Gen. Butler spoke for about two hours about the Air Force reorganization which is now his "baby," and no one was bored. The time simply "flew by" and everyone was most impressed. Somehow, Gen. Daugherty was Gen. Butler's mentor, for Gen. Butler affectionately referred to Gen. Daugherty as "Uncle Russ," and so did some other high ranking officers.

The guests stayed two days, and visited the buildings of SAC command, as well as a B-52 and the new B-1 bomber. Sen. Fears boarded a B-1 bomber, and went through the aircraft. He was most impressed at the weapons officer's station. This blind panel is loaded with radar and instruments for the weapons officer to drop his bombs and fire his missiles. This aircraft is designed to follow the terrain at very low level, to avoid radar defenses and to sneak up on the target. The pilot doesn't even fly the aircraft. It is flown by radar, a ground sensitive altimeter, and connecting autopilot. The weapons officer sits behind a bulkhead and can't see the terrain ahead. The whole crew must depend on the accuracy of the instruments, and have faith in the Lord. Fears decided he couldn't handle the stress of flying in this aircraft in actual combat. This replaces the B-52 in SAC operations.

During the return flight on the KC-10, the crew refueled a B-1 Bomber in the air and this was another tense time for Sen. Fears. After the midair refueling, the KC-10 landed at Dulles Airport and all deplaned. Fears had met several interesting people on the flight and kept in touch with a number of them. Sure enough, the Air Force reorganization was adopted under the leadership of Gen. Butler. Even the Military Air Lift Command was reorganized and placed under the Combat Command. Fears got a ride to Spain in a C-5 out of the Naval Air Station in Norfolk. The name is now the "Combat Support Command."

Gen. Butler has since retired, and President Clinton wanted to appoint him as Director of CIA, FBI, National Security, or something like that, but it is believed that Butler didn't want a political job. In Fears' opinion, Butler should have been a U.S. Air Force Chief of Staff.

It's a small world, for the Colonel in charge of Base Engineering (a Civil Engineering Graduate from VPI who had been a Squadron Commander of a C-135 tanker squadron) was on Gen. Butler's staff, and was stationed at Omaha. This young man was one of twins born in Accomac, and entered the Air Force right out of ROTC from Virginia Polytechnic Institute. His father died in a nursing home in Onancock, Virginia. This Colonel's name is Jack Miles, and he is now retired. Sen. Fears located Col. Miles by telephone on the Omaha Base when he was there, and invited him to the club for a drink and to meet Gen. Butler. Miles refused by saying, "There are too many Generals there for me. I don't want to get too familiar with the CO – might regret it," which can be true!

There is another Air Force Ace in Accomac who flew F-86s in the Korean and Vietnam conflicts who is a retired Air Force Colonel named Bill Nelson. He was born in Accomac. He has a son, also a twin, for whom Sen. Fears tried to get a cadet scholarships at VMI. Anyhow, this young lad graduated in ROTC from VMI, couldn't enter pilot training because of eye problems, but did qualify as a Navigator-Weapons Officer, and served in B-52s. He is now a Major and his father, Col. Nelson, tells the Senator that his son is now part of a B-1 Bomber crew as the weapons' officer. He has got to be a very brave young man to sit behind that blind panel without seeing outside, and trusting the pilots and the complicated navigational instruments. But then his father was a brave pilot in combat, and was always on operational flying status piloting a jet fighter aircraft until he retired from service.

There are no more "old bold pilots," for President Kennedy made certain of that. Now you are either promoted, or you are mustered out at a young age; so if one doesn't make General by the time he's fifty years old, he is retired if he has twenty-eight years of service or more.

After Fears returned full time to his Accomac, Virginia, office to practice general law with Westcott B. Northam, Esq., he was elected to the Virginia State Senate. Although he did not own part of an aircraft anymore, he continued to fly as a pilot and rented aircraft from a fixed base operator in Melfa, Virginia, either a Piper 140 or a Cessna 172, when he needed to travel to some distant place.

Then the FAA changed the rules so that one had to undergo a check ride with an FAA inspector every two years to keep the license active, and had to undergo a physical exam by an FAA medical doctor about every two years even for a private pilot's license. To maintain a commercial license, and an instrument license, it was costly and very time consuming. So about 1975 Fears stopped flying altogether because of the expense. From then on, he even had more fun in aircraft.

As a retired Lieutenant Colonel with Class A privileges, he was able to fly in military aircraft on a space available basis. He made trips to Florida and Memphis on C-9s, and rode to Germany and England on C-141s and C-5s. These are huge aircraft for carrying freight, but do have some passenger seats available occasionally.

One trip to Roda, Spain, he flew on a C-5 from Norfolk Naval Air Station. He visited the pilot's compartment, which resembled a penny arcade with all the instruments, lights, and buttons. The pilot weighed about 115 pounds, and had a ponytail. The U.S. Air Force Captain flying the plane was an Air Force Academy graduate, and turned out to be female. Several years before, while imbibing at the bar in the Officer's Club at Oceana Naval Air Station, Fears had a drink with a female Navy Lieutenant with pilot's wings. She was the "spin instructor" on the base – teaching the hotshot F-14 pilots how to recover from a flat spin and other maneuvers. Fears thought she must have had cast-iron inner ears to accomplish this feat. Anyhow, being an old chauvinist, he couldn't believe the females could do this, but has now changed his mind, and has no resentment toward having these ladies participate in combat.

Chapter 8

LAWYERS

When William Earl was a student in Yale studying engineering courses, he was pursuing these courses because they encouraged him to get a job on graduating. Studying law was a "no-no," for in the '40s it was a "father and son" game. The ethics laws prohibited a young lawyer from advertising and most law graduates were glad to find a place in a law firm as a clerk, just to get their feet in the door. There were few blacks and women in the courses or in the profession. William Earl remembers talking to one Henry Kellogg on the train from New Haven to New York. Henry was a real snob for he was a rich kid, being from the Kellogg Corn Flakes family. He was a senior in the Yale Law School, and had been placed in a New York law firm like Case and White, but at no salary. He was entering as a young clerk and it would take two years before he was paid anything. They likely hired him hoping he could be a "rainmaker" and bring in the Kellogg company business, which he probably did. Fears knew another real bright student named Bob Von Mehren, an honor student in Yale undergraduate school, and on his way to Harvard law school. William Earl learned later that Von Mehren had graduated from Harvard Law School, and had been hired by the New York law firm of Plimpton and McLean. Von Mehren did his time as a "legman," and is now a senior partner and head of the litigation section. The big father and son firms had all the law practice, and it was a closed shop for "nobodies." William Earl paid his dues in the Army Air Corps for three years, and thought that with an engineering degree and a law degree the world would be his. He had a semester of law at the University of Cincinnati while working for Wright Aeronautical Corp. as an engineer, and returned to this school to finish the law degree after the war. Cincinnati was a nice city in which to live, but it really was a closed shop with family law firms owning all the practices. William Earl tried to get into one of the few Patent Law firms in Cincinnati, but no luck. He did get hired by Alcoa in Pittsburgh because he had the engineering background, and the next year by International Nickel Co. for the same reason. These were both jobs with little future; so this is the main reason William Earl moved to rural Virginia where he built his own practice, and made a living for his family. He later learned that Patent Lawyers were a "dime a dozen," and there were hundreds of smart guys with science and/or engineering degrees, and law degrees working in the U.S. Patent Office where they were buried in "go nowhere jobs." Also, there were several of these working for corporations doing nothing but patent novelty searches and writing patent applications, and were buried in very non-exciting jobs. William Earl, in his rural general practice, was never bored again for he "hit the ground running," trying murder cases, and all kinds of criminal and civil cases – beating the old law firms at their own game. William Earl's first partner was one Wescott B. Northam, Esq., who had been a Patent Lawyer in the U.S. Patent Office, and then a patent lawyer with Westinghouse. He too had been stymied, and finally moved back to his home area with a wife and two kids and started practicing in a "cubbyhole." He ran for Prosecuting Attorney against William Earl, who was then the County Prosecutor, but he didn't win, but he did cost William Earl his job by splitting the votes so that one Norris Bloxom, Esq., another home boy, won.

William Earl bought an old office building in the Courtyard from a man named Herman Watson, who owned an oil distributorship and a lot of cheap real estate in the '50s. The purchase price was the grand old sum of $3,000 on a note for that amount at 3% interest, and William Earl practiced in this office for several years. Across the street was a dirt lot with an old windmill which provided water for the county buildings. He was able to buy the old house and this lot near the jail. William Earl paid $1,200 for the property bought from an estate. He gave the lumber to another struggling "come here" named John A.H. Davis, who started an insurance and real estate business. Davis was an import from Berlin, Maryland, and had married a local girl as had William Earl. Davis tore down the old house in exchange for the old mantelpiece and the lumber. These items he put in a house in Locustville, Virginia. William Earl had to dig up two large tree stumps, and fill in an old outhouse pit, and then he built a block office building on the lot, in which he practiced law until retirement. This was built in 1961. He brought in Northam, and the firm's name was Fears and Northam. Northam won the County Prosecutor's job by beating Norris Bloxom, Esq., who had defeated William Earl in 1959. This partnership lasted for several years, and Fears won the State Senate seat in 1967 by popular vote. The Virginia Senate elects the Judiciary. William Earl had a difficult political fight to elect Northam to the District Court bench, but won the fight, and Northam was elected District Court Judge in 1979. He remained on the bench for ten years and then retired on an income of probably $75,000, for he had bought his military time, and his twelve years as the County Prosecutor with the retirement system, which gave him over 30 years retirement time. The old adage about "knowing people in high places" certainly paid off for Northam. William Earl still practiced law in the building with a new lawyer named Robert Turner, Esq., and Northam is enjoying his retirement.

When William Earl settled in Accomac in the '50s, a lawyer couldn't advertise – he couldn't even hand out a card unless the person requested it, for the ethics laws prohibited this.

When William Earl settled in Accomac, Virginia, there were only about six practicing lawyers, and these were relatives of other practicing lawyers. There were no "come here" lawyers in the practice. It was a sacrilege for a "foreigner" to open an office against all odds – William Earl did it! There were only 40,000 people in both Accomack and Northampton Counties, with two county seats and two courthouses. In

Northampton County there were only about five homegrown lawyers. Northampton County was more of a "closed shop" than Accomack County. William Earl, while the County Prosecutor, and then in the State Senate, changed things considerably, and "rattled the old boy network cages" somewhat. The population has not increased, but the character has changed. Many New Jersey and New York retirees invaded the Eastern Shore to escape crime and the rat race in the eastern cities. There are now two social sets: the "locals" and the "come heres," and it is a better place to live for both sets.

Some lawyer in northern Virginia filed a suit in the Federal District Court, after he had been charged with an ethics violation of soliciting business. The case went to the U.S. Supreme Court back in the early '80s and to everyone's surprise, and especially the staid old law firms, the Court ruled that a lawyer could advertise as any other business. So now the yellow pages are loaded with full-page ads, and the TV is full of commercials proclaiming the prowess of each lawyer and each law firm. New law schools have started up and the old ones have expanded. Every bright boy and girl now wants to be a lawyer. They are forming new firms like crazy, and the law schools are brimming with "A" students. A "B" student hasn't a chance of entering a highly touted law school like Harvard, Yale, or Virginia. A "C" student is a candidate for a course in plumbing or painting houses. The great TV programs like Perry Mason and Matlock, with all the publicity (and the millions and millions made on the O.J. Simpson trial), have whetted the appetites of all the bright undergraduates to enter a law school. All the bright homeboys have finished law school, and have invaded Accomack and Northampton Counties. There are now more than 40 practicing lawyers, not counting Legal Aid lawyers (which is a breeding ground for new lawyers trying to cut their teeth on practice in each community). Just imagine in a rural area such as Accomac with a ratio of one lawyer for every 1,000 people. The average net income in Accomack County usually doesn't exceed $10,000 per year. The "glitch" is that most of the homeboys coming home have old family money, and they don't have to earn a living practicing law.

Pick up any telephone book and peruse the yellow pages under lawyers, and you will find full-page ads from new lawyers and law firms, and not from the old established reputable law firms. In the small Eastern Shore telephone directory, one will find the big city lawyers from Norfolk, Virginia Beach, and Richmond with full-page ads, listing local telephone numbers of runners bringing in clients for a runner's fee. The ads read as follows (just for a few): "We sue owners of dogs that bite"; "We sue drunk drivers"; "Accident Injury – I'll put the law on your side"; "I'll help injured people"; "Tell them you mean business – The Hurt Line"; "Hurt – I'll get you as much as I can, as fast as I can"; and so on. Many also advertise the millions of dollars they have collected in big verdicts. William Earl feels that these people have cheapened the practice of law, and the public generally feels that lawyers are a bunch of charlatans. William Earl feels they remind him of a bunch of vultures sitting in a tree waiting to pounce on the carrion. Also there is a lot of anti-Semitic feeling because most of the personal injury lawyers advertising as such are Jewish from the big cities. Finally the Virginia Bar Council has adopted an ethics rule that prohibits lawyers from following an ambulance to the hospital and confronting the injured party with a contract just before he or she goes under anesthesia. William Earl has developed a healthy disrespect for lawyers, and especially the new ones touting their wares. William Earl's son is a Medical Doctor, and he is proud that his son is really out there doing good and helping the poor public. The irony is that his grandson, the son of his daughter, is a lawyer. William Earl has tried to discourage him, but the grandson has delusions of grandeur, after watching too many TV programs about being an International Lawyer. Sounds good but William Earl has found out, in his international travels, that the foreign law firms hire American lawyers overseas just to run each office – for England, France, and especially Switzerland, won't admit American lawyers to their courts. England has a division of practice. There are

Solicitors, and Barristers, and it's a "closed shop." William Earl's grandson has graduated from law school now. He didn't have an "A" on his undergraduate record, but has a bunch of "B"s and "C"s. An investigation at University of Virginia finds that the Admissions Committee is requiring a 3.8 grade point average, and an 90+ percentile grade in the Law School Aptitude Test. What this amounts to is that the University of Virginia is filling the classes with rejected "A" students from the Ivy League schools, and there is no room for an average Virginia resident student anymore; Thomas Jefferson didn't intend this!

When William Earl started working for Wright Aeronautical Corporation in Cincinnati, he decided he was interested in patents, and in Patent Law; so he convinced the superintendent of his plant to put him on the second shift. This was January of 1943. William Earl then visited the University of Cincinnati Law School admissions office, and talked with the Dean of the school personally. At that time, there was no LSAT requirement anywhere. This was a later gimmick to help weed out unqualified students. Anyhow, he told the Dean he wanted to study law. The Dean asked him, "Where did you get your undergraduate degree?" and William Earl replied, "Yale University School of Engineering." The Dean simply stated, "When do you want to start classes?" and that was that. William Earl started classes in June, and finished a semester of law before entering the Armed Forces. When he was separated from the armed services, he immediately returned to Cincinnati, and finished his requirements for his degree under two years, and graduated in the upper third of the class with a "B" average. One of his professors, a "crusty" old adjunct professor practicing law in Cincinnati, stated to the class, "You 'A' students will make professors; you 'B' students will make Judges; and you 'C' students will make money." This is true! William Earl voted for the funding and the accreditation of George Mason Law School in Arlington, Virginia, when he was in the State Senate, because one of his young friends was a student, and a professor was a Commander of one of his Reserve Units. His name was Gen. Conrad Philos, who was an adjunct professor. The student is now the Prosecuting Attorney of Accomack County, and was the law partner of Fears for several years. The County Prosecutor, in undergraduate college with Fears' son, had played more than he had studied, and was a "C" average student, but did well at George Mason Law School. Now George Mason is requiring high grade point averages of students, as well as high scores in the LSAT (for the uninitiated this acronym stands for Law School Aptitude Test). In reviewing the brochure for his grandson, Matthew, who studied law, he finds the old professor was right; the professors at George Mason are honor graduates of Yale and Harvard University Law Schools, with now some kind of Master's Degree from some other place. They each have been on the law school law review, and have published a paper or two of no great importance, but that is the "name of the game" to become a law school professor. William Earl wishes he were still in the Senate where he could do something constructive for the average undergraduate wishing to enter any graduate school in Virginia.

William Earl's son wanted to be a Medical Doctor. He had served in the U.S. Army as a Second Lieutenant in the Infantry during the Vietnam conflict, and had a very difficult time entering any Medical School. His mother, Belle, graduated from MCV (Medical College of Virginia) and is a retired Medical Doctor. His grandfather graduated from the University of Maryland, and was still practicing medicine when he died at the age of eighty-three. Brad couldn't get into medical school in Virginia because his undergraduate grade point average was too low. He took a very difficult year of studies as a graduate student at James Madison University, and got a "B" average and so the University of Virginia Medical School admitted him. Brad did graduate from medical school, and practiced medicine in Northampton County for about 16 years, as an Obstetrician-Gynecologist, and was head of the department. William Earl was in the Virginia State Senate when all the Vietnam Veterans were being discharged, and many of them wanted to go to Virginia graduate schools. However, the schools were taking out-of-state undergraduates because they could get the high grade point graduates from Ivy League schools, and could collect the high nonresident tuition to make the trustees look good financially. William Earl felt that State-supported graduate colleges in Virginia should give priority to Virginia residents, for State-supported colleges should be for Virginia taxpayers' children. William Earl learned that the University of North Carolina colleges and universities, and the University of Delaware, restricted those graduate colleges to 15% nonresident students. So, with some sentiment in the Virginia General Assembly, he introduced legislation that would restrict Virginia State supported graduate schools to 15% nonresidents. An avalanche descended on him in the Education Committee in the Senate. All college presidents and deans descended on the committee against the legislation, and all the media editorials lambasted William Earl for his alleged stupidity. The senior Senator, Sen. Edward Willey from Richmond, and Chairman of the finance committee, said publicly to Fears, "What are you trying to do, destroy quality education in Virginia?" To which Sen. Fears replied, "No, I'm trying to get Virginia students into Virginia Graduate Schools, which I believe Thomas Jefferson, the founder of the University of Virginia, intended when he established the University." Anyhow Senators Edward Willey and Hunter Andrews were both powerful adversaries, and the bill was defeated in the Education Committee. Sen. Willey is now deceased and Sen. Andrews is still living, although he was defeated for re-election in 1994. Sen. Willey had a son named Edward Willey, Jr., Esq., who practiced law in Richmond, and because of his father's clout and prestige the son represented some of the most affluent people in Richmond, but made bad investments for them to lose about 40 million dollars, and thereafter shot himself. Sen. Willey died before this happened, which was fortunate for this would have broken his heart, as he doted on his son and his son's wife. If the reader recalls, this Willey widow was the one who was involved in the harassment flap with President Clinton. This too would have been a great disappointment to Sen. Willey. Everyone admired him greatly, and Sen. Andrews was a fine leader. Andrews knew more about Virginia government, especially finances, than anyone. He was such a curmudgeon however that he could not get elected Governor of Virginia, but he should have been. Sen. Fears didn't like Andrews personally, but would have voted for him for any public office, for like all those "in the know," Sen. Andrews was very smart, and was a great leader, even though many people disagreed with his governmental philosophy at times, such as this education bill for the benefit of good Virginia students.

For several years after the education bill was defeated the admission committees were sympathetic to Virginia students, but they are right back at it again. A family with wealth named Bayly-Tiffany, from the Eastern Shore of Virginia, left a scholarship to the University of Virginia to help Virginia Eastern Shore students get an education. The Tiffany will specifically restricted the scholarship money to Eastern Shore of Virginia resident students, but it was learned that the officials were using the money for the "brainy" non-resident students from out of state. George Walter Mapp, Esq., threatened the University trustees with a lawsuit and it worked for a while, but William Earl still believes they are using the funds to support nonresident students. After his bitter experience with the legislation attempt, he's leaving the Bayly-Tiffany problem to other disgruntled parents and grandparents of the affected students from the Eastern Shore of Virginia.

There are too many lawyers, and too many schools turning out law graduates like "Chiclets from a gum factory," and the public and businesses in this country are fed up with lawyers. There is no business, person, or property safe from the hordes of lawyers. Statistics show that the U.S. has 70% of the world's lawyers, and in Washington there is one lawyer for every 500 residents. One can hardly blame all the young lawyers who open offices, now that they can advertise their services. None of the young lawyers want to work for the large law firms either. To survive in this climate, a young lawyer has to be a "rainmaker" and bring in clients with money connections, or be brilliant as an associate, and do all the work for the senior partners. The young lawyer might get to be a senior partner in ten years, but now with the increased life span, they each work to support the retired senior partners and their surviving spouses. William Earl's advice to all the young lawyers is to go out on their own, open an office and "hit the ground running." We don't really need any more lawyers, but we do need good and able carpenters, plumbers, electricians, bricklayers, plasterers, motor vehicle mechanics, and the like, but the youngsters all want to carry briefcases, and not get their hands dirty. William Earl is taking computer courses at the Community College, and is reading books entitled "Windows for Dummies," and the like, for there is still hope that he can make a living in his twilight years in something besides the practice of law. When friends ask him if he is still practicing law he replies, "No, I don't practice law anymore; I already know the law." The cliché about "Old lawyers don't die or retire, they just lose their briefs" is certainly true (and this at least gets a laugh), for the application of the law by a lawyer isn't fun anymore; it's treacherous. The politicians, clients, family, friends, schoolmates, and anyone looking for an "easy buck" will sue a lawyer for almost any reason, and can usually win the suit in front of the present juries. The practice of law for the general rural practitioner commenced in the 1970s to be a burden, for legislatures began to meet every year, and changed the laws so much that one had to spend large sums just to keep up with the codified law changes. Then, in Virginia and some other states, intermediate courts such as Virginia Court of Appeals were established, and a new set of publications such as the Court of Appeals books hit the program. William Earl while in the State Senate did not vote for the establishment of this Court, for plaintiffs' lawyers do not appeal, for the plaintiffs cannot afford to do so. Most plaintiffs' cases are accepted by lawyers on a contingency fee basis. Only the "fat cats" can afford the appellate process anyway. Anyhow the better grade law students started to specialize in one specific field of law, and tried to enter the urban laws firms, and more and more law schools came into being in every state. It is true that the U.S. has 70% of the worlds' practicing lawyers. Now no one is safe from a frivolous lawsuit and your life, liberty, and the pursuit of happiness are all at risk. The big urban law firms are seeking young, bright, hard-working lawyers to grind it out 16 hours per day; so that the senior partners can play more golf, and perhaps enjoy an early retirement. The quickest way to a senior partnership is to marry a senior partner's daughter, or be the son or daughter of a senior partner, or be so brilliant that one can become a "rainmaker" (this is being a person who can bring lots of business to the firm). Unless a law graduate has exceptional ability, it is a delusion to think the average student can enter a large law firm and expect to become an early partner. When we reached the 1980s with the advent of the computer, the hard working associates and the junior partners now do most of the work and only dream of becoming senior partners.

Chapter 9

ISTRES, FRANCE

After combat was over in England, Fears' bomb group was assigned to a base in Istres, France, to fly in a project known as the "Green Project."

These were interesting times in Istres. We used to load up an airplane with airmen – because of the conditions, the CO would allow us leave to visit Paris, Rome, Africa, and England for some fun. The enlisted men occasionally rode a truck to Marseilles for some drinking, and to visit a really plush whorehouse. The officers flew to Cannes on the Riviera for some rest and rehabilitation. We carried side arms in shoulder holsters in Marseilles and Casablanca, for a couple of soldiers had been murdered, stripped, and thrown into the sea or bay.

My Squadron Commander visited Paris on leave, picked up a beautiful Mademoiselle, and caught the "clap." Had he reported on sick call his career would have ended, for at that time officers were not supposed to do such things. Our Flight Surgeon was upset because he had been drafted from a lucrative surgical practice and stuck in the war. His name was Capt. Kearney and he was from Chicago. His base clinic had a vertical sign which read: "Capt. Kearney's Kold Kapsules: Kures Kolds, Klap and Kleptomania."

He visited the Lieutenant Colonel with the clap, and shot him in the ass with the new penicillin every three hours until his ass resembled a pincushion. Needless to say, the young combat Lieutenant Colonel never went anywhere again on leave until he returned to the United States – won't mention his name for he may still be living (or perhaps his wife is).

The Green Project mission involved setting up an air base on an old desert bed, and all personnel lived in tents, slept on cots covered with mosquito netting (for the mosquitoes would carry one away), took cold community showers maybe once a week, brushed one's teeth from a flack helmet, and drank "battery acid" (cheap grapefruit juice), and ate powdered eggs and greasy bacon for breakfast.

The bomb racks and gun turrets were removed from the B-17 G aircraft, and replaced with plywood seats. Also, oxygen systems were removed so we couldn't fly above ten thousand feet. We flew exhausted combat personnel from Marseilles to Port Lyouty, Africa, where they were off-loaded to C-54 aircraft and flown home via South America. We then flew exiled French citizens back to France. The red dust was so bad on the engines we stuffed Kotex (requisitioned from the WACS) in the air intakes when the aircraft were on the ground. Occasionally, we flew a trip to Dakar, Africa, and to Monrovia, Liberia, across the Western Sahara Desert. We flew between uncharted mountains, and there were plenty of thunderstorms to create a lot of "puke" from the airsick passengers, and to increase one's "pucker factor," but Fears wouldn't have missed all this for the world. All WWII types love to tell war stories, especially to each other.

One nice summer night, 1st Lt. Fears drove his jeep to Istres and removed the distributor cap and disconnected the battery so no one would steal it. The French like street dances, and as Fears could speak some French, he joined in the fun. After a couple of shots of cognac, he accompanied a very small French girl to her room. After hanging his pants and coat over the only chair in the one room in the old French house, he got into bed with the young girl. There was a loud banging at the door, and a G.I.'s guttural voice said, "You get that son of a bitch out of there, or I'll kill you both!" Apparently she had a G.I. American boyfriend, and Fears didn't want to get killed or Court Martialed; this might have ruined his temporary career. The French windows have no screens; they have only lattice blinds which close. This was on the second floor, so Lieutenant Fears gathered up his clothes, put on his shoes, and jumped out the window right smack into a rosebush. He drove back to the base without a conquest, got into the cold shower, and lathered with a bar of old yellow lye soap, and scrubbed all his wounds. His friend, Lt. Jim Casagrande, came into the shower after his evening out and asked Fears, "What happened to you?" To which Fears replied that he had "tangled with a wolverine."

In spite of the red dust ruining the aircraft engines and the scare of crashing in the Sahara, all went fairly well. In fact, an entire crew was lost, including one of Fears' friends, in a crash in the fog while they were landing in Lyon, France. Also, in spite of having red dust up one's nose, in one's ears, and in one's lungs, all personnel made the best of it. There was some pleasure in an occasional flying visit to some place in Europe, and some pleasure in the camaraderie with good friends. William Earl wouldn't have missed the experiences for a better and cleaner life. Before going on any short leave, one had to clean his dress uniform in 100-octane gas taken from the wing tank of a B-17 G.

After all this, William Earl returned to the U.S. via one of Kaiser's Victory Ships. This took two weeks and everyone was seasick except the aircrews, who were accustomed to *mal de mer*, when they sailed through a North Atlantic storm. Fears tried to reenter law school in the east, but no school would give him credit for the courses he had already completed at University of Cincinnati. He gathered his wife and belongings in a trailer and ended up in Cincinnati where a nice little apartment was found near the law school. This school was glad to have another Yale graduate, and another veteran in the class. In fact, one member of his class was a Lieutenant Colonel, with DFC and other decorations for valor.

William Earl has always worked at hard jobs to exist. He had worked as a bellhop, soda jerk, and a "barker" at an illegal game in Berlin, Maryland, just to earn food money. He lived with his grandmother, Alice Virginia Fears, in Ocean City, Maryland, and had to care for her since she was almost an invalid and, of course he had to work long hours at this time. Aunt Myrtle did little but pay his tuition at Friends Seminary in the wintertime.

Lt. Fears finally was discharged from the Air Corps in September 1946, and still had no clothes. The Lieutenant had to wear his uniform until he could afford to buy new civilian clothes. Uncle Edward would give you the "shirt off his back" – but he would take yours too, so he took all of Lt. Fears' civilian clothes. Lt. Fears, by telephone, was reentered in the Law School in the University of Cincinnati for the Fall Semester. He came by to see his wife, Belle, who had just graduated from the Medical College of Virginia with an M.D. degree and had finished her internship. She was practicing with her father in Accomac, Virginia, who was a rural family physician, and she was staying with her parents. They had married when Lt. Fears was commissioned in 1944. Lt. Fears had sent his $404 per month total net income home to Belle, and she had saved $5,000 of it. Our Lieutenant caught a train in Wilmington, Delaware, and had ridden all night in a coach with some other discharged servicemen. All of them had "post traumatic stress syndrome" so the whiskey bottle was passed around. Lt. Fears doesn't remember anything except that he had unconsciously gotten off at Pittsburgh, but the conductor had taken care of him and put him back on the train. The next thing our Lieutenant recalls is coming back alive with black coffee just before arriving in Cincinnati. He had puked all over his uniform, had a terrific hangover, and was generally a mess.

There is one lesson our Lieutenant learned fast; that is, one should have started with a bomb group early in combat, flown lots of missions and survived it all rather than being killed, badly wounded, or be taken a prisoner of war to get promoted in the Army Air Corps. Our Squadron Commanders were all veterans of over 35 combat missions, and each had signed up for a second tour each. Our Group CO was a West Pointer, had over 40 combat missions, and had been wounded twice. He was a full Colonel at the ripe old age of 28 years. The war was winding down, and although Fears did fly with a combat crew on several combat missions, the War with Germany was over in May 1945. The last mission flown was to Pilsen, Czechoslovakia, to hit the "Skoda" ball bearing plant. A first-time crew was blown up by a direct 88-mm antiaircraft shell, on their first and last mission. What rotten luck!

These were real heroes, not the survivors. Fears had hoped to return to the States and be assigned to the B-29s in the Pacific Theater at the German war's end, but no such luck. He was assigned as a replacement Engineering Officer to the group assigned to the Green Project in Istres, France. Each aircraft had to be hosed out after each trip because of the puke from the passengers each way. Fears finally got assigned to a Group Commander from the States, who really appreciated Fears' ability as the then Group Engineering Officer, and gave him a superior rating for the six months, and immediately promoted him to First Lieutenant. The "big-eared ugly duckling" had finally found a commanding officer who judged him for his ability – not his looks. The trip home by boat was in July 1946, landing in Ft. Dix, New Jersey, from where Fears was separated from the service in September of 1946.

After completing his cadet training, he was commissioned a Second Lieutenant in June of 1944. Because no one could buy a new car, he hitchhiked to Accomac, Virginia, and married his teen-aged sweetheart, Betty Belle DeCormis. After a week's honeymoon, he reported immediately to Kelly Field in San Antonio, Texas, for his first duty station – after a cinder-laden, slow, troop train ride on the Southern Railroad to Texas.

He led a nomadic life, going from base to base after this all over the U.S. for various phases of training. Then came the trip he wanted: he was shipped to England on the troop ship Mauritania and, after sweating out the German submarines, arrived as a replacement in the 92nd Bomb Group of the 8th Air Force, called the "Hollywood Air Force" because Col. Jimmy Stewart and Maj. Clark Gable were serving with them.

Like everyone facing 85% casualties, Fears flew several combat missions over Germany and thanked Heaven that the war ended in May of 1945. But then Fears was shipped to Istres, France, and assigned as an Engineering Officer. His job was to oversee aircraft maintenance and to keep the aircraft operating on a mission called the "Green Project." This place was an abandoned German air base located in a valley covered with red dust blown everywhere by the French "Mistrals."

Chapter 10

BLACK & WHITE CONFLICT

William Earl Fears was born and attended grammar school in Jonesboro, Arkansas, where there was racial prejudice continuing from the Civil War. In the 1920s, the blacks lived in one part of the town in sort of an isolated "black ghetto" and the whites didn't mix socially with the blacks. The schools were segregated, and although the white high schools were good enough to get students into the University of Arkansas, or Arkansas State College, the blacks had very poor schools, and poor jobs in the community. William Earl, when he was a youngster, had a very uneasy feeling about this relationship and occasionally played with blacks near his neighborhood, but his mother told him this was not the thing to do. William Earl wondered why in those days, there were black housekeepers, cooks, and waitresses, but no black managers. The toilets and waiting rooms were segregated, and there was no mixing in the restaurants or public swimming places, which were lakes or gravel pits for the white boys and girls.

William Earl lived with his family during the Great Depression in Sarasota, Florida, for a couple of years, and segregation there was even worse than it was in Arkansas. In fact, William Earl can't recall seeing one black person in a public place or on a public beach. When William Earl attended the Friends School in New York City, there were a few blacks in the school, for the Quakers probably have never been racially prejudiced. The Quakers are God-fearing people, and are kind to everyone (except for that "bad apple" Hon. Richard M. Nixon, who was a Quaker and who was proved to be a pardoned criminal). The social aura of New York City was a different matter, for William Earl noticed that the "rich whites" such as the Vanderbilts, Rockefellers, Morganthaus and the Kennedys all lived on the East Side, on Madison Avenue and the like, in townhouses and luxurious apartments, and the blacks lived in Harlem, or in the Puerto Rican section on the upper East Side or the Bronx. William Earl tried to associate with some blacks and Puerto Ricans whom he had met and liked. He noticed when he visited the Harlem area there seemed to be resentment of the fact he was "white" in that area. No one "mugged "him in those days for he was a teenager, and crime wasn't rampant in Harlem at that time.

At Yale, there were races from all over the world, but there were very few "African-Americans" there. The place catered to "rich white boys" from Exeter and Andover Academies, and occasionally a "smart white boy" from a public high school. There was one black in Fears' calculus class from New York City, but this student came from a fairly wealthy African-American family in Harlem and was an excellent student. In fact, this black student got a perfect score in calculus on his final examination. William Earl doesn't recall what happened to this student, but he must have been successful someplace, because he was highly respected among the students and the faculty, and was a brilliant student.

William Earl served in the U.S. Army Air Corps as a First Lieutenant in the 92nd Bomb Group in England, and later in the General Assembly of Virginia, but then the Army was segregated. There was an all-black fighter group stationed in Italy, and they flew F-51s as fighter cover for Fears in the B-17s, and the bomb group was surely glad they were there. These were college-educated blacks who were trained at Tuskegee Institute in flight school. William Earl met some of these pilots in Rome on a rest and relaxation leave. They were intelligent, attractive and better attired than Fears' white associates. The Army ground troops were also segregated, and the blacks seemed to be relegated to the Quartermaster Corps driving trucks or delivering materials to the combat troops.

William Earl finally moved to Virginia in 1951 and opened his office in Accomac, Virginia. There was still much racial prejudice, but not as much as in New York City. The blacks helped elect William Earl as the County Prosecutor in the '50s, and helped elect him to the State Senate in 1967. Fears was one of the first politicians to vote to repeal the poll tax and made several close black friends in the community. In fact, William Earl supported and helped elect a black as the Clerk of the Court in Accomack County. He lost many prejudiced white friends in supporting a young black lawyer for the Juvenile and Domestic Relations Judgeship in Accomack County – and it was one hell of a fight, but the defeated State Senator Fears still had friends in the legislature who supported Judge Bryan Millbourne for the office. Fears also convinced the black caucus in the General Assembly to support Millbourne. William Earl felt this African-American deserved the "brass ring," for he was definitely qualified for the office. William Earl has observed forced affirmative action over the years, and in a way isn't for the allocation of positions as a quota for blacks. If a black is as qualified as a white he should be given the same consideration, and if he or she is better qualified he should be given the position. William Earl feels though that when a black supervisor gets into an organization they are prone to employ blacks to fill every position under them. The black clerk of court usually employs a black each time a white retires, and the black Judge immediately employed a black clerk to replace a white girl, who was rightfully discharged for wrongdoing. William Earl needs to contact Federal Agencies in DC often, (such as the IRS, the Social Security Administration, and the Veterans Administration) and all the employees now seem to be black. He feels that they are really poorly trained employees and lack knowledge in handling his matters. He feels that the black supervisors have been hiring blacks who are less qualified than white applicants and this he resents.

William Earl, having been a State Senator, was asked by the father of a budding Eagle Scout to address the lad's ordination as an Eagle Scout before a group of scouts and their friends and relatives in a church in Parksley, Virginia. The thrust of the speech was to study hard, stay home and help the parents, and behave oneself – the usual stuff which bores young people, but which the parents lap up. Anyhow, as part of the speech, William Earl pointed out that he had never heard of a Greek or Jew being on welfare, nor having illegitimate children. He stressed that they worked and studied hard, possessed high moral standards, and helped one another.

William Earl, at one time, belonged to the AHEPA, a Greek society dedicated to helping Greek immigrants entering the U.S. Some of his Greek friends coaxed him into joining the AHEPA probably for political reasons, but Fears after a while realized that this was a great organization to help Greek immigrants get started. William Earl personally knows a leading Greek citizen in Williamsburg who can hardly speak English. When he immigrated to the U.S. he started washing dishes in a restaurant, but now he owns hotels and restaurants in Williamsburg. He is a millionaire, and another Greek immigrant in Virginia Beach now owns a restaurant and a motel on the beachfront. He was honored by the citizens of Virginia Beach one year as the "King of the Neptune Festival." Anyhow, since there were no Jews or Greeks in the Parksley audience, Fears felt like he was in a refrigerator, and there were no compliments on this great speech.

When William Earl was growing up in Arkansas, Florida, Maryland, and New York City, there was no such thing as "aid to dependent children." If a girl got pregnant in high school, the boy and the girl both got expelled. There was no such thing as food stamps, no allowance for fuel oil or electricity, or any kind of welfare except through charitable institutions. William Earl as a teenager mowed lawns with a push mower for 50¢ per day, and worked as a lifeguard for $20 per week. One simply had to work to eat, and there certainly wasn't any Medicaid, Medicare, or SSI for Social Security benefits.

At first William Earl thought all these things were helpful to the really needy, but now he feels that this has developed a new culture, especially among the minorities. Probably it is because the minorities had a weak culture before all these "goodies" developed. The minorities can progress if they will study hard, develop high moral standards, and relate to the family group, but they are hesitant to do so. People like the late Ron Brown, Congressman Bobby Scott, and a few others have achieved the respect of all whites and blacks. But the whites are alienated by the likes of O.J. Simpson, Louis Farrakam, Jesse Jackson, and other so-called black leaders.

William Earl listened and watched the "Million Man March" in DC promoted by the Islamic leader, Farrakam, and felt this man was so bitter at the whites that his sole purpose was to turn all blacks against all whites. Then came Jesse Jackson, for whom William Earl had respect, but he "rabble roused" the masses into thinking that the reason they hadn't progressed is because of "white supremacy." Fears lost respect for him. The black culture has literally taken over the American culture, for the dress now of all the young people is influenced by the black culture. The black athletes now have taken over all professional sports such as boxing, basketball, football and baseball. This is all right for they are better in these sports, but the money they make is ludicrous. The black music culture has permeated the American music culture so that rap music is all that teens – both blacks and whites – listen to.

William Earl misses the days of pressed woolen trousers, and "weegens," and coats and ties at Yale for dinner. He misses the old days of Cole Porter and Gershwin music, and the day of professional sports when the players were paid well, but the tickets to the game were affordable. He misses the days when the areas in which he lived didn't know what "crack" was. No one can explain to him (in his office between the jail and the Courthouse) why nine out of ten of those committing crimes are minorities, and why nine out of ten in prison for felonies are minorities.

The sociologists will rationalize that all this is because the minorities never had the benefits of growing up in a healthy environment, and that they had no opportunities. If so, why do all of us see on every nationwide news program a leading black commentator, and why do half of the TV sitcoms portray all-black casts, and why do we have the black colleges such as Norfolk State and Virginia Union University all asking for more money; and at the same time insisting on quotas for admission of blacks to the University of Virginia and other state supported schools? The military units are now integrated, and we have plenty of minority Admirals and Generals. They got the "brass rings," and they probably worked for and deserve them.

Colin Powell was a family man, had high moral values, studied hard, and that is why he was No. 2 in his graduating class at the Army Command and General Staff College, and he deserved his "brass ring." But why should many blacks act loud in public, try to beat me into parking spaces to prove a point, push their way into a queue such as in a subway waiting area, and cruise up and down the shopping centers with a "boom box" in the car so loud that it startles people?

There is still strife and conflict in the military between the black and white gangs, and there is still conflict in politics between the blacks and whites. In 1945 William Earl, on one of his flights to Monrovia, Liberia, learned of the beautiful new city of Leopoldville in the Congo. The rubber plantations were flourishing, and the blacks and whites there in 1946 were all relatively prosperous, but the "Maumaus" wanted it all, so they simply went into Leopoldville with machetes and killed all the whites. Now the rubber plantations are gone, and the city is again grown up into jungle. President Mandela seemed to be a reasonable President for South Africa, and things are reasonably quiet there but William Earl has the uneasy feeling that if the "Zulus" and the members of the "African National Congress" ever join, and are armed with automatic weapons, as they are in Yugoslavia, the whites will be annihilated as they were in Leopoldville.

When William Earl came along in the '20s, there was little opportunity for him to get a college education, and the social separation between the "haves" and "have nots" was very distinct. In spite of hardships he did get a college education, and made a chance for himself. The blacks continue to complain of being suppressed, and not being given opportunities to advance. In this generation they have a better opportunity of getting a "piece of the action" than many poor whites, because of scholarships reserved for blacks, and corporate vacancies reserved for blacks.

William Earl visited Rio de Janeiro and saw many Brazilian children about eight years old begging in the streets, and scrounging in the garbage dumps for food. He understands that the generation of lost children in Brazil are brain damaged from lack of good nutrition, and there is no "welfare" there. Here in Brazil about 35 Portuguese families own about 90% of the wealth, and especially the property. Now the "poor" are destroying the rain forests to find a better way of life, but they are really destroying themselves and all of us.

In India there is a terrible caste system, and the "light-skinned" people are prejudiced against the "dark-skinned" people. In Yugoslavia the Christians and the Moslems are bitter enemies, and in Africa the tribes are killing each other in places like Rowanda. There has always been racial or religious prejudice all over the world, and it appears there always will be. The worst example is the conflict between the Israelis and the Arabs. One can hardly blame the Palestinians for in fact, they were pushed out of Jerusalem by the Jewish immigrants in the '40s because the Jews claimed the land from biblical precedent.

There will always be conflicts as it has from the time of Christ. The point William Earl is making is that the U.S. was developed by "minorities," who were suppressed and persecuted in their countries of origin. Is there any doubt that the immigrants cheated the American Indians of their lands? The blacks have as much chance of getting the "brass ring" as William Earl does. The blacks blame the whites for slavery, and forget that the blacks of different tribes in Africa captured other tribal blacks in Africa, and sold them to the slave traders who were probably British Captains. William Earl feels that we should all forget the past and get on with the future, and if a person works for it and deserves the "brass ring" he or she should get it.

One of William Earl's best friends in politics is the ex-Governor of Virginia, the Hon. L. Douglas Wilder, a black who was elected to the Virginia State Senate, the office of Lieutenant Governor, and the office of Governor. He could not have won either office without white voters voting for him because he was the best-qualified candidate in all three cases. Fears served with Wilder in the Senate and was in fact his desk mate. Fears supported Wilder and personally campaigned with him in his district in which there were old-time prejudices. Wilder proved himself as a good Governor and Virginia maintained its "AAA" bond rating. Wilder did not show favoritism to blacks and didn't increase taxes on the whites to support black projects. In fact, because of this, ironically, Wilder helped defeat Fears for reelection in 1991. In the black community around Williamsburg and Newport News, they stayed away from the polls and simply didn't vote because they weren't pleased with Governor Wilder, and they knew Wilder and Fears were friends. Fears knows this because the President of the Young Democrats, a black, supported Fears and visited the black polls on Election Day. He reported this problem to Fears in the late afternoon that day.

It's the age-old problem in politics: "If a politician doesn't give the electorate what they want then they are against him or her." There is truth to the corny old adage: "Here I stand behind the tree – tax the others but don't tax me." If minorities will "knuckle down" and work for it they can realize the fruits of the "American Dream" just as other races have. Great examples are the Koreans, Vietnamese and the Cuban immigrants who have recently immigrated to the U.S. A Korean immigrant was No. 1 in the graduating class at the Air Force Academy, and the Cubans have become prosperous in the Florida business community; a Cuban was even Mayor of Miami. Incidentally, ex-Governor Wilder has a daytime talk show in Richmond on a local radio station and is teaching Political Science at Virginia Commonwealth University. The blacks and other minorities have better opportunities for advancement in this country than any other country, and William Earl wishes they would stop complaining and stop being so prejudiced against the Caucasians, more so than the whites are against them. There are opportunities for all races in the U.S.

Dr. Belle and William Earl over the years have developed a one-acre lawn with rose bushes, a large garden, and twenty-four bantam fruit trees forming an orchard, and all of these need care, not to mention the house and garage. One day, in the '70s, two teenaged "black lads" came to the door and wanted to work. William Earl put them to work and showed them how to use the riding mower and other tools. These lads had another brother who also did some work for William Earl. They were about a year apart in age. The older brothers, Larry and Craig, were school dropouts, and over the years got into trouble with the law. In fact, Larry and Craig served time in the penitentiary for felonies. It is said that Craig has several illegitimate children by different girls, and continues to be a troublemaker. Larry is in trouble much of the time, and it is understood that he also has some illegitimate children.

Perry, the younger brother, finished high school (at the insistence of William Earl) and was employed by Perdue Industries (with the help of William Earl) in a chicken processing plant in Accomac. Perry got a girl pregnant and married her. This didn't last, probably not Perry's fault, for the lady had been married before and had another child whom Perry treated as his own. William Earl handled Perry's divorce case for no fee because he is so fond of him. Perry still works for William Earl on many household repair jobs, and maintenance of the orchard and the yard. William Earl has taught Perry many things and he is like one of the family. He works for the Fears' after his work has ended at Perdue Industries, and on Saturdays when he isn't working at the Perdue plant. Perry has his lunches and dinners with the Fears' in the house with them, and he prays before each meal. Perry is a very religious person and a fine young man with good qualities. The lad's mother and father are hard-working people and have raised other children. 'Perry has progressed well, has good morals, and a great attitude but the other two boys will probably clash with the law again in the future. The parents of these boys did the best they could do in raising their children. One daughter is a Deputy Sheriff for this county and is reputed to be a great employee. Anyone, including a black from a large family, can do well in life if he or she will simply follow the rules and customs, and adapt to the circumstances. It's mostly luck and circumstance! Without the prejudice and possibly some effort, all can fit into society as good useful citizens. Perry is now a supervisor in one of Purdue's departments, and will probably advance further. William Earl told Perry, "Don't die before I do Perry, for I need you too much since I am an old man now." Perry is "true blue" and one of William Earl's favorite people. They are friends, and close friends at that!

Chapter 11

IRS, CONGRESS, MONEY & STOCK BROKERS

William Earl sincerely believes that those who are wealthy have manipulated the system along the way to get ahead, just as the old railroad and "robber" barons of the '30s did. Everyone knows that Carnegie, Morgan, Schwab, Vanderbilt, and Kennedy – the old patriarchs – manipulated everyone to get so wealthy and Heaven only knows how many Chinese and African-Americans were actually slaughtered along the railroad trails. That bad history of the old "robber barons" is long forgotten, and the Carnegies, Vanderbilts, Morganthaus, Kennedys and all the old wealthy families are now highly respected, and with all the money and power they can get anything they want, including political offices.

You also have the "nouveau riche," and this is a different ball game, but Fears feels that they were not completely honest with the system or they couldn't have accumulated all that wealth from "scratch." Fears has always tried to pay his taxes fairly. He prepares his own income tax returns. In 1979, just after a re-election of Fears to the Virginia State Senate, the IRS (and the IRS does this every now and then – that is, target a group of taxpayers such as lawyers or doctors) audited Fears and other Senate members' tax returns.

When Fears was just one day out of the hospital, an IRS agent visited his office for an audit. William Earl explained that he was just out of the hospital from an appendectomy. Fears said, "Your timing is atrocious." The agent smiled and said he would come another time, but Fears said,

"No, I want you to audit my records now. I don't want to sit around here worrying about you." Everyone fears an IRS audit for they always find something wrong so the agent can prove to his or her supervisor that the job is being done, and the agent is worth his or her "salt." Women agents seem to be more aggressive and more annoying than men, but I guess that's to be expected. They are trying to prove their equality to men in the workplace. Sen. Fears isn't convinced that they should be in the IRS with all that power over the mortals trying to get by.

Unless one is born with riches, an inheritance or an angel in the family, or someone outside the family gives one a nest egg to start something; then one has to be a genius of some sort, or be lucky to be at the right place at the right time. Bill Gates, who started Microsoft and made billions by the time he was forty, had something "on the ball" because he started his software ideas at the right time. So did Ross Perot. These men did have some basic formal education though, for Gates at least finished three years at Harvard, and Perot was a graduate of the U.S. Naval Academy. Then there is the other "lucky" type such as Gen. Collin Powell, but even he had a degree in Chemistry, and excelled in Military Science. He simply learned not to aggravate any of his superiors except one old "crotchety" General somewhere in the Dakotas whom all military personnel knew as something of a "nut," and he interfered some against Powell. Gen. Powell, though, usually was simply in the right place at the right time.

Fears recalls a cadet named Dawkins, who graduated first in his class at USMA, was Captain of the football team; an All-American player, president of his class and president of the Student Honor Council. He even went to Oxford on a scholarship and the "Brits" let him play on their "rugby" team, where he was also a star. Everyone said he would someday be Chief of Staff, but somehow into oblivion he went because he wasn't "Calluchi's" associate, or was at the wrong place at the wrong time. Every "guy" or "gal" in Fears' area inherited his or her wealth, or someone gave him or her a "nest egg" to start, except Fears himself and a few others.

The Senator was born in Arkansas on a farm and, like President Clinton, had to "crawl up the steep road" to accumulate any wealth. The lawyer who won the Circuit Judgeship over Sen. Fears had plenty on the "intellectual ball," but his wife inherited a pile of money from some elderly gentleman in Florida (could have been a relative but Fears thinks he was just a good friend). Anyhow, after Judge Tyler's wife inherited this wealth, Tyler built a brand new expensive office, bought a new Cadillac automobile, and brought the "richest" young lawyer in town into practice law with him. This other fellow is named Revell Lewis, Esq., and as soon as he graduated from law school Judge Tyler made him an immediate partner, for he is a "rainmaker."

Lewis' father, William Lewis, had inherited his wealth from his father, and had enough "smarts" to invest his inheritance in "Holly Farms" chicken processing company early on. The father got to be a Vice President of Holly Farms, and sold his interest to Tyson Foods for a fortune. Billy Lewis bought his son Revell the biggest mansion in Parksley, Virginia, on his graduation from law school. Since Billy was President of the local Central Fidelity Bank, he immediately put his favorite son on the local board. The other son of wealthy Bill Lewis received a brand new Jaguar V-12 automobile, and went into the grain business with his father. Now Billy Lewis and his son are making another fortune in the grain business as Associated Farms, Inc. The successful Judge Tyler appointed Billy Lewis (who had also named Lawyer Tyler to the local bank board, and played tennis with him), when Judge Tyler won the Circuit Bench Judgeship to the Board of Directors of the Chesapeake Bridge Tunnel Commission. Fears had "pushed through" the second bond issue for the Authority, over the objections of the leaders of the General Assembly, and got that second bond issue approved. The Finance Chairmen of both houses and the Governor didn't want this bond issue for they were trying to get an education bond approved, and were afraid of the Chesapeake Bay Bridge Tunnel Authority Bond issue, for they felt it would give them too much competition. Fears wanted this appointment to the authority, and felt he could be helpful to the tunnel authority, but Judge Tyler appointed his friend Billy Lewis, after the death of the Hon. Lucieus Kellam, the father of the Chesapeake Bridge Tunnel.

It is also to be noted that before Judge Tyler defeated Fears for the bench election, he was a partner with Revell Lewis, Esq., and another rich fellow named Henry Custis, Esq., whose mother owns half of Baltimore. The firm's name is now Custis, Lewis and Dix (it was Tyler, Custis, Lewis and Dix before Judge Tyler was elected to the bench). This rural community only has about 40,000 people, most of them poor, but these inherited rich fellows created a land and building development bonding company, on the main U.S. Route 13; built a million-dollar office for themselves and furnished it lavishly. Fears calls it the "Taj Mahal" and claims the firm has a huge vacuum cleaner to suck in all the wealthy clients.

Now with the combination of State and Federal Taxes taking 50% of the average self-employed taxpayer's income, it is almost impossible to accumulate enough money, over and above living expenses, to gamble on investments to try to accumulate a small estate. A lawyer practicing with his own office must pay 15.3% of his net income in "self-employment taxes," which is unconscionable. It appears that all those who accumulate wealth had a start with some money, which Fears calls the "critical mass." Take Ross Perot: his wife gave him money from her inheritance to get him started in the software business. In Accomac, one lawyer married a very wealthy lady, and that is how he got his money power. Another lawyer inherited his uncle's practice and his office building to get a start. Mind you, both these gentlemen are leaders of the community and were fine lawyers, but money does attract money. These types are never satisfied for they want it all. It is reputed that somehow two of the local lawyers placed their wives on some kind of payroll, and paid social security taxes on them for years. Now the spouses have been drawing benefits, for they are each over the age of 65. Also, both were drawing Medicare benefits for medical problems but both have died. No wonder the system is going bankrupt. The point is that those who have a start with a nest egg can afford to be entrepreneurs, but those who start from scratch with families to support either must be genii, or have great natural talent such as Frank Sinatra, and even then someone in power had to give him a start.

Another guy who was born in Accomack County opened an office in Accomac to practice law about the same time as Sen. Fears did, but had the local contacts. About four of these contacts were Presidents of local banks, and they made sure only their sons (or other relatives) who were lawyers were placed on their bank boards. These powers would not appoint one Dick Hall, Esq., or Bill Fears to their boards, for they wanted to "hog" all the real estate business, and they did. But Dick Hall's father had made money in real estate in Ocean City, Maryland, because he married a lady with money. Dick Hall, Sr., was a known alcoholic in the Depression Era, and he and Dick Jr.'s mother were finally divorced. Dick Sr. made sure Dick Jr. had his college tuition paid, furnished Dick Jr. a car in college, and generally "doted" on him. Dick Jr. was not without brains, however, and luck, for he had been an attorney with the U.S. Treasury Department after he got his law degree, and had learned a lot about income taxes and how to use all the exclusions and exemptions. Some barrier islands, known as Smith and Hog Islands, were deficient for taxes owed to Northampton County amounting to about $40,000, so Dick Jr. bought them for taxes; then a development company bought the islands from Dick for $750,000. The development company failed, but not before the Nature Conservancy bought the property and guaranteed Hall's mortgage. Dick Jr.'s father then built him a large house on the Chesapeake Bay, and Dick had his "critical mass" to start operating. As an entrepreneur, he took an option on a farm at a crossroads in Onley, Virginia. Acme Stores, Inc., committed to a 20-year lease on a store as the nucleus, and Hall then started building a shopping center with local inexpensive non-union labor. Everyone in the area in business thought he had lost his mind. Dick knew what he was doing and parlayed the $750,000 into a very active shopping center, killing businesses in two towns, and along the highway. He then built a McDonald's, a Burger King and some other buildings which he rents for a percentage of profits. He even built a Comfort Inn motel, and a restaurant (which he also rents for a percentage of profits), which adds to his "Midas touch." Now he has his "critical mass" of wealth to grow with. He was irritated at the "powers that be," and even started a Building and Loan Association with some other money guys and that is now a savings bank and doing well. The bank built a new building on Dick's shopping center property, and he is now retired as Chairman of that Board of the bank. He even has an oil portrait of himself hanging in the lobby as if to say, "kiss my ass everyone." (This reminds me of the huge portrait of Gen. George Patton hanging in the lobby of the Patton Hotel in Garmish, Germany. This is directly across the street from the old SS Headquarters where all the SS Officers rested and recuperated when Germany had all its military power. Patton said he wanted the large portrait so he could get to look across the street to tell the Nazis to "kiss his ass.")

On top of all else, Dick's father died, left him some property worth another fortune, and then his stepmother died leaving him another fortune. How lucky can one be financially? Dick has stopped practicing law, and he and his wife drive Lexus 400s or BMWs and he owns a half-million dollar yacht, which he captains himself. Dick learned about navigation and seamanship as a trained Naval Officer in WWII. Vicariously, Fears envies Hall, for Fears feels if he had the "critical mass" and his present knowledge he too might have got even with the powers holding them both down.

William Earl finally was able to accumulate a little money and tried many ways to use it to make more, but nothing seemed to work. Had he simply bought real estate in the '60s he could have tripled his savings, and had he simply put his savings in deferred tax accounts or annuities he would have at least doubled his investments. But his friends in the stock brokerage businesses, and other financial advisors talked him into investing in the stock market. After dealing with many brokerage houses and his friends, the brokers, Fears has learned so many disastrous lessons he figures he is now a fair financial advisor himself.

The latest fiasco was recently announced on the TV show "60 Minutes." It seems that the very reputable brokerage house, Prudential Securities (or was it Prudential-Bache?) caused many elderly people to lose their life savings. They had an investment called "PB Energy Growth Fund" which was a flop. They told all the old folks that the investment was safe, and that the investors would make money. Fears and his wife each bought $5,000 worth of this "dud." Fears, as a lawyer, was educated enough to file an arbitration request and recovered his wife's money. The arbitrator thought she was a "dummy" and had been taken advantage of, but William Earl lost about $1,200 over time – for the arbitrator decided he should have known what he was doing!

William Earl has invested in "touted" stocks in firms such as Merrill-Lynch, Wheat First Securities, Prudential Securities, Paine Webber and other companies on each commission broker's advice. He feels that no one should listen to a broker when they tout the red-hot stocks and try to give investment advice. One should do his or her own thing. Once a broker for Merrill-Lynch talked Fears into buying commodities, since Fears lived in the country where they grew agricultural products. William Earl invested about $1,000 to start with, and then pyramided the purchases in such things as sow bellies, soy bean oil, wheat and corn. He made a paper profit of about $3,000 in a week, but the broker didn't explain to him that if the market dropped more than five points, trading would be discontinued. The market did drop, over five points, even though Fears had taken the precaution of placing a stop-loss order in at one point below the market value each day. William Earl lost all his gains plus about $3,000 more before he could sell out. What a hard lesson to learn. Unless one is actually a farmer hedging on his own product, one should avoid the commodity exchange probably.

The only appreciation of investments William Earl made was on his own decision, or on sheer luck. In 1960, he was trying to get on the Board of Directors of a small family-owned bank in Chincoteague, Virginia. He purchased 35 shares of stock from an estate, and held it for years, but never got elected to the board. In 1990, the F&M National Bank of Onley, Virginia – run literally by its president, another wealthy lawyer named George Walter Mapp, Esq. – bought the Chincoteague Bank. Fears received 420 shares of stock in this bank in exchange for his 35 shares. Now a son-in-law of Mapp (whom Mapp had put on that board) approached Fears to purchase the 420 shares at market price, but Fears smelled something "fishy" and didn't sell. Then suddenly the bank board merged the F&M Bank with the Mercantile Bank of Baltimore, and Fears learned why the son-in-law probably wanted to buy his stock. Fears received 3,400 shares of Mercantile Bank stock worth $90,000 on the market. It only paid a 2% dividend so Fears sold the stock, paid the capital gains tax, and finally found one "brass ring." But by then he was over 70 years old, and bought treasury bonds with the cash. Fears learned later that the son-in-law had bought all the stock in F&M he could, and made a fortune in profit. His wife, Mapp's daughter, already had more than a million-dollar trust fund left to her by her grandfather, one of the founders of the Smith-Douglas Fertilizer Co., which was later bought by Borden Chemical Company. This really taught Fears a great lesson, for after that he realized that the "inside traders" have a great advantage – but sometimes this can be illegal.

Families like the Kelloggs, Fords, Vanderbilts, Forbes, etc., have probably made their money on knowledgeable "inside trading." Somehow it seems to be legal, but even though Fears is a lawyer he hasn't figured out how it is. Anyhow, Fears now studies investments himself, not depending on alleged financial advisors and alleged stock-brokers for investment advice. There are plenty of phonies out there on the marketplace.

Now the way Fears invests is to gather all the financial advisory sheets he can, listing all the stocks touted by all brokerage houses or mutual funds, and when several of them are touting the same stock, then he buys it. As soon as the mutual funds start selling it, then sell it. This way one, without inside knowledge, may make some profit. But don't forget that with every gain someone has to lose. At 81 years old, as Fears is, the best investment advice for the aged is to now buy U.S. Government notes or bonds, or buy AAA-rated State Municipal Bonds.

Fears feels that if the government goes bankrupt then the country will also go "broke," as it was in 1929. Since Fears started using his own judgment, he has accumulated a little retirement "nest egg" of his own.

Most of one's retirement income in old age only comes from "just plain luck." Fears started working in 1933 when the Social Security Administration only took 3% of one's earnings. There was no tax on self-employment income, no food stamps, and no aid to dependent children. Food was distributed to the needy from surplus agricultural commodities. Now the Social Security tax on Fears' self-employment income is 15.3% and this is just a hidden tax so Congress can cover all its allegedly great programs, and pay legislators $140,000 per year, with a million-dollar retirement package.

Fears recalls when his friend Hon. Tom Downing was in Congress. Tom got paid $15,000 per year, with few retirement benefits. Tom had to continue to practice law to make a living, and that's the way it should be. We should not have professional politicians, but citizen legislators. Anyhow, when Fears started in the Virginia State Senate, he received a salary of $1,800 per year, and when he was defeated in 1991, he was making about $18,000 per year. Now it is a "professional legislature" and not a voluntary citizens legislature. Fears has reached the age of 81 years, but "lucked" into a $1,200 per month income from social security, $800 per month from his U.S. Army retirement and $1,000 per month from the Virginia State Senate. His wife, Belle, receives some from Social Security, and some from the Virginia Supplemental Retirement System for her 12-year service as a local health director. All these retirement incomes were not planned, and were just "plain luck." The planned investments didn't work out because Sen. Fears kept listening to the financial gurus. If Fears' and his wife's combined savings had been invested in annuities, the pair would probably be millionaires.

Fears was the father of the Virginia "State Lottery Law" which passed the Virginia State Senate, and he toured the state of Virginia debating the issue. Ironically, this project helped defeat him because most of the Southern Baptist and Methodist preachers were opposed to the lottery.

The lottery benefits have gone for good causes, and to Fears' delight the big winners have been poor people who really do need the money. The rich do not play the lottery as they feel it's stupid, since the odds of winning the "big pot" are now fourteen million to one. It's true that more people are likely to get killed by lightning. This lottery does give people a little hope, and especially Sen. Fears. He buys tickets every week hoping to win the "big pot" so he can tell all the inherited rich people, whom he usually dislikes, and his political enemies, where to go. Guess this will never happen, but Sen. Fears continues hoping and buying lottery tickets; guess his motive is too bad to win.

Sen. Fears doesn't believe any statement made by any political office holder. All appear afraid to be forthright, and they will tell every special interest group what they want to hear. If an honest man told the public that he agreed with "Roe vs. Wade," agreed with the "Brady Bill," was for eliminating food stamps and aid to dependent children, and for eliminating taxpayer federally funded scholarships – that person would not be elected or re-elected. The very intellectually honest ones, such as Jimmy Carter, Warren Rudman, Mario Cuomo, and Bill Bradley are all out of office or don't want to run for office. No one is sure of the great Gen. Colin Powell, but if he did run for public office the news media would surely discover that he "threw a rock at a bird" when he was five years old. The public wants to be told what they want to hear, not the truth. It is amazing that the Republicans won these last elections for they somehow have convinced the electorate that they are going to save the country and the world, and that the Democrats are "big spenders." How could anyone believe that "trickle-down economics" would have worked? The very rich don't invest their wealth in starting businesses or hiring new workers. They do like Doris Duke did; that is, invest her wealth in tax-exempt bonds or bank CDs. The great actor President Ronald Reagan and his buddy Congressman Dan Rostenkowski got us into the five trillion dollar deficit with passage of the so-called tax reform act of 1986, not Jimmy Carter or Bill Clinton. The book about "President Reagan Sleeping Through History" is interesting reading and, of course, Rostenkowski has been proven to be a liar and a convicted criminal. Many of us agreed with the fair, the great, and those "gimmee governments" who helped develop the "freebie" institutions. We created a new dependent society who uses their food stamps to buy food, but use their own money to buy beer, whiskey and cigarettes. We created aid to dependent children so that promiscuous mothers, and irresponsible and putative fathers could have more illegitimate children; we fostered a new industry in which the taxpayers have to support the elderly in nursing homes under Medicaid; we encouraged children to kill each other in "gangs" and in "turf fights" over drugs. When Sen. Fears was born, there were no "freebies" – no Medicaid or Medicare, no food stamps, and no aid to dependent children. Families took care of the elderly and disabled. In fact, there was no such thing as unemployment compensation or maternity leave. Everyone worked for a living and used his or her money to support the elderly family members and the infirm. Doctors and lawyers were devoted to their professions and did this because this is what they wanted to do, not make lots of money. If the government could get all the "cheating" health care providers, and the "cheating" lawyers, out of the taxpayers' pockets no one would have to worry about Medicare failing, and the budget would be balanced. Sen. Fears may live long enough to see a balanced federal budget, a credit in foreign trade, Israel supporting itself, and the great giveaway society abolished. Ever notice that one can't get windows washed, can't get the yard mowed, and can't get the crops harvested anymore? Everyone wants to go to college at the taxpayers' expense, and everyone wants to carry a briefcase instead of a lunch box or toolbox. One of these days the United States won't be able to pay its debts; all the "goodies" will be cut off, and we'll have a change of government, or perhaps a civil war between races, or the haves and have-nots, or the industrial leaders and the workers. Don't know when, but one of these is surely coming in one way or the other in the equitable reckoning of things.

Chapter 12

EVER BEEN REALLY SCARED?

Most people have had at least one experience in life wherein they have been really "scared to death." William Earl has had a couple of very exciting ones. He credits these with some of his gray hair at an early age. Besides having a pistol stuck in his ribs a couple of times, which created some gray hair, his two most scary experiences are years apart but never to be forgotten.

William Earl had just bought a brand new Ford Thunderbird convertible. It was all black with a red leather interior. This is probably the first new automobile he had owned in his own name and he was very proud of this vehicle. He bought it through the local Ford dealership, which was owned by an old friend of the family – especially of his father-in-law, Dr. DeCormis. The man's name was Harris West, a self-made wealthy lumberman who had money enough after the Great Depression to buy this dealership. The car was beautiful, and only cost William Earl $4,500. When it only had 5,000 miles on the odometer William Earl drove it through the Virginia Peninsula and up Rte. 17 through Gloucester, Virginia, heading for Baltimore, Maryland, on business.

On Rte. 17 in King George County, Virginia, while William Earl was driving at the speed limit of 55 mph, an elderly man and his wife in an old Pontiac sedan suddenly pulled out into the path of the Thunderbird; they were trying to beat William Earl into a left-handed intersectional road. Here they were, immediately in front of William Earl and he had nothing to do but "scotch" his brakes and slide into the front of their car. The traffic in the other lane was heavy coming south and Fears couldn't turn there. To the right were a deep ditch and some light poles, so he couldn't turn there. It took a second or two before the crash. It was before the seat belt laws, but William Earl had his seat belt "locked down" tightly because he knew traffic was heavy. His life passed before him and he wished he had been a better Christian, but there it was: death facing him, for he knew no one could survive this – a head-on collision.

The crash came, and the rear of the Thunderbird spun around so the car was facing the opposite direction. Fortunately, the front bumper was very sturdy steel, and the big V-8 engine absorbed the impact. The other driver had got so far as to be in a turn so the vehicles didn't impact "plumb" head on, but rather hit a glancing blow. William Earl threw up his right arm to cover his face from broken glass and settled down with a badly bruised elbow, caused by hitting his arm against the steering wheel and bending it inward.

When William Earl finally settled down, he got out of his car and yelled over to a service station crew to call an ambulance and a state trooper. Someone yelled back that this had been done. William Earl went over to the other car, which had a demolished front end, just like his new Thunderbird. The old couple had crashed into the windshield with their heads, breaking it and cutting themselves. There was blood all over the front seat, and the two of them were grotesquely lying across each other. William Earl thought they were dead. The ambulance arrived, loaded them in, and sped off to the local hospital. Fortunately, they were both alive.

Immediately after the accident, a Virginia State Trooper arrived on the scene and checked the collision evidence and interviewed William Earl. The outcome of the investigation was that the trooper gave the other driver a warrant charging him with "failure to yield the right of way." Fears had to appear at trial to testify, and the Traffic Judge found the other driver guilty.

Based on the state trooper's report and the outcome of the traffic court trial in King George County, the old folks' insurance carrier wanted to repair William Earl's '62 Thunderbird convertible. But William Earl wanted no part of it repaired. He had to threaten the insurance company with a combined personal injury and property damage suit to get them to buy him another '62 Thunderbird, which they did from a dealer in Portsmouth. This replacement car was a beautiful white machine, with red interior, and had an insert for the rear seat to convert it into a sports two-seater. It had real chrome wire wheels, but they caused William Earl to prematurely get rid of the car later.

A year later, a young Richmond, Virginia, lawyer filed suit in King George Circuit Court for the other driver and his wife against William Earl, claiming William Earl was negligent in driving too fast. Scott Anderson, Esq., of Richmond defended William Earl and the Allstate Insurance Company in the trial before a jury of King George County citizens. Fears had $50,000 maximum liability coverage on each person. After all the evidence was in, the young lawyer from Richmond, representing the man and wife, came over and offered to settle the suits for $4,500. Fears got Anderson aside and told him he only had $50,000 coverage on each, and unless Allstate would agree in writing to assume the excess verdict amount, if one happened, then he wanted the cases settled. Anderson made a phone call to the Allstate authorities and returned to tell Fears they had agreed and told Anderson to go on with the trial. The verdict was for William Earl in each case. William Earl figured the other parties would get a verdict because he was a young lawyer driving a brand new "hot shot" Thunderbird convertible. This old couple even knew the jurors personally, but the jury fooled William Earl with a verdict for him, based on the facts and the law.

After the jury verdict in these cases, William Earl was leaving the Courthouse to go to his automobile, and was on the walkway in front of the Courthouse when one of the jurors called out to him. The juror came up to Fears and wanted to know how his cousin so-and-so on the Eastern Shore was. They had a discussion about the area and William Earl remarked, "I thought surely you would have given a verdict for that couple since they are from over here, and the members of your jury personally knew them. I am a stranger, and a lawyer with a quality automobile." To which the juror commented, "Ah! That old man is the biggest liar in the county, and everyone knows it and you certainly didn't cause that accident." Justice was done! When William Earl was elected State Senator, he got a law passed, and adopted by the Virginia General Assembly to place sanctions on a plaintiff and his or her lawyer for filing a frivolous law suit.

Now William Earl really loved the white Thunderbird. Since the despotic Judge Walter, the only Circuit Judge in Accomack County, made life so miserable for William Earl he took a job in Washington, DC, to make a living. He used this beautiful Thunderbird to commute to the Eastern Shore on weekends, and kept it in a garage serving his apartment in DC, but with all the closeness of parking and other bumps and bangs it got nicked considerably. The chrome wire wheels also caused some problems.

Twice while Fears was driving on the high-speed beltway around DC he had tire blowouts and spun around in the road, scaring the hell out of himself and other drivers. It proved to be that the wire spokes dug into the inner tubes and a blowout would suddenly occur. Instead of having the patience to let the Ford Motor Co. correct the problem by trading those spoke wheels for disc wheels, William Earl spontaneously traded the Thunderbird for a white "American Motors Marlin." The price for the trade was small – William Earl learned later that the dealer wanted this wonderful Thunderbird for himself. William Earl drove the Marlin for several thousand miles, and then gave it to his daughter for her commuting to the University of Georgia where she was attending college. He then bought himself a new Chrysler from a close personal friend in Accomack County.

After many years working in DC, William Earl finally returned to Accomack County to practice law, after his nemesis, Judge Jeff Walter, passed away. He sold his Harley Davidson Tour Glide motorcycle for $6,000 with only 5,000 miles on the odometer, after having paid $9,000 for it. This bike is now worth $15,000. That isn't bad enough, but the wonderful '62 Thunderbird convertible became a collector's item and it is now worth $25,000. Oh well! William Earl, following his usual practice, "sells low and buys high." Now he wishes he had both vehicles for the sport of riding in (or on) them, but it is too late. He also owned a third interest in a four-place Cessna aircraft, which was bought from a friend for $5,000, and sold for $5,000. This aircraft is now worth $50,000! Isn't this great luck?

Our new Second Lieutenant in WWII wanted to get into combat action as quickly as possible for he was only an assistant engineering officer at Hensley Field, Texas, and had additional duties as a Squadron Adjutant and Mess Officer. He read the Army Air Corps Times searching for some program which would get him to a combat theater quickly so he signed up for the Combat Gunnery Officer's program and was sent to Harlingen, Texas, and then on to Laredo for training. This was a brand new program in the Army Air Corps. After graduating from these courses, our happy warrior was shipped on the Mauritania, a troop ship out of Ft. Dix, New Jersey, to the European Theater and held at a replacement depot in Liverpool, England, until he was assigned to the 92nd Bomb Group in Northampton, England. This was February 5, 1945.

After about a week's training, he went with a combat crew on a B-17 G to Kiel, Germany, to bomb some marshalling yards. It proved to be a radar-directed bombing mission so the "flack" was not accurate, and our P-51 escorts kept the fighters off the Group formation. Our new warrior was scared to death, just like all first-timers in combat, but came home with this lucky crew for another time. This position designated Fears as an Assistant Operation's Officer, but the job was really quite useless. But at least our hero had made it to combat and felt as important as a Second Lieutenant could, and there were a lot of new Second Lieutenants in this Bomb Group.

In February of 1943, William Earl was a private in the U.S. Army in a voluntary induction program, he already had experience in building Wright aircraft engines and had a degree in engineering from Yale University. In classification he ended up in the Army Air Corps as an Aviation Cadet. He was assigned for training in Maintenance Engineering and after months of training all over the U.S., he arrived at a small base in Dallas, Texas, as the Assistant Engineering Officer and Squadron Adjutant. He knew he would be stuck here for the duration so he signed up for the new program called "Combat Gunnery Officer." The Mauritania was supposed to be so fast that the German supermarine "packs" couldn't catch it to fire a torpedo. William Earl knew better and kept his fingers crossed hoping they didn't get torpedoed.

Our personnel landed in England and were shipped to a replacement depot. William Earl was assigned to the 92nd Bomb Group which was flying B-17s in combat on daylight missions. William Earl, being a brand new Second Lieutenant, was assigned to the 407th Squadron as the Gunnery Officer, and was assigned to fly occasionally on a combat mission. He kept asking the Squadron Commander when he could go on a mission, and was finally listed on a crew for a mission to Kiel, Germany, to bomb some marshalling yards. At 3:00 AM one morning, he was rousted out of his bunk and he dressed in his long underwear, for this was February and it was cold and damp in England. He walked down to the operations hut, suited up, checked out his oxygen mask and a flack suit with a flack helmet, in addition to a parachute with harness. He went to the briefing and learned where they were going, and the other necessary information for the mission. About 4:30 AM he was taken by Jeep carrier out to the hardstand to the assigned aircraft with the crew and climbed aboard.

It was foggy and the weather was bad, but the Group took off anyway with about 36 planes headed for the "buncher" (a signal area where all came together in formation). After the Group was formed, the 407th was flying low squadron in the Group, which made it more accessible to the German fighters. They headed for the target of Kiel,

Germany. Nearing Kiel, the "flack bursts" commenced all around them. William Earl suddenly realized he could get killed, maimed, or become a POW and for the first time he was really scared as hell.

The group flew over the target on the first pass, dropped its bombs, and then got out of there in a hurry with the flack still following them. There may have been fighter attacks but William Earl was too busy to notice them, and he was happy to get back to the base and end up at debriefing where everyone was interrogated by intelligence officers about the mission. William Earl returned to his barracks after the 8-hour mission mentally and physically exhausted.

The thought of being a warrior suddenly evaporated and now he could only think about getting this war over so he could get back home alive. On the inside of his barrack's door were some pictures of various officers, and he was told these were the photos of those in his barracks who had finished the required number of missions. At first the required number was 25, then 30, now 35! He couldn't see how anyone could finish 35 missions and still be alive. After what he had seen on his first mission, to live through 35 seemed to be impossible.

The "Memphis Belle" was the B-17 with a crew that first finished 25 missions and returned to the U.S. to promote the sale of War Bonds. William Earl knew that the 100th Group, commanded by Col. T.S. Jeffreys of Buckingham County, Virginia, lost all of its aircraft over the Kiel target at one time. Col. Jeffreys is now a retired Major General. William Earl met him in Buckingham, Virginia, and they now exchange letters.

The 100th Bomb Group lost all of its B-17 aircraft again on the raid to Münster, Germany. This was a retaliatory mission to punish the Germans for obliterating an English village. Münster, like the English City, was a historical city with archives of the history of Germany. Münster was practically destroyed with the "firebombs," but the toll on the 8th Air Force was great also. Following that raid, many an airman was buried in the Cambridge England Cemetery, the American airmen's cemetery in England.

The last mission flown by the 92nd Bomb Group was to Pilsen, Czechoslovakia. The British had flown in a Beaufighter the day before and dropped leaflets telling the Germans to get the civilians out of the ball bearing factory named "Skoda," for we were going to bomb the factory the next day. This was in April, and was our last mission. Of course, the Germans didn't remove anyone but the Germans, and they were waiting for us with all the flack batteries they could muster. There were some fighters there too, and for the first time the crews of the 92nd saw a Messerschmidt 260 in action. This was a twin-engined jet fighter which cruised at about 500 knots. It had a 30-mm cannon mounted in its nose and fired on another group in the bomber stream. One unfortunate crew, a brand new crew from the 402th Squadron on its first mission, was hit directly by flack and the aircraft blew up in midair killing everyone aboard. All aircraft got plenty of flack hits. Then the surrender of Germany came in May of 1945, and the 92nd flew no more combat missions. Hurrah!

About the middle of June, William Earl was shipped with all equipment, all 92nd Group men, and all aircraft to a place called Istres, France, to a base abandoned by the Luftwaffe. The group, along with the 384th Group, was to set up operations for a mission called the "Green Project." Our joint mission was to strip all the guns and the bomb racks from the operational aircraft, cover the open ports with aluminum skin, and construct plywood seats in each waist lengthwise, which we did.

The oxygen supply was also removed for we were not to fly the aircraft over 10,000 feet altitude. We were assigned to use the crews stuck in Istres to support the mission. We started to carry ground troops from the staging area in Marseilles to Port Lyouty, Africa, where there was a large Naval Base with long runways. The ground troops were then loaded on C-54s and flown to the U.S., and each B-17 aircraft returned with a load of exiled French civilians to Istres air base where the civilians could be transported to their homes in France. We also dispatched a plane about once a week to Monrovia, Liberia, via Dakar, Africa, where we had small bases and small contingencies.

On one of these trips to Port Lyouty in a B-17 with Fears aboard, they ran into a violent thunderstorm in the Mediterranean, and since this aircraft had no oxygen on the ship the crew had to fly through a thunderstorm at 7,000 feet. The radio operator had a "fish antenna" on a long aerial wire reeled from the aircraft. Lightning struck this antenna burning out the radio operator's short wave radio, and scaring the daylights out of the operator, and all aboard.

There was "St. Elmo's Fire" circling the propellers because of an electron buildup around the spinning propellers. Lightning was frequent and bad, and the aircraft had to be flown manually with the auto pilot turned off, for it was like riding a Brahma bull to keep the aircraft level. When one reached for the metal gang throttles which controlled the four engines, sparks would fly from one's fingertips to the throttles. The instruments were "precessing" and sometimes not reading properly. This trip scared the daylights out of everyone on board, but fortunately on the return flight to Istres it was uneventful. Oh, yes! William Earl was as frightened as anyone, and during this 30-minute storm he thought the aircraft would spin in if things got worse, but it didn't.

First Lieutenant William Earl Fears was now the Green Project combined group Engineering Officer. Istres air base was located on an old desert bed with no green foliage growing anywhere and the personnel had to bring in their water by tanker. Living was very prim-itive and all had to live in tents. There was one hanger building which William Earl and his engineering crew fixed up, patched the bullet holes in the roof, and made into an office area. After all the abandoned land mines left by the Germans were cleared, they started work on the aircraft inside this enclosure. Fears even put a cot in there and slept in the hanger out of the red dust that was blown around by the "Mistrals" all the time. Gauze had to be stuffed into the air intakes on the engines for the red dust could wear out an engine in 250 hours.

This base was situated in a valley and the "Mistrals," sometimes with winds as high as 100 mph, would blow through this valley covering everything with red clay dust. William Earl had thought about making the Army Air Corps his career, but not after this year's experience. The aircrews were really "bitching" for they were afraid to fly the aircraft across the Mediterranean, and – even worse – across the Western Sahara from French Morocco to Dakar, Africa. William Earl had a meeting and told the crews that the aircraft were as safe as ever. To prove his point, he went as a crewmember on a flight to Dakar.

The Operation's Officer of the Group, one 1st Lt. "Jimmie" Casagrande, with Lt. Fears and Lt. Purvis as navigator, headed for Dakar to pick up some personnel. On the way down they came upon the Atlas mountains and, according to the aerial map, one high mountain wasn't even on the chart so this crew flew the aircraft through a valley to reach the flat Western Sahara. About halfway across the desert, the oil pressure gauge indicated zero on the right outboard engine. The cylinder head temperature and the oil pressure gauge remained normal, and the manifold pressure and the RPMs on this engine remained normal; so the engine wasn't feathered. Nevertheless, it frightened William Earl. He doesn't know about Lt. Casagrande and Lt. Purvis, but William Earl will never forget this experience.

Chapter 13

HOW TO GET INTO
POLITICAL TROUBLE

William Earl was elected to the Virginia State Senate in 1967, and was sworn in on January 8, 1968. The old "Byrd Machine Boys" were bitter because their old friend, Sen. E. Almer Ames, had been defeated by the "maverick upstart" Fears. The old Clerk and the Assignment Committee in the Senate put Fears over in "coffin corner" of the Senate chamber by the window. At least Fears could look out at the birds and squirrels in the Capitol green. A "crusty" old Senator by the name of Bill Stone came over to Fears' desk. William Earl thought he came over to welcome him to the Senate. Uh, uh! He came over and told William Earl that he had defeated their friend who was supposedly the most respected man in the Senate, and he resented it. Stone then stated, "Young man, my advice to you is to sit over here and keep your mouth shut." Fears said, "Sen. Ames must have been doing something the electorate didn't like or he wouldn't have been defeated. I'm going to try to do what my voters sent me up here to do, and I surely hope you and the others do not interfere." Stone spun around and positively rushed back to his seat.

The next four years, Fears felt like "a whore at a family reunion" and didn't get anything accomplished. But he surely did enjoy voting against legislation he didn't believe should be passed. This was a redistricting year and old Sen. "Peck" Gray, who was the caucus chairman for the Democrats, got rid of Williamsburg and James City County, and purposely gave them to Sen. Fears. Sen. Herbert Bateman, one of the "darlings" of the Senate (now a deceased ex-Congressman and then a Democrat), wanted to get rid of the upper end of Newport News, for they were mostly Republicans and Herbert, at that time, was a great Democrat. He later switched to the Republican Party so he could run for Congress. Anyhow, Fears inherited everything the powers didn't want and knew well he would probably be defeated in re-election.

Fears ran hard in 1972, with both a Democratic opponent in the primary and a Republican opponent in the general election. He won – to his surprise and everyone else's. Old "Peck" didn't want Williamsburg and James City County, for the William and Mary students were then voting, and the Vietnam War was still in progress, which prompted Congress to give the 18-year olds the right to vote. "Peck" stated, "I don't want those crazy college students voting in my election for they are all liberal nuts." Anyhow, they must have voted for William Earl, because he won.

That next term, old "Peck" died from cirrhosis of the liver, and some of the old "Byrd Machine Boys" got defeated. Fears got along fine with the new Senators and gradually over the years moved to the center of the chamber, finally being seated next to the Majority leader Sen. Hunter B. Andrews. He got to be the Chairman of the Commerce and Labor Committee, and a senior member of other committees, and finally was placed on the Rules and Finance Committees. He was the No. 2 Senator in seniority when he was defeated in 1991.

William Earl blames his defeat on the things he accomplished, and the redistricting in 1991 that added another 10,000 constituents to his already lopsided district. By this we mean he lived on the Eastern Shore of Virginia with a population of little more than 40,000, and ended up with 120,000 in the peninsula counties of Gloucester, York, James City, and the City of Williamsburg, and a bigger chunk of the City of Newport News. This gave him 160,000 constituents, and the 10,000 added were mostly Republican voters. He also blames his defeat on the many legislative programs he voted for or against in the General Assembly.

The way to get re-elected to office is to tell every special interest group and all voters what they want to hear; never vote for any tax; and never vote for a controversial bill. Most of his Senate colleagues have either retired or were defeated. Some of the senior members who were not defeated are Hon. Virgil Goode (now a U.S. Congressman) from Rocky Mount, Virginia; Charlie Waddell from Loudon County (now an Assistant Transportation Director); and Madison Marye from Shawsville. Also, there is Joe Gartlan from Fairfax County, who has since retired. Virgil Goode, Esq., never voted for any kind of tax; always voted against the budget bill each session; and never voted for the referendums on alcoholic beverages by the drink, any bond referendums, and certainly not for the lottery. He always played to the gallery and would have never been defeated. He is now a U.S. Congressman and it is believed a Republican. Charlie Waddell always gives his constituents what they want, and always is on the "side of the angels." Madison Marye's claim to fame is the "forced deposit legislation on beverage cans and bottles," which he annually introduced. The environmentalists love him dearly, but this bill has never seen the "light of day" in the Virginia legislature.

William Earl can't recall any other meaningful legislation introduced by Sen. Marye. Hon. Joe Goatlin came roaring into the Senate with all the "do gooder" bills for women's rights, child protection, strong regulation for day care centers, and all the "apple pie and motherhood legislation." Joe has done more to increase the cost of the government, and put more burdens on private organizations, than anyone in the General Assembly. He gets this legislation through because he is smart, shrewd, and pushy; not to mention that he is also a "workaholic." The really intellectually honest guys have either been defeated or retired.

Hon. Hunter B. Andrews, who was the most honest person in the Senate, was defeated because he made too many constituents mad. Several of his areas wanted to elect school boards, for Virginia either permits the Board of Supervisors or the Circuit Judges through an Electoral Board of School Trustees to select the school board members.

This had more to do with Andrews' defeat than any other legislation. Fears and Andrews represented overlapping counties and cities and Fears stuck with Andrews. William Earl feels that Andrews was absolutely right. The system in Virginia is a good system to insulate the school board members from the public so they will not play politics. Anyhow, the enabling legislation was adopted by the "yes men" in the General Assembly, and now under the present system the complaints are even louder.

Under the elective system, every disgruntled mother who thinks her child should have gotten an "A," when the child didn't deserve it, will run for that school board. To emphasize the point, those in public office in the Virginia Senate who were really intellectually honest have been defeated or retired. The same attitude exists in the U.S. Congress. William Earl feels that Bill Bradley and Warren Rudman were very intellectually honest representatives, and they both simply got disillusioned and quit. Bradley later ran for President of the U.S. The public needed them, but the public didn't realize this. It used to be that the electorate sent representatives to the legislatures to do a job, and before the television commentators started having such an impact the electorate allowed the legislators do the job as they saw it. Now every voter thinks he or she can do a better job, and they are really defeating their own purposes. The quality of the representatives in the State Legislatures, and in the U.S. Congress (in the opinion of William Earl, speaking from years of experience) is not as good as it was 25 years ago.

The State of Maryland and the District of Columbia have had a lottery for many years. Accomack County, Virginia, is on the Maryland border, and many people were going to Maryland to play the lottery, but while they were there they also shopped for groceries, clothing, and the like; even automobiles and high priced items. William Earl philosophically doesn't believe the states should be in the "gambling business," but since they are and were in Maryland and DC, he felt that these states were "bleeding" money from Virginia. So he introduced the "lottery referendum" in the State Senate.

All prior Governors, and then-Governor Balisles, were opposed to the "Lottery Legislation." Sen. Fears appeared on TV stations to debate such notables as the perennial candidate Marshall Coleman, Esq., and others in opposition to the lottery, but the lottery referendum was accepted by the people by a heavy majority vote. Now it supplies the Commonwealth with about 400 million dollars per biennial budget. The rich people don't play the lottery for the odds are too great, but the poor people have much hope and do play, and occasionally one of the poor folks wins. What a lift for them! They buy new homes, new cars, and put their children through college. When William Earl learns of these needy winners, it takes the sting out of the argument that this is a tax on the poor and is a regressive tax. Anyhow, this is a piece of legislation blamed partially for Fears' defeat, where the blame should be rightfully placed, and all the staid religious people, including the Protestant ministers turned on William Earl and helped defeat him for reelection in 1991. William Earl thinks it is a great program, and the ones in government who were opposed to the legislation, such as Governor Balisles, surely don't mind spending the money on their "pet projects." In other words, the hypocrites surely are proud to spend the money and this goes for all those in the General Assembly who were so-called "great Virginians" and therefore opposed the lottery legislation.

William Earl was one of the "ringleaders" who supported the enabling legislation so that Virginia could enjoy "liquor by the drink," and the other "sin" legislation ("paramutual" horse racing and betting) for Virginia has bred some of the best race horses in the world, and he believed in the industry, but again the religious fanatics got into the act and punished him for supporting this legislation, which also helped defeat him in 1991. But the urban areas are now vying for arenas and coliseums, sports centers, and public racetrack locations. They seem to have forgotten the moral and religious implications now that the areas are becoming prosperous.

"Liquor by the drink" did more for Virginia's prosperity than any legislation in the past 50 years. There are large coliseums in Virginia Beach,

Hampton, and Richmond, and William Earl has been long forgotten for his efforts in this great "sinful" but prosperous legislation. Most of those "Great Americans" who voted against all of this legislation are still in the General Assembly (or in the U.S. Congress, for obvious reasons) and really doing little there other than telling their constituents what they want to hear. To stay there, "just don't rock the boat!"

In the rural areas of Virginia, old junk cars were piling up all over the landscape and no one seemed to be doing anything about the problem. A very nice lady by the name of Amine Kellam of Northampton County, Virginia, called the "junk lady" by those critical of her, kept pushing Sen. Fears to introduce legislation to do some-thing to solve this unsightly problem. This lady is wealthy, and comes from a very fine family. In fact, her father was a beloved country physician and her mother was an accomplished violinist. She worried Sen. Fears so much that he introduced a bill to provide each juris-diction with a $12 payment from the state coffers for every junk car the county or city picked up, had shredded, and delivered to the junk metal buyers in the cities. Peck Iron and Steel Co. proved to be the best place to sell the cars. This company would send a compactor to an area, compact the cars, and deliver them to the shredder in Richmond.

Sen. Fears had to first find the state funds to do this, so he got a bill through the General Assembly placing a $1 additional tax on auto-mobile titles to supply the money, and then got the "junk car" recycling legislation passed. Accomack and Northampton counties disposed of 9,000 junk cars through this legislation, and most of the other areas in Virginia also benefited. In fact, Accomack County realized a $50,000 profit for their efforts one year. Mrs. Kellam received state and national awards for her efforts, and Sen. Fears lost many votes to his opponent who accused William Earl of being a "big tax" proponent. Anyhow, Sen. Fears got no awards, and most people don't even know such a clean-up law exists. Sen. Fears in the legislation inserted a provision placing the funds in a separate account for this purpose, and intended to repeal the tax after all the junk cars had been removed from the landscape. The fund had accumulated a five million dollar amount, and Sen. Edward Willey, the old crusty chairman of the Senate Finance Committee, needed money to balance the budget one year so he simply "bled" the fund of this money to do so, over Sen. Fears' objection.

The next session Fears had a floor battle to increase the payments to the cities and counties to $50 per shredded car – because of the increased costs over the years, the jurisdictions had lost interest in doing the job. This also kept Sen. Willey from taking the money to balance the budget. Sen. Willey is now dead and the legislation is still working well. A new industry has been created for the junk dealers in picking up the cars and shipping them to Richmond to the shredder for a part of the $50. This is just another example of a legislative program developed by a member of the legislature for the good of all, but legislation which penalizes the patron for placing another tax on the public. The public doesn't give a damn about cleaning up the junk; all they can remember is that Sen. Fears put a new tax on them.

Over the past 15 years, the number of operating automobiles and especially pickup trucks has doubled on the highways, and since we now have an affluent society, every high school student drives an automobile to school instead of riding the bus. Now, as was bound to happen, the accident and death rate on the highways have increased considerably. A new organization was formed called MADD ("Mothers Against Drunk Drivers") and they have made a powerful impact on the political process.

William Earl doesn't blame them for being aggressive in their causes for each member has lost a loved one in an auto accident. But they have blamed alcoholic beverages for the problem. Young people, and especially young single boys and men, have caused a high percentage of the accidents and deaths because of speed and reckless driving. It isn't all caused by alcoholic beverages. The insurance companies have the statistics to prove this. Anyhow, alcoholic beverage consumption has been blamed by the MADD group for almost every death on the highway, which just isn't true. They have been so aggressive the members of congress and the state legislators have been frightened by them so much that legislation is now in effect to try and solve these problems. The jails are full because of mandatory incarceration laws prohibiting driving with small amounts of alcohol in the driver's tested blood percentage. The MADD folks got State Sen. Bobby Scott to introduce legislation to lower the blood alcohol content to 0.08% for an automatic conviction for operating an automobile under the influence of alcohol, for the breathalyzer machine test actually is a presumption for conviction. This may have cut down some on the number of accidents, but many people – such as social drinkers, and even Priests – are convicted of drunk driving by being stopped at road checkpoints and tested. These people are perfectly able to operate an automobile without danger to others. Scott introduced this legislation by an amendment to another bill on the floor of the State Senate knowing that all the "scared ones" would be afraid not to vote for this amendment.

Sen. Fears was the only one who stood up in the Senate and argued against this bill. He made a long speech. He pointed out the weaknesses of the legislation and demonstrated that we will be "throwing the baby out with the bath water." During this speech, with tongue in cheek, he stated that, "If we continue to pass such legislation you are going to take the sport out of drinking – and driving."

This created much laughter in the Senate; the amendment passed anyhow, but was killed in the House Committee. Had the bill gone to the Senate Committee it would have been defeated before it reached the floor for a vote. Anyhow, even though Sen. Fears meant this as an oxymoron, the press had "grist for the mill," and literally "crucified" the Senator for his comments.

This comment by William Earl caused the loss of many votes, and was a big factor encouraging the Republicans to hold a "telephone booth convention" the day before the cut-off date to nominate William Earl's opponent, who defeated him in 1991. This winning opponent did reintroduce the legislation in 1991, and all the "fraidy cats" voted for it. The law now in Virginia is 0.08%, and a lot of fine people are being arrested at roadblocks, and the MADD group is now a heavy political power. Sen. Bobby Scott is now a Congressman, and Sen. Fears is now a "has been" politician. Sen. Fears, again with tongue in cheek, threatens to form a new organization called DAMM ("Dads Against Mad Mothers"), and threatens to spread red, white and blue bumper stickers to advertise his organization. Or maybe it should be "Drunks Against Mad Mothers." The 0.08% legislation may have had a good effect on decreasing the accidents and deaths on the highways, but William Earl doubts this. In fact the Republican oppenent, Sen. Thomas Norment has been arrested and found guilty of drunk driving under his own bill. Sen. Fears believes that alcoholics will be alcoholics, and they will continue to drive even if they are jailed for life. He feels that this restrictive legislation probably only hurts the good citizens. MADD is here to stay and perhaps they are doing some good. Had William Earl been a "yes man" to all the "do gooder" legislation and voted against tax laws, and the budget each year, he would now probably be the Senior State Senator in Virginia!

The Federal Government has or had a program for the construction of state residential care homes for veterans of all wars, and their surviving spouses, under which the "feds" contributed two-thirds of the funds for construction to match the state's one-third. Almost all states built state veterans' homes under the program except Virginia. William Earl tried unsuccessfully for years to get a bill through the Senate Finance Committee to provide matching funds for Virginia to build a veterans' care home but could not succeed. Most of the members of the finance committee were veterans of WWII or the Korean conflict, and very conservative. People like the chairman, Sen. Hunter B. Andrews, a veteran of WWII from the Navy, told Fears, "The veterans don't deserve any more than other people – why should we vote for this money?"

Fears disagreed and kept trying each year. William Earl was the one with the "guts" to sponsor the lottery referendum legislation in the Senate, and the referendum passed. The public voted for the lottery law by a majority and, of course, the lottery became a reality in Virginia. Gov. Gerald Balisles, the then-Governor of Virginia, opposed the lottery legislation, but did sign the bill for it was only a referendum, and Balisles didn't think the public would vote for the law anyway, but to his surprise they did! He appointed a Lottery Board of his friends, including ex-Senator Bill Parkerson, who was also opposed to the lottery program, as well as the other new members of the board who were opposed. He wouldn't name anyone suggested by William Earl, although Sen. Fears was recognized as one of "fathers of the lottery."

After the state had accumulated about $500 million of lottery money Gov. Balisles sent a bill to the floor of the Senate spending all the money on his "pet projects." Before the bill hit the floor for debate, Sen. Fears quietly got all the veterans' representatives he could muster, and told them to wear their hats, badges, and medals to the Senate gallery on the day of the vote on the bill. Sen. Fears amended the Governor's bill to include a first item of $7 million for the veterans' home from the lottery funds. The Senators had to vote before all the veterans in the gallery; so the body voted for the amendment after Fears gave a "scathing presentation." They didn't dare vote against the amendment for obvious political reasons. The vote was 21 to 19. Then Hon. Hunter B. Andrews, the Majority Leader and the Chairman of the Finance Committee, went around the floor and "scared the hell" out of everyone and got enough votes to send the bill back to the Finance Committee, and tried to kill the amendment. Again all the veterans groups put so much political pressure on the members, the amendment was passed by the Finance Committee. The bill then went to Balisles, after the House had accepted it, and Balisles signed the legislation.

Fears believed that Andrews and Balisles planned to get rid of the problem by technically delaying the federal action until the project failed. Sen. Fears found a man in Washington who was a "Veteran of Foreign Wars" activist, by the name of Walter Sanford, and got him interested in the project. Walter knew everyone in Washington familiar with this program and started "pushing" the program through the Washington bureaucracy.

Then Gov. Wilder was elected and he named an African-American lawyer from Arkansas as the Secretary of Personnel. She had gone to law school with Gov. Wilder. Wilder, being a veteran of the Korean conflict, told her to "push" this program through with the Federal Government. Her name was Hon. Ruby Martin, and she did a great job in conjunction with Walter Sanford. The matter went through all the technical hurdles, and the project was finally approved.

Wilder appointed Walter Sanford as Chairman of the "Virginia Nursing Home Board," and the "Virginia Veterans Care Home" was finally built on a site donated by the City of Roanoke next door to the Veterans' Hospital. It is a beautiful home housing about 200 residents. It is now run by private enterprise, and isn't free unless the veteran is totally indigent. In other words, the home substantially supports itself. It cost about $18 million to construct the facility, which was completed in 1992. Sen. Fears was defeated in 1991 and wasn't even invited to the dedication. All the hypocrites who had voted against the home, and Wilder, who supported it, showed up to take the credit. Hon. "Dickie" Cranwell, who was the biggest hypocrite of all the General Assembly members, in whose area the home is located, received great accolades. But he had been of little help to Sen. Fears to get the project through the General Assembly or through Federal Authorities. "Dickie" is still in the house and is, in fact, the Democrat Minority Leader.

Walter Sanford and the VFW members finally recognized Sen. Fears as the real "father" of this project. The American Legion gave Fears no credit, for he had opposed the referendum in the General Assembly to memorialize the U.S. Congress to vote for a constitutional amendment making it a crime to deface the American flag, and they were furious at him and Sen. Andrews for killing this meaningless legislation. Congress voted against the legislation for the same reasons Fears and Andrews voted against the resolution in the State Senate. The political hypocrites, after they realized the nursing home was a reality, tried to force the General Assembly to name the home after one of their favorite sons, a deceased Congressman named Dan Daniels. He was a great conservative son of old Virginia from Danville, who had served in the Virginia House of Delegates, and would not have supported the legislation anyway. Sen. Fears and Gov. Wilder both knew this and stopped this attempt. The home was named the "Virginia Veterans' Care Home," as it should have been.

Finally, poetic justice triumphed, for the Home's Board of Trustees had a plaque made of brass with the inscription, "The Bill Fears Room – WWII Combat Veteran – Virginia State Senator – and Attorney at Law." This plaque is on the wall of the activities room in this new veterans' home. Sen. Fears did get "one little brass ring" of recognition for his efforts. He got another from the Eastern Shore Community College for his efforts on its behalf. He was the guest of honor at graduation, and was presented with an honorary degree in 1993 as an "Associate in Humane Letters," not that he ever wrote a humane letter. With all these plaques and $1.00 he figures he can get a good cup of coffee, but it was not good enough to give him the Circuit Judgeship. Oh well, that's life isn't it?

A political office holder simply cannot honestly commit him or herself on every issue before every special interest group, and continue to get re-elected. When William Earl first was elected to the Virginia State Senate, the requirement for blood alcohol for a DUI conviction was 0.15% and the MADD organization was just becoming powerful. William Earl voted to lower the blood alcohol content to 0.10% because he felt that this was about right, but then the MADD people kept pushing for 0.05%, which is ridiculous. Why not just have total prohibition, and then put everyone in jail for driving with alcohol on his or her breath? The MADD people gave the Senator no credit for voting for 0.10% however.

Then there is the "Right-to-Life" anti-abortion group. Sen. Fears told them he was personally opposed to abortion at any time, but that it had taken the Justices of the Supreme Court years to develop "Roe vs. Wade," and this was in his opinion the best solution to the problem. He told the group that he didn't feel it was right for government to tell a female what she could do with her body, and we should simply leave her to Heaven. These special interest groups are very uncompromising. A political office holder must do exactly what they demand or they will simply vote against the person in block. It's too bad there are so many organizations involved in the political process with so many single issues. Sen. Fears feels that these people will ruin the electoral process in the future, and all office holders will have to be "intellectually dishonest" to get re-elected.

William Earl isn't an ardent environmentalist, and tries to be prag-matic about jobs for people, since he was a product of the Depression Era. But while serving in the State Senate, he did something that was well ahead of the times. In 1979, when the Arab oil producing companies tried to break the U.S., William Earl tried to help the farmers and the environment. He introduced legislation to give the ethanol producers an incentive to produce and sell ethanol-enriched gasoline. The legislation provided a 9¢ per gallon tax refund from the Commonwealth of Virginia for ethanol-enriched gasoline producers. This is gasoline with a 10% ethanol addition (by volume) to a gallon of gasoline for use in automobiles. As we are all learning, this is kinder to the atmosphere in reducing air pollution, and actually helps an engine perform better. Even now, William Earl adds ethanol to his gasoline. It is hygroscopic and absorbs water in gasoline to help prevent water buildup in the fuel system, and actually helps clean out any sediment in the system. Now the gasoline producers have spent a fortune to try to convince the public that alcohol is bad for the fuel system and the automobile's performance but this is simply not true. The legislation was adopted by Virginia, and several ethanol plants were constructed providing many jobs. The farmers had a better market for their grain products, and "wood waste" was used in the distillation process. All was going well until the "sharpies" found a way to ship in alcohol waste products from out of state, and started refining this into 100% ethyl alcohol, and of course tapping the tax coffers of Virginia.

Sen. Edward Willey, the crusty old Chairman of the Senate Finance Committee, and his sidekick Sen. Hunter B. Andrews, who really ran the Finance Committee (for Willey was quite inept in understanding complicated matters), introduced legislation to repeal the Fears ethanol legislation. There was a heated debate in both houses, but the tax benefit for the ethanol producers was phased out over a period of two years, and the legislation expired. The law should have been amended to eliminate the "charlatans," and the philosophy should have remained in Virginia. Now that Sen. Fears is no longer in the legislature, California has learned the wisdom of the ethanol legislation. Los Angeles is requiring its use to help eliminate air pollution and an industry is being developed there. Virginia had the "golden opportunity" under the Fears law to do something good for the environment, to help the farmers in financial trouble, and to stop the Arab oil cartels from taking advantage of the U.S. again. We can all remember the $1.60 per gallon gasoline lines, and in Europe a gallon costs $4.00. One of these days we will probably see $3.00 per gallon gasoline in the U.S., and it isn't far off. This could destroy the economy of the U.S. Sen. Fears isn't remembered for his farsightedness in this legislation, and now Sen. Willey is dead, and Sen. Andrews has been defeated. One of these days the production of ethanol will return, and our pioneer from Virginia will be remembered – maybe!

Chapter 14

MOST INTERESTING TRIALS

William Earl was quite bored with his first job as an engineer in a casting foundry for the Wright Aircraft Engine Manufacturing Co. in Cincinnati, Ohio, and afterward even more bored with his job as a Patent Attorney with Alcoa and the International Nickel Co., but having a wife and a couple of children he had to earn a living and ignore the boredom. He always rationalized that if he didn't pursue a gainful occupation he would be "chopping cotton" in Arkansas. Oh well – things got interesting in the general practice of law in the country. He opened his own practice and went right into trial work, and worked directly with people, and not the "flakey" scientists. There was no Bill Gates around to make life even more interesting. Hon. Jeff F. Walter, the local Circuit Judge, and his old cronies wanted to get rid of Fears anyway; so the Judge appointed Fears to defend a Puerto Rican migrant farm worker charged with capital murder. It seems the farm laborer, while living in a migrant labor camp, knifed a black night watchman in the labor camp to death by cutting him 17 times, practically into pieces. The Puerto Rican couldn't speak English so Fears hired an interpreter who was married to a local girl; he was from Mexico, and was attending college in Virginia. The interpreter was great, but Fears had to pay him $50 for services rendered. At this time, juries were handpicked by jury commissioners appointed by the Circuit Judge, and there was no such thing as the "Miranda" warning. If someone was killed by a knifing, especially a night watchman, the killer simply got the electric chair. Judge Walter thought this would be the end of Fears' practice. However, Fears was able to prove that the night watchman had told the Puerto Rican's lady friend in the camp that if she didn't have sex with him she would have to leave the camp. In Puerto Rico this is probably good cause for killing someone, and when the jury heard this from the girlfriend they gave the accused life imprisonment instead of death. In Virginia, the jury assesses the penalty on a "not guilty" plea. In other states, the Judge gives the assessment after the verdict. Fears got the Puerto Rican out of prison in five years provided he would return to Puerto Rico, which he did. Instead of costing Fears his reputation it really helped him with his criminal practice, for the newspaper headlines "played it up" very well for "Counselor Fears." Fears was paid $25 for defending this indigent by the Commonwealth of Virginia. During this time, only capital offenses were defended by appointed counsels who were paid a great fee of $25.

Sen. Fears thoroughly enjoyed general law practice, and especially trial work. This is diversified, and the thrill of waiting for a jury verdict after a trial well tried is really worth more than making money. Fears got good enough at trial work that he has been rated by Martidale-Hubbell, a biographical and demographic rating directory used by most lawyers to pick lawyers in other jurisdictions when needed. Fears has the highest rating given, namely "a-v". If he had started work as a "leg man" for a big law firm, it would have taken years, and Fears would have to have been a "rainmaker" to get to be a partner, and to get to try interesting cases. Furthermore the retired senior partners of big firms are living longer, playing more golf, and spending all their time on their yachts. All the junior partners and the associates are doing is "working their asses off" to support the retired senior partners of the big firms. Now that young lawyers can advertise, because of a recent Supreme Court decision, Sen. Fears' advice is for young lawyers to open their own offices, with perhaps other fledgling lawyers if one is really self confident, and go to it. When Fears opened the one-room office in Accomac, in a county of only 32,000 people, there were only about six practicing lawyers; now there are more than 40, and at least five firms of more than one. The more law practiced in a community though, the more legal business is "stirred up" – not that this is really good for the country. Sen. Fears feels that there are entirely too many lawyers in the legal business, and that the law profession has little respect by the public except when that person complaining about lawyers needs one. Fears has had several law partners; one is now a retired Judge, one is now the full-time elected County Prosecutor, and one now has his own office with a woman lawyer associate who isn't a bad trial lawyer herself. Fears had a young partner, but Fears is now at the age where he has retired. He wouldn't take a case just to make a fee, probably knowing his client couldn't win, but only took a case when he felt the case had merit, if he felt he had at least a 50/50 chance of winning before a Judge or Jury. This way he maintains a reputation with the courts trying the cases on relevant issues, and did not try to "muddy" the case with a "shotgun" style of trying to inject confusing or irrelevant evidence. This makes the practice even more fun when one can select which cases one wanted to try in court.

There were two characters from Chincoteague, Virginia, who were allegedly duck hunting guides, and were paid to carry out big city duck hunters from Baltimore, and the DC area, to hunt ducks on the barrier islands across the Bay from Chincoteague. There were plenty of ducks there. A man from DC came down for two years consecutively for duck hunting, and our "host guides" took him home to their houses, where our hunter stayed overnight and ate breakfast with the guides each morning. The hunter kept urging our guides to furnish him some dressed frozen ducks, boxed, so our hunter could carry them back to his alleged corporate friends in DC for a duck feast. For two years our guides couldn't be inveigled into furnishing the ducks, but one year after legally hunting our hunter from DC was returning to DC empty handed. He again coaxed the guides into furnishing him some fresh dressed, frozen, wild ducks. It is against the Federal Law, and in fact is a felony punishable by three years in the Federal Penitentiary if convicted. These cases are tried in the U.S. District Court in Norfolk, Virginia. The guides finally, after another breakfast at one of the guide's homes, agreed to get the hunter some ducks packed in ice. The great hunter thanked them with all his heart and returned to DC. Three months later our guides were served with "Federal Felony Warrants" for illegally selling wild ducks to the hunter from DC. It seems our hunter was a federal game warden, and had been stalking the guides from Chincoteague for several years. The guides, one being a great duck hunter from Chincoteague by the name of Walt Clark, Sr. (the name of the other can't be remembered), hired the supposedly best trial lawyer then in the county, Lawyer Fears, to defend them. Fears chose a jury trial, and used the "grounds of entrapment" as a defense. The Judge was a really common sense Judge named Hon. Richard Kellam, who never graduated from law school, but read the law in his brother's office. The Kellams were political leaders in Virginia Beach, Virginia. Hon. Richard Kellam was first a Virginia Circuit Court Judge, and then a U.S. District Court Judge. Fears chose a jury, and went through the lengthy Federal Pre-Trial Procedure, and finally to trial. During the "voir dire" of the jury, Fears recognized an Eastern Shore native named Pat Foley. Foley started to speak to Fears, but Fears shook his head. He surely wanted to keep Foley on the jury for Pat Foley was a pretty good duck hunter in his own right. The Court actually gave Fears an instruction on entrapment defense, which most Courts won't do, and armed with this instruction, Fears only argued a couple of minutes. He argued that, "Here this game warden is at my clients' breakfast table eating my clients' food, inveigling, begging, cajoling with all kinds of lies as reasons to convince my clients to violate the law so he can snag them to make a great name for himself." Fears further argued that it reminded him of "poor little lambs in the slaughterhouse being led to their deaths by the old conniving Judas Goat." The jury was out about five minutes, and acquitted the Chincoteague guides. The trial made headlines in the Virginia Pilot and even named Fears as the lawyer. With this kind of advertisement it helped Fears' criminal practice. The local Circuit Judge, Hon. Jeff F. Walter, acted disgusted and told Fears he should be ashamed of himself for freeing these terrible, dangerous criminals.

During the good old days of morality, most girls and boys at least up through high school were virgins, but the world has changed. In the early days there were protective statutes for young girls during their puberty, and they were protected from the male animal. Virginia even had a statute making it a felony for a married man to seduce an unmarried female if she was of previous chaste character, but the statute was repealed by the General Assembly in 1995. All states have statutory rape laws protecting young girls. In Virginia, if the male is over 18 years old and has a sexual relationship with a girl under 16 years old, he is in a "heap of trouble" as a statutory rapist even though the girl may have consented. Fears represented a young divorced male, aged 23, who spent the night with a 14-year-old high school girl. The girl's father was a really rough Chief Petty Officer retired from the Navy, and the girl's mother was a native Hawaiian lady. The 14-year-old girl was large in size, and was built like a Green Bay Packer. Anyhow, the girl showed up in court looking 25 years old with a slave bracelet on one ankle and a man's large class ring hung around her neck on a golden chain. The girl admitted she had consented to sexual inter-course the night before and had objected in no way. On cross-exami-nation she admitted the class ring belonged to a sailor, and that the slave bracelet belonged to another man. She also admitted she had had sexual intercourse with these men before the affair with Fears' client. After arguments before the jury they acquitted Fears' alleged rapist in about five minutes. The father of the girl came up to Fears' counsel table and struck at him, but Fears ducked the blow without being harmed. The Judge wanted to know if Fears wanted to take any action against the Chief, but Fears declined saying, "He is an irate father and I can hardly blame him, so don't charge him with anything."

This father had been hunting for the man and his daughter that night of the incident, and I'm sure would have killed the man if he could have found him, for he had a huge double-barreled shotgun loaded with buckshot. The evening after the trial Fears went to the movies, for his wife was away. After the movies, Fears pulled up in his driveway and got out of his car. He saw a man out of the corner of his eye, and thought he heard the hammers on a shotgun cocking. Instantly Fears fell to the ground and rolled into the bushes. The guy standing by the corner of Dr. DeCormis' office was not the Chief, but he wanted to know what happened to Fears (by now both parties recognized each other). Fears replied, "Oh, I just fell over the border around the plants in the dark." But his heart was pounding a mile a minute. He didn't even tell his wife about this for surely his pride would have been damaged by her laughter.

After this "scary" episode with the rape case in which the Chief Petty Officer scared the hell out of Lawyer Fears, Fears ran for State Senator. While campaigning, he came across a crew-cut gentleman sitting on some front steps in a town. Fears approached him without recognizing him and was told, "Don't bother me and get the hell away from me." It was the father of the 14-year-old girl, years later, after he had retired from the Navy. Years passed and the Eurasian daughter had married, and had at least one child. Her son was then a teenager and for some reason resided with his grandfather in Chincoteague. The grandson had gotten into trouble with the law and was charged with breaking and entering. Guess what? The Chief (grandfather) called Lawyer Fears and asked him to represent the grandson who was about 15 years old. The Chief told Fears he was hiring him because he had done such a good job defending the man accused of raping his daughter.

Fears took the case and, because the lad was a juvenile, was able to get him sentenced as a delinquent and placed on probation in custody of the Chief. It all worked out; Fears was now in the good graces of the Chief and the teenaged grandson apparently stayed out of trouble thereafter. Now that the years have passed Sen. Fears has no idea what happened to the Chief, the beautiful Eurasian daughter, nor the grandson. But Fears will never stop being surprised with lifetime events. It's all in the game! Knowing the Chief, I'll bet the lad got some heavy punishment outside the Court.

Lawyer Fears really loves his trial work. During his Senate career, Fred Carter, Jr., a very intelligent African-American – a licensed mortician practicing with his father and mother in Gloucester County, Virginia, in the funeral profession, and also a Deputy Sheriff for the county – befriended Fears during his first election effort for the State Senate. This black was a real live wire and respected by blacks and whites for being good for the community. His mother, also a licensed mortician, had received her undergraduate degree from Yale University, which was unusual for a southern black woman before the '60s. The entire family took Fears under its wing and went all out to help him win the election, which he won with a majority vote in Gloucester County. As time went on, the favor was returned, for Fears helped get Fred on the Virginia Mortician's Board, helped him in a family real estate hearing in Gloucester County Circuit Court, and helped Fred become a lobbyist in Richmond. He also was ordained as a Protestant minister, and preaches in a church in Newport News, where he now lives.

Fred's wife is also a mortician and another live wire. They have two very bright children; the girl is a licensed lawyer in Newport News, and the son was last known to be in law school at William and Mary Law School, and a class officer. In 1991, Fred called Lawyer Fears and asked him to represent his son, who was a senior at the University of Virginia, and an honor student. There had been a "sting" operation on the campus and several students had been charged with drug offenses. All had pleaded guilty, and received reasonable punishments, but they had been branded with a record as felons, which is tantamount to a destruction of one's career. Fred's son had been charged with two separate charges of distribution of cocaine. These charges had gone to a grand jury, and had "stuck" with indictments. The Judge was a stern stickler for prosecution of crimes, and the juries in Charlottesville are reputed to be the toughest in Virginia on drug offenses. Fears wanted to discuss plea-bargaining with the prosecutor handling the case. He was an African-American, but this attempt was "no deal." The prosecutor thought he had an ideal case and was going for the limit on these charges – so there was no choice but to request a jury, and plead "not guilty." There was a lot of preliminary fencing by discovery, and request by Fears for prosecutorial evidence, and many interviews with the accused, the father and mother, and several witnesses. Fears prepared as best he could, and even hired an expert witness to identify voices on a tape recording used by one of the undercover officers during the alleged delivery of narcotics by the accused, and during the arrest.

Sen. Fears asked the fledgling woman lawyer (who was a daughter of Fred Carter) who had just passed the Virginia State Bar Examination to assist him in the trial, for with her at the counsel table as the sister of young Carter, the accused, it could make a favorable impression on the women on the jury. Fears introduced her as co-counsel in the case to the Court and the jury, which produced a nervous reaction from the Chief Prosecutor from Charlottesville, along with the Assistant Prosecutor, and the detective who handled the investigation. Fears liked the idea of the detective sitting at the prosecution's table before the jury for, as you will see, this was most favorable to Fears' defense. Young Carter's father (Fred Jr.) and his mother were placed immediately at the defense counsel table – also for good impression, for Fred Jr. is over 6 feet tall and, along with his wife, might make a very good impression on this conservative Charlottesville jury.

The jury consisted of a couple of elderly women, a couple of blue-collar African-American men, and a mixture of other young men and women. Knowing full well that Judge Sweat, like most Virginia Judges, was not prone to give an instruction on entrapment, nor allow closing arguments on the same, Lawyer Fears introduced young Carter's parents to the jury, and introduced the attorney sister as such, and began with an opening statement accusing the officers of "setting young Carter up" and entrapping him into passing the cocaine to another student whom Carter knew. The evidence disclosed that the officers had hired another lad who was an acquaintance of young Carter to go with an undercover detective to convince Carter that they were friends, asking Carter where he could get some "coke." Carter had none, but told them he knew a fellow living in DC, who had visited the fraternity house frequently to date one of the girls on campus, who might get some cocaine. Carter obtained the cocaine, and the next weekend the alleged friend – who was wired with a recorder – and the youthful undercover detective dressed as a student appeared for the cocaine. Carter gave it to them, and they paid the going price, which Carter allegedly gave to the contact in Washington, DC. This happened twice within about three weeks, and the second time Carter was arrested.

Fred Jr. posted the required bond for his son's release from jail. All went well at the trial, and the principal witness testified that he had pending charges against him, and that he hoped for more favorable treatment if he acted as the undercover witness in the purchase of the cocaine from Carter. Then the detective testified that there was a "sting" operation being conducted on campus, which had resulted in arrests of several students and others on campus. After the prosecution had put on its case, young Carter made a superb witness, and so did Fred Jr. and his wife, the parents of young Carter.

During the trial, young Carter's sister, the fledgling lawyer, cross examined one of the Charlottesville detectives and did a pretty good job of it. Then instructions were offered to the Judge in chambers by both sides and, as Fears suspected, the Judge would not allow an instruction on entrapment. But Fears knew from opening arguments that the jury already was thinking about the unfairness of the arrest process. The case was argued well on both sides, and the jury retired. In about two hours, the jury returned to ask the court a question. The question was not significant. When they retired to the jury room again for deliberation, Fred Jr. told Fears, "They are going to acquit my son."

Fears asked Fred Jr. how he knew and he stated, "An African-American fireman gave me the eye." Fears tried to pass this up as nonsense, but Fred Jr. said that in slavery days the people working in the mansion house couldn't talk to one another, or to the owners, so everything was said with the eyes. Fears told Carter that this was a long time ago. After about five hours of deliberation, the jury came in with the verdict. Fears rose with his client, young Carter, with his heart about to "burst from his chest." The jury read the verdict of "not guilty on both indictments." What a wonderful day to have saved a young man's career. This is called practical country justice. Incidentally, the two elderly white women on the jury wanted to convict.

It is believed that young Carter attended law school and did well. He should make an excellent trial lawyer, for he now has good practical personal experience. His sister, the lawyer, now has her own practice in Newport News, and is doing much criminal practice. What a wonderful "brass ring" for lawyer Fears, young Carter, and the then-fledgling lawyer on her first winning case. Fears charged an expense fee only and Fred Sr., the mortician, promised to bury Sen. Fears and his wife Belle, *gratis*, when the time came.

While Sen. Fears was serving in the Virginia State Senate, he had a housewife in Williamsburg who had campaigned for him in one election *gratis*, and was a great campaigner and fundraiser. He had had a young man who was quite "prissy" – and was an extreme idealist – the year before as an aide; so Fears hired the housewife as his principal aide and "plunked her down" in his office to run it. She did a great job, and worked for him in the Senate for 18 years until he lost the election in 1991.

This fine lady has several children. One is a CPA, another is a mathematician working for a defense industry in Washington, DC, and a couple more bright young men who got in and out of financial difficulties. Her youngest son had some birth difficulties, but is quite intelligent, but has since been a burden on his mother. He fell in love with a 15-year-old "wild" girl and got her pregnant, and married her. The child of this love affair is a beautiful blue-eyed blonde who is also quite intelligent. The marriage between the two eventually broke up for the wife was allegedly quite promiscuous.

The aide to Sen. Fears (the grandmother) took this little girl into her home and raised her. The mother tried, through court action via a divorce proceeding, to get custody of the child, and Fears represented the grandmother and father, and fought hard to keep this beautiful child out of the "clutches" and influence of this promiscuous mother. He had to defend and try the case in Gloucester County before an "old school" Circuit Judge. After a two-day trial, the Judge awarded the physical custody of the child, who was about five years old, to the grandmother (Sen. Fears' aide) but gave visitation privileges to the father and mother.

The grandmother took this girl in, gave her everything comfortable and, being a devout Catholic, enrolled the child in Walsingham Academy, a very fine Catholic School in Williamsburg, and paid her tuition. The child – under protest – visited her mother every weekend. The mother remarried; she now has two young children. According to this grandchild, she was afraid of the stepfather, claiming he touched her where she shouldn't be touched.

The child did very well in school. Sen. Fears was rather accepted by her as her "grand-godfather" and, in fact, he paid for some piano lessons for the girl, and gave her gifts. The child was an honor student in Walsingham Academy, until she reached the 9th grade. Then "up jumped the devil" – she lost all her baby fat and grew into a tall beautiful girl of 15. She met a boy of 16 who resided in a trailer park and attended Lafayette School. According to the evidence, the boy was in some kind of "vampire cult," and introduced the grandchild to narcotics, and seduced the girl in the home of her mother and stepfather. The girl was in love and had got a "bite of the poison apple," as many do in this day and time. She says the stepfather entered the den and then excused himself while the girl was having a sexual interlude with the 16-year-old boy in her mother's home. The child returned to the grandmother's home and wanted to dye her hair jet black. She had the appearance of being under the influence of narcotics one Sunday when she arrived after a visit with her mother. What a mess!

The grandmother was really upset and forbade her from seeing the seducer, rapist, or whatever, and kept a close rein on her "protégé." The girl left the grandmother's house one night without permission, and went to her mother's home where she met her youthful lover again, and refused to return to the custodial home of her grandmother.

The girl's father had married again, and has a boy child and is working in North Carolina. The grandmother called him and told him the problem. The father came to Virginia and took his daughter with him to North Carolina where she lived for a while. He enrolled her in a small high school there for the remainder of the year, and the girl was No. 1 in her class. She did well there, and her "loverboy" now has a new girlfriend in Virginia. Would you believe it – the mother had filed suit to get custody of this mixed-up child probably just to be spiteful with the grandmother. The grandmother is now frequently financially embarrassed, has borrowed money, and has spent all her savings on the grandchild to give her a good education and a better life. But with her mother's genes, the child could have destroyed herself.

Sen. Fears then entered the second suit with a cross petition to get custody for the father, and to stop the mother from getting her "clutches" on the child, which would probably really destroy the girl. Young teenaged girls are many times so very foolish, and this is one of those times. That's why there are so many illegitimate children born to teenaged mothers. Sex is a wonderful thing, but it can also be a very destructive thing, and this is one of those tragic times. Sen. Fears certainly did all he could to salvage this young girl's life, but it's difficult when they think they are in love, and have had a taste of the "poison apple." The girl has worked, graduated from high school, and is doing well in college now.

The practice of law can be somewhat dangerous, too. A District Court Judge in Louisa County was blown away by a sawed-off shotgun blast by an assailant while the Judge was on the bench. Now all courtrooms are protected by metal detectors, and police officers actually search everyone entering courtrooms anywhere.

When Lawyer Fears started the practice of law, one could enter a courtroom freely without any problem. In the '50s, he represented a black woman in the Juvenile Court, for child support and spousal support, against her husband. The Court ruled that the husband must pay a certain amount of spousal and child support, and the husband was furious. He claimed she deserved nothing because he claimed she was playing around, but he couldn't prove it to the court.

Fears had a small single practitioner's office right in the courtyard, but the office had no back door for cowards. This irate husband entered town the next day, came into Fears' office, closed the door, and stuck a pistol in Fears' stomach. He told Fears he was going to "blow your white ass away." Lawyer Fears was absolutely petrified with fear, but with a lot of talking he convinced the man that the decision by the Court was only a civil decision and nothing criminal, so the man could not be incarcerated, although the Court can jail an errant husband for contempt for not complying with a decree. Fears said, "Man, if you kill me in this state they'll 'fry' you in the electric chair for first degree murder, and all you have to do in this case is make up with your wife and support the child." Finally, the husband cooled down and put the gun away. With some more talking, Fears really proved he could talk his way out of a grave problem. When the man left, he was almost smiling. After the man left, Fears never complained to the police, nor did he request a warrant of any kind. He was simply glad the experience was over, tried to understand the man's lack of education and judgment, and also felt as a coward should – that if he did anything drastic the husband might return and finish the job. What an experience – from then on Fears tried to be a little kinder and more considerate to the defendants in his cases, and always hoped the opposing party would arrive with his or her own lawyer.

It's a good thing that Lt. Col. Fears had learned some martial arts while in his last year at Yale, and during his training in the Army Air Corps, for this was required at both institutions and especially for self-defense. During the '70s, Fears represented an attractive woman from Virginia Beach, and we had better call her "Alice" for reasons you will later understand.

She lived in an expensive house in Virginia Beach, was given a new Lincoln Continental every year by her husband, and was raising two teenaged daughters from a prior marriage. Her husband, let's call him "Jim," was very wealthy, owning large hotels in a city in Michigan, and also in Reno, Nevada. Jim kept a couple million dollars worth of jewelry in the house at Virginia Beach, which Alice wore frequently to the "ritzy" parties they attended.

Jim came to the Beach on Tuesday or Wednesday each week and left again on Thursday and spent the rest of his time in one of his hotels in Michigan. Alice figured he had a lady friend there so she played around a bit too. Jim came home one night and followed his wife to a nice dark lot and saw her exchanging kisses with a male friend. When she got home later, he didn't confront her but quietly packed up the jewelry claiming he was financing a new enterprise, and had to use the jewelry as collateral. She accepted the explanation, but the next week he "sneaked" down and took the Lincoln, which was in his name, back to Michigan. Fortunately, Alice's name was on the house deed at the Virigina Beach Clerk's Office. The marriage broke up and Fears represented Alice, which was quite an experience. Fears had heard rumors that Jim was part of the Michigan organized crime group, and that was where his wealth came from.

One evening, Lt. Col. Fears drove to the Little Creek Naval Base to the officer's club for a drink and dinner. It was wintertime, and Fears had on an overcoat and fortunately leather gloves. It was dark in this parking space by the water's edge. He parked his car and another sedan parked right beside him. When Fears exited his car, a man got out of the other car. The man was wearing an overcoat, was middle-aged and well dressed. It was not Jim, for Fears knew Jim personally. The man stuck an automatic pistol in Fears' stomach and ordered Fears to get into the other car. This scared the hell out of Fears but he wasn't going to get into that car. Lt. Col. Fears "chopped" the guy's gun hand, and simultaneously kneed the guy in the balls as hard as he could. At the same time, with the other hand, he struck the guy in the Adam's apple with all his might. The guy went down, and Fears kicked him about the head until the guy was bloody and probably unconscious. He then picked up the 38-cal. automatic, and threw first the clip into the water, and then the pistol itself.

Fears then got back into his car, which was a black Lincoln, and drove off the Base, across the Chesapeake Bridge Tunnel, and to his home in Accomac. He didn't dare report the incident to anyone, and read the Virginia Pilot for about a week to see if the guy was found dead or had reported the incident. Nothing was in the papers, but Fears searched his car each morning when he left for his office to see if there were any explosives wired to anything. Fears also kept his house blinds drawn at night in his den at home for about a month, and kept a 45-cal. automatic, which resembled the one he had used in the armed service, close at hand in his car, in his office, and at home, just in case. Fortunately, Fears' wife, a local Health Director, left early for work each morning and came home late in the evening, or she would have realized that something was wrong.

This didn't end the episode with Alice, for she had always had a large bank account with Jim. But as her life became confused she had written several bad checks in small amounts to pay for necessities. She then took a trip to Florida to try to forget some of her troubles. When she returned from Florida she was immediately arrested for the "bad checks."

In Virginia, if a bad check (insufficient funds) is over $200, it can be a felony, but if under this amount it is a misdemeanor. A misdemeanor can be punished with up to a year in jail. Poor Alice had five such back check warrants, each for under $200, waiting for her when she deplaned in Norfolk. She paid off all the bad checks immediately, but still had to appear in the Police Court in Norfolk. The arresting detective was really sympathetic with Alice and told her the Judge would probably fine her and place her on probation. No such luck! The Judge gave her six months in jail. On the way down to the holding cell, poor Alice went to pieces, and the detective got a bondsman to bail her out until an appeal could be taken. This Police Judge was a strict, pompous old man. He parted his hair in the middle, and slicked it back plastered to his head. He wasn't well liked by any of the lawyers in Norfolk. At her hearing, Alice was not represented by a lawyer and waived that right. Alice's 19-year-old daughter telephoned lawyer Fears in Accomac asking him to help her mother.

The judgment was well within the 10-day appeal period. Fears visited the Police Judge in chambers, and filed a motion for a re-hearing. The Judge was his usual strict self and told Fears to appeal the decision to the Circuit Court and discuss the matter with the Prosecuting Attorney, one Joe Campbell, Esq. Now Joe is a wonderful, understanding, compassionate person. Joe summonsed the detective to the conference and the detective stated: "Joe, this woman doesn't belong in jail. She's made good on the checks, and has enough trouble in her married life." Joe agreed to charge her with disorderly conduct and assess the fine of $50, and the Circuit Court Judge agreed.

Fears was in the State Senate at the time, and when Joe Campbell was nominated for a Circuit Court Judgeship in Norfolk, Sen. Fears was delighted to vote for him in the State Senate. Now Joe liked booze and had to get dried out once in a while, but he had the reputation of being a very good and respected Judge in spite of his alcoholic weakness. While on the bench, an ex-prosecuting attorney for Virginia Beach had some sort of traffic charge in Norfolk. Somehow Judge Campbell had the wrong name placed in the order on this lawyer, and somehow the Judge was accused of some kind of criminal offense. Judge Campbell was charged with a crime, and in a plea bargaining agreement lost his seat on the bench. Sen. Fears doesn't know the present status of Judge Campbell. Fears wishes Judge Campbell the best in life, and feels that all this "monkey business" about Lawyer Sciortino's name was a tempest in a teapot.

Alice has remarried a Navy Chief – Fears received a Christmas card from her about 25 years ago. She seems to be happy, Hon. Joe Campbell seems to be doing well, and Sen. Fears is still admitted to practice law. Incidentally, the crusty old Judge is now deceased, and probably his family, if he had one, misses him terribly.

In another case, there were two young men (David and Wayne) working together on David's house. David operated a repair shop that did body and fender work on automobiles and Wayne was a carpenter. David was trying to get his house in order so that his fiancée and he could move in. The girl was going to have a baby. David was to work on Wayne's automobile, and Wayne was to help with the carpentry work on the house. David did pay some for Wayne's labor charges, and paid with credit cards for materials. Both seemed to be getting along well together, but then after a while there developed a conflict over money, and the details are so complicated and convoluted it is too boring to relate. One day, a heated argument developed between the young men over money. David had a 9-MM automatic pistol on a bed headboard upstairs in his unfurnished bedroom. David told Wayne he would go up to his bedroom to get a checkbook and pay Wayne on the account. Wayne followed David upstairs, and a heated argument ensued. There was a fistfight. Somehow David got the gun and fired at Wayne. David claims he sat there a long time after he had shot Wayne in the side of the neck. David claims he didn't intend to kill Wayne, but decided Wayne was dead. Right at that moment, if David had called the Sheriff's office, and an ambulance, he probably could have been acquitted of any felony charges. But instead he buried Wayne's body in a hole already dug for plumbing pipes, and then used Wayne's credit cards to buy materials for the house from some Salisbury, Maryland, supply houses. He then drove Wayne's truck to Wayne's house in Parksley, left the keys on a table in the house, and turned on a light. All this was an alleged attempt to cover the alleged shooting. Things continued with everyone in Wayne's family and the law officers looking for Wayne.

In the meantime, David checked into a motel in Salisbury and called his father, a very fine man with a good reputation from Chincoteague, Virginia. The father contacted lawyer Fears who advised the father to bring David to Fears' office in Accomac. In the meantime the officers had discovered Wayne's body, and had discovered the credit card purchases on Wayne's credit cards. Warrants for capital murder and robbery of the credit cards were outstanding. The Court refused to bond David out before trial. Fears admonished David several times in his office not to make any comments or statements to anyone – not to officers, nor fellow inmates in the jail, and simply tell the inquiring officers to see Fears. The "Miranda" warning was explained to David, and basically this is the law protecting an accused from making any incriminating statements or giving a confession of any kind without the presence of counsel. David supposedly told a fellow inmate, an African-American, all about the shooting, and of course the prosecutor simply used the inmate's testimony to help convict David. The prosecuting attorney was one Gary Agar, Esq., who had been Fears' law partner. Gary was elected as county prosecutor and was then on his own. This trial was well publicized in the newspapers, and on TV and radio stations. David was well liked in Chincoteague and Wayne was well liked in Parksley. This turned into a geographical fight between the people of the towns of Parksley and Chincoteague. Wayne's family in Parksley were nice people, and well respected by their neighbors. David had a lovely sister in college, and a fine father and mother who also were well respected in Chincoteague. The Circuit Judge was from Parksley, but it is doubtful he leaned one way or the other. The jury was picked carefully by both sides. The prosecutor pushed for "Capital Murder," and the death penalty, but Fears, at the end of the prosecution's evidence, moved the Court to reduce the "Capital Murder" charge, which the Court did and legally should have. The trial lasted four days, which is a long trial for a rural area in Virginia, unlike the O.J. Simpson trial. (Had the Simpson trial been held in Virginia, the Court would have excluded the TV cameras and would have insisted on only one lawyer on each side trying the case. The trial would not have even lasted two weeks.)

Lawyer Fears spent many hours interviewing David and preparing him for trial, and gathering any favorable evidence. There were reliable character witnesses to testify as to David's good character; however, David had pledged the 9-MM as collateral to a friend in Pocomoke for some materials earlier; and unfortunately a week before the shooting had got his gun back from this friend. This was introduced by the prosecution at trial. Fears was able to prove that David had been the victim of vandals before, and this was the reason for the need for the pistol, for David also slept in the open house under construction on just a mattress to protect his open property. The courtroom was packed with Parksley citizens on one side of the room, and with Chincoteague folks on the other. Fears tried to get the Court to give an instruction on manslaughter, but the Court refused. The Court stuck to the textbook standard on the degrees of murder. The testimony of the inmate "did David in;" otherwise, the jury's verdict could have been for acquittal or manslaughter, and after all the preparation by Fears, David made a very poor witness on cross examination. The jury brought in a verdict of first-degree murder, and assessed David a penalty of life imprisonment. David's father had paid all he could in attorney's fees to Fears, amounting to about $10,000, which was a small figure for the amount of time expended to try this difficult case.

Everyone in Parksley is still mad at Fears for defending David. Anyhow, Fears declared David an indigent for the appeal, and an appointed appellate counsel named Terry Bliss, Esq., was appointed for the appellate work. Fears helped behind the scenes with the lengthy transcript. Fears was positive the Court had erred in not granting an instruction for manslaughter, and felt the Appellate Court would send the case back for a new trial on error. The case was argued before the Court of Appeals by Miss Bliss, but unfortunately one Judge Joseph Baker wrote the opinion in the Appellate Court that there was no error. One has to know Judge Baker is a "tough" judge on criminal appeals; so Fears still felt there was error and the case went on up to the Supreme Court through Ms. Bliss. The Supreme Court did rule with the Court of Appeals, and denied a writ of error. Fears and Bliss both feel the apellate court was in error in not granting a new trial because of the missing instruction on manslaughter. Well that was that, and everyone on David's side tried to get the best out of the trials and hearings. The unfortunate lesson to be learned from this case is that if David had simply called the law officers and an ambulance immediately he would have probably been a free man. The Jury convicted him not of the initial shooting, but the attempt to cover up by burying the body and using Wayne's credit cards to try to make people believe Wayne was still alive. The cover-up was not the crime, but it essentially caused the conviction of David for murder when the actual shooting incident could have been proved an accident; not really a crime.

No matter how hard a defense lawyer tries to protect his client and try a case, the usual defendant will try really hard to mess it all up. It isn't easy being a criminal defense lawyer. The prosecution always has the upper hand, for he or she has all the personnel in the world to assist, and the opportunity to build a case with the taxpayer's money, but the defense counsel has to spend more than his client's funds, and really work very hard to defend the case. This, to Fears, is an anomaly in the law that "the prosecution must prove its case beyond a reasonable doubt." The guy with plenty of funds (such as O.J. Simpson) gets acquitted, but the guy with no funds has a tough job.

William Earl had an Uncle Alfred who was a leech and a convicted felon, and a great "bull-shitter," and who always had delusions of grandeur. Aunt Myrtle inherited from her husband, Gen. Frederick Humphreys, a huge five-story mansion on Riverside Drive in New York City, and a lovely waterfront farm near Ocean City, Maryland. Uncle Alfred was convicted of armed robbery in Texas when he was about 19 years old, and back then served five years on a Texas road gang cutting brush and fighting rattlesnakes. He survived, and came to New York to live with Aunt Myrtle and Uncle Frederick. It was during the Great Depression for he could not find a good job – for that matter, he wasn't really qualified. He worked as a salesman for Garwood Heating Co., now defunct, trying to sell furnaces. The only one he sold was to Uncle Frederick, which was installed in the mansion house on

Riverside Drive. Later Uncle Frederick, who was President of Humphreys Homeopathic Medicine Co., hired Uncle Alfred as some kind of "gofer" in the company. Still later, Uncle Frederick became an alcoholic, and the board of directors forced his retirement. Of course Uncle Alfred was then fired too. Uncle Alfred became the "gofer" for Aunt Myrtle and Uncle Frederick, living in the mansion in the Winter, and at the farm in Maryland in the Summer. Of course he was supported by Aunt Myrtle.

William Earl had a father in Trumann, Arkansas, who lived to be 93 years old, and remarried a widow (Mary) in Trumann after William Earl's mother died. Earl Sr. and his second wife both had retirement incomes, and they were both over 80 years old. William Earl told them that if they got married the wife would lose her pension, but Earl Sr., affectionately known as "Pappy," said he didn't think it was right to live in sin; so they got married, and moved into a nursing home in Trumann, Arkansas, together. Later this second wife died, and Pappy became very lonely. He talked William Earl's younger brother, Carl E., and his wife Frances who lived in Memphis, Tennessee, into taking him out of the nursing home, because he was tired of "rabbit food," and wanted some ham and eggs for breakfast. He lived with brother Carl E. for five years, and nearly worried Carl's wife Frances to death, for she had to care for him. About 1993, Earl Sr. became so disoriented in Carl's home that he had to place him in another nursing home where he died at 93 years old, with old age complications.

Aunt Myrtle contacted her lawyer nephew William Earl in the '70s to come to New York from Virginia to seek his advice. William Earl found her in a wheelchair with a fractured hip. She would not enter a hospital to get the broken hip repaired, although William Earl told her he would pay the medical bills if she would do so. Aunt Myrtle was a stubborn woman, and by then quite paranoid. No wonder, with Uncle Alfred living with her, and taking all he could get. In other words, Aunt Myrtle was property poor, and probably didn't have enough food to eat. The hip healed by itself.

William Earl suggested that Aunt Myrtle allow him to establish a trust with him as trustee, and allow him to sell the farm in Maryland, the house and furniture in New York City, and to invest the funds in a trust account, and to buy a retirement home in Florida or New Jersey in an elderly village where transportation was furnished. Then she could employ an in-house maid, for William Earl found out that he could sell the farm for $750,000 and the house in New York (not counting the provincial French furniture) for about $400,000. In 1970, this was good money. He prepared the trust agreement and sent it to her in New York for her signature, but Uncle Alfred told her that her nephew William Earl was trying to steal everything, and she wouldn't sign the trust agreement. William Earl even put a provision therein for support of Uncle Alfred in the same retirement home and support for him in his lifetime, if any estate was left after Aunt Myrtle's death. Things remained static for years, and in 1980 Aunt Myrtle died in a nursing home in Cambridge, Maryland, where Uncle Alfred had placed her. She was blind and incompetent; so the doctors there later told William Earl.

One day William Earl received a call from his father, Pappy, in Trumann, Arkansas. Pappy told his son that Uncle Alfred had come by and visited him. Uncle Alfred showed Pappy his will, leaving everything he owned to Pappy. William Earl was suspicious, and told his father that Alfred could destroy the will upon leaving Pappy's presence. Pappy then asked his son to see what had happened to "Sis' estate," for she had just died in the nursing home. William Earl flew up to New York, searched the records in the Orphan's Court in New York City, and found that Uncle Alfred, under a power of attorney from Aunt Myrtle, had sold the New York mansion for $400,000, and had qualified as Executor under her will which had been executed 20 years before. Under Aunt Myrtle's will she had devised all her properties to a Bank Trustee and Uncle Alfred, and the Trustees were to sell all the real estate, invest the money and pay to each of her nine heirs the income equally for life each. She devised Uncle Alfred all the personal property. Uncle Alfred rightfully owning the personal property had auctioned off in the mansion and all the lovely French provincial furniture, and had kept the money.

William Earl filed a motion with the New York Orphan's Court, and got Uncle Alfred disqualified as the Executor, but it was too late. Uncle Alfred and his lawyer in New York City had already "bled the estate dry" and it was impossible to find any of the cash. Then William Earl checked the records in Worcester County, Maryland, and found that Uncle Alfred had gotten Aunt Myrtle to sign deeds to the Maryland property over to him, and Uncle Fred (in Berlin, Maryland) jointly. He was again very clever, for Alfred knew that Fred, under joint ownership with survivorship, didn't realize that if he died before Alfred then Alfred would get it all. William Earl got his father, and his brother, Carl E., to join with him in suit against Uncle Alfred, and Uncle Fred (who would be just a paper respondent.) Uncle Fred was 10 years older than Uncle Alfred. William Earl tried to get his other cousins who were heirs also under the will of Aunt Myrtle to join as plaintiffs in the suit, but they wouldn't; so William Earl with his father, and brother Carl as plaintiffs filed an Equity Suit in the Worcester County Circuit Court to set the Maryland deeds to Uncle Alfred aside for fraud and incompetence of the grantor. Uncle Alfred hired one Ray Coates, Esq., who practices law in Snow Hill, Maryland, as his lawyer. William Earl was already admitted to practice law in Maryland by examination. The usual *lis pendens* was also filed in the Clerk's office to freeze the property so Uncle Alfred and Uncle Fred couldn't sell it. The usual pretrial preliminaries with interrogatories and discovery were filed, and answered by both sides. The Circuit Judge in Worcester County had taken the Maryland Bar Examination with William Earl, and the parties knew each other fairly well; so Fears filed a motion for a pretrial conference. Uncle Alfred showed up with Uncle Fred and Uncle Fred's two sons (William Earl's cousins) to testify for Uncle Alfred. In chambers, Judge Prettyman asked William Earl what would be his evidence. William Earl explained to the Court that Aunt Myrtle's medical doctors and attending nurses in Cambridge, Maryland, would testify as witnesses that at the time of signing the deed Aunt Myrtle was absolutely incompetent. Lawyer Coates knows the Fears family and the Judge very well. He might have also known that Aunt Myrtle was incompetent.

The Judge suggested that Coates settle the case with William Earl. Coates agreed as settlement to get Uncle Alfred and Uncle Fred to convey a one-third interest in the Maryland farm property to Pappy, and to convey $60,000 in cash to Pappy. William Earl knew that if Pappy died, his second wife, Mary, and her family would inherit what William Earl had worked so hard for; so he had the one-third interest in the farm put in trust with the property going to William Earl and brother Carl on the death of Pappy. Also, since Pappy and second wife Mary were in a nursing home, William Earl placed the $60,000 in trust and paid the income each month for the support of Pappy and Mary. Then later Uncle Fred and cousins Willie and Frederick found out that Uncle Alfred had lied to them, had married a 50-year-old lady by then, and would have died with two-thirds of the farm in his possession. They convinced William Earl to represent them; so William Earl filed another suit (in the names of Fred, Frederick and William Alexander Fears) to set aside the remainder of the Maryland property, and for a share of the estate money to the relatives. In the meantime Uncle Alfred was disqualified as Executor of Aunt Myrtle's Estate, and William Earl had the felony records from Texas on Uncle Alfred, which would have been devastating to his great pride in Maryland, if the trial was held and the records introduced to discredit him. Anyhow, Uncle Alfred conveyed the other two-thirds of the farm to Uncle Fred, and all agreed Alfred could keep the money on the New York house and property sales. Everything was static for years. William A. had hired his own lawyer, a professor of law from Baltimore, who took Willie's case on one-third contingency fee. This matter languished for years, for Uncle Alfred had by agreement, a life estate in one-third of the farm, and collected the farm rent and paid the taxes. Somehow Frederick had gone into bank-ruptcy and had tied the property up in his daughter's name, all without

William Earl's knowledge. Uncle Fred died leaving his interest to cousins Willie and Frederick, and then Pappy died in the early '90s.

Then along came a buyer, a very wealthy young man who is an heir to the Perdue Farms fortune. He wanted to build a house on the 160-acre farm, and William Earl, Carl E., and cousins Frederick and Willie all agreed to sell the farm to James Perdue for $1,300,000, and were to deal with Perdue's lawyer in Salisbury, Maryland. William Earl (the lawyer in the Fears clan) convinced the others to sell the property on an installment sales basis over five years to spread out the capital gains taxes over five years. All agreed and the agreements were signed. Because Willie and Frederick had appeared in Court the first time to defend Uncle Alfred (until they too learned he was a "ne'er do well") William Earl wouldn't represent them against Uncle Alfred until they signed a note for $5,000 each out of any sales proceeds as attorney's fees, to which they agreed.

When Perdue's attorney did the title search he felt the property wasn't clear in the names as to the sellers without releases from cousins Edward and Alice (these were the children of Uncle Edward, who had long been dead.) If you recall, they wouldn't join as plaintiffs in the suit against Uncle Alfred and, fortunately, William Earl had their refusal letter in his files. Cousin Edward approached one of William Earl's lawyer friends (he thought), named Steve Smethurst, Esq., from Salisbury, to tie up the sale with claims from him and Alice. They wanted one-fifth of the purchase price for their releases. William Earl felt like they deserved nothing. He told Willie and Frederick to "stonewall it" and to let Steve Smethurst, Esq., file a suit – for he knew Steve couldn't collect a nickel for his clients. William Earl wrote to Steve and told him he would settle for nothing, and to go ahead and file a suit for his clients. He also knew from experience that Steve would want a big retainer, which he also knew Alice and Edward wouldn't be willing to pay. Willie and Frederick paid Alice and Edward $7,000 each to get releases from them so the sale could go through. This held up the sale for a year. Willie said he wanted his money to buy a Corvette and some cowboy boots, which he had wanted all his life. Frederick had a new wife and wanted to buy a recreational vehicle and take her (a retired schoolteacher) to Alaska. William Earl took part of his money and bought his grandson, who was entering college, a new Mustang since his grandson had studied hard. Also, the grandson wanted to study law, and William Earl felt that Matthew deserved the new car from his grandfather. Willie and Frederick paid William Earl promptly the $10,000 for attorneys' fees from both from the estate of their Aunt Myrtle.

Uncle Fred, Uncle Edward, Aunt Myrtle, and finally Uncle Alfred are all now deceased. Willie is enjoying his Corvette, his "shit kickers," and some happiness; Cousin Frederick is enjoying his recreational vehicle, his new wife, and his trips to Alaska, and William Earl's brother is $245,000 wealthier, but he hasn't offered anything to his brother William Earl for all the successful hard work. Guess he feels that William Earl owes him for keeping Pappy for five very difficult years. Cousin Edward has telephoned William Earl and "cussed him out" for allegedly costing him what he feels is his right of inheritance. William Earl is simply glad that he went to law school, for this amounts to poetic justice for him, and he feels that he did get one little "brass ring." Also, he learned legal advice for others, to wit: "Trust a stranger but don't trust family members when it comes to money!" Now Edward is deceased, and the rightful heirs have their inheritances to enjoy. However, cousin Eddie is also now deceased, and so is cousin Frederick.

Chapter 15

A Visit to Alaska

William E. Fears (now the name used instead of "Earl Fears, Jr.," so no one would continue to call him "Junior") who served in the military up through the rank of Lieutenant Colonel; served for 24 years as a State Senator; and is now retired from his law firm which was Fears and Turner; is now 81 years old and in a depressed mental state, as all elderly people should be at this time in life. When in the Senate, he was called Senator Fears everywhere he traveled until he lost his bid for reelection. Now he is thought of as "Bill Who?" – even his children, at the dinner table, refer to him in the third person (as Art Buchwald says) as the "village idiot." The community appointments are now back in the hands of the born here, raised here, "good ole boys"; so, being fed up with provincialism, tired of local boredom, and greatly disappointed because he didn't get the local Circuit Judgeship, William Earl desired a change of scenery.

He had two unused American Airlines, "old age" coupons, and asked his wife to go with him to Alaska, but she didn't want to go. Incidentally, these senior citizens' coupons are very reasonable, for they were bought for about $600 for four coupons. The Fearses had two coupons each left after a trip to San Diego, California. Unfortunately, Dr. Belle Fears, William Earl's wife, didn't want to make the combined "air-boat" trip to Alaska because she has motion sickness on aircrafts and boats, so Sen. Fears started his voyage to Alaska alone. Also, Belle has some kind of unusual heart trouble, and has to wear a "scopalomine patch," for motion sickness, which has other bad side effects. The patch leaves her "goofy" and she is "out of it" for a couple of days.

Sen. Fears, in his law practice, first had to take a deposition of a Dr. Krop in Virginia Beach. Dr. Krop is an Orthopedic Specialist, and his deposition is necessary for a trial to be held in Accomack Circuit Court. This was a very important personal injury case, for a lady in Accomack County who suffered injuries in an automobile accident, primarily had a badly broken arm. Dr. Krop charges $500 per hour for deposition testimony. Heaven only knows what he charges for personal appearance testimony in the Circuit Court of Accomack County, which is about four hours driving time round trip from Virginia Beach. The defense counsel is a young handsome "whipper snapper" – a real "smart alec" from a Virginia Beach law firm.

This smart alec defense lawyer aggravated Fears so much during the deposition that Fears wanted to smack him, but he held his composure and finally finished the deposition. This young lawyer graduated from Rev. Pat Robertson's law school, named Regents Law School, in Virginia Beach. This school was founded by the Rev. Pat Robertson, who has degrees in Law and Divinity from Yale University. He probably learned he could get more money from the widows in church donations than he could in practicing law. (Shades of Jimmy Swaggart, Rev. Angle, Rev. Oral Roberts, and all evangelical preachers!) Fears feels that Robertson started a law school so he could place his "right wing Christian coalition disciples" in some government jobs, and control the government. This is a good idea except for us broad-minded, liberal thinkers. Now Robertson's father was a great U.S. Senator, and did much for Virginia politics, but Fears feels that Pat is doing a lot of harm to good government. Fears would like to fly Robertson's beautiful tan and brown, four million dollar Lear Jet parked in the Piedmont Aviation hangar at Norfolk Airport. Guess the little old widows' donations paid for that jet though. Rev. Pat Robertson has built a financial empire in Virginia Beach called the "Christian Broadcasting Station," and has started his own Regents University. The Rev. Falwell has built his church empire in Lynchburg, and has his own university called Liberty University. Sen. Fears figures that most of the money is donated from rich and poor widows who have been promised access to the "Promised Land." The only one of these evangelical types for whom Sen. Fears has any great respect is the Rev. Billy Graham, for he doesn't seem to be a despotic opportunist, but really and truly is a man of God.

Anyhow, Sen. Fears took the deposition and checked in as a space "A" guest as a retired Lieutenant Colonel at the Oceana Naval Air Station Officer's Quarters and, after partaking of two "stingers" and a chicken sandwich at the Officer's Club, argues with a Navy Captain, who happens to be a Wing or Squadron Commander. The Captain feels that we should apologize to the Japanese for the A-bombing of Hiroshima and Nagasaki. The Captain thinks we went too far, but Sen. Fears feels that no apology should be made. He agrees with President Truman after the terrible "Bataan Death March" and the beheading of Gen. Doolittle's flyers on the B-25 raid from the "Shangri La." These executions were done by the Japanese publicly in Tokyo. Fears believed we saved many lives of the Japanese and Allies by strategic nuclear bombings. After a very fine debate – no winner, no loser – in front of other personnel, including two female Lieutenants, Sen. Fears went to bed for a good night's rest. Incidentally, the food, drink, and the quarters were not free, as many taxpayers think. The room cost $16 per night, and it would have been empty if Fears hadn't occupied it, so in a way the retirees help support the programs.

Lt. Col. Fears doesn't appreciate the Japanese taking advantage of the economy in the U.S. by beating us in competition, and owning much of the real estate and businesses in the U.S. We are naive to think the Japanese there will open all their markets to our exports. It's the fault of the U.S. citizens in believing that Japanese automobiles are of better quality than U.S. automobiles. Lt. Col. Fears doesn't buy any Japanese or German products, but only U.S. products, if he knows it. He still remembers the days of WWII. This generation doesn't care, for they all have the "me only" complex, and surely not "ask what you can do for your country" philosophy.

After a good night's sleep in the Officer's Quarters and a good argument in the Officer's Club with the Navy Captain, Fears heads for the Norfolk Airport to catch his first leg flight of his trip to Alaska by flying American Airlines to Seattle. First, there is a change of planes in Dallas, and it is a circus to find one's way and to rush to change planes. But it's a lot more exciting than stagnating in the little village of Accomac looking at the same old provincial faces. This is all an anti-climax after the death of the Hon. George Willis, whom Sen. Fears helped prevent getting the full-time District Court Judgeship for Accomack and Northampton Counties.

Judge Willis was a Naval Officer during WWII. He was wounded in the foot and as a result had a pronounced limp. He had married a lawyer's daughter in Northampton County, and then practiced law with his father-in-law, one Quinton Nottingham, Esq. Because of inherited money, and a terrible disposition, he had all the qualities that other lawyers didn't care for. He was arrogant, pompous, opinionated, and just plain spoiled. Because of his family connections, the local powers that be with the appointive power named him the part-time County Court Judge, to pay a political debt to Quinton Nottingham, Esq., for 20 years of support. This was before the General Assembly designated the position as a full-time District Court Judge. No lawyer really wanted him to get the Judgeship, but some played hypocrite because they thought he would get the position in spite of Sen. Fears' opposition, because this is the way it had always been. Judge N. Westcott Jacob, the appointing authority for the interim appointment admitted to Sen. Fears that "Willis was an ass," but said he "had to appoint him because he had been a part-time Judge for a long time" and somehow was in Judge Jacob's support group. Willis' supporters had been Judge Jacob's supporters when he received his interim political appointment from the Hon. Mills Godwin (first a Democrat, and later a Republican) so the great Hon. Henry Howell, the "populist," wouldn't get elected Governor of Virginia. Fears supported Henry Howell for Governor against the "change of party" candidate Hon. Mills Godwin, who had first been elected Governor as a Democrat, and then ran as a Republican to defeat the Hon. Henry Howell, who had been a "populist" State Senator. It probably would have been good for Virginia had Howell been elected Governor.

One has to be an accomplished navigator to enter the right place in a commercial airport such as Norfolk, but Fears finally got to the correct entrance. Now one must enter a three-story parking garage, and go round and round each floor trying to find an empty space. Finally, in the poorly lit garage, one is found somewhere in the third level. (Good thing Fears isn't senile or he would not have been able to locate the car upon his return.) It used to cost $2 per day, and now the rate is $7 per day. All these new charges are irritating, but the most irritating is the $9 airport charge on the "old men's cheapie" tickets. This is a new and outrageous fee. Next is $4.50 for a Danish roll and a paper carton of orange juice. Good thing our traveler is getting social security benefits, to which he should be entitled since he has been working and paying the tax since he was 16 years old. Now the great revolutionary Gingrich did try to put this income on a "needs basis." Surely hope this professor never becomes President in the future. Many, including our traveler, think the President and Congress should be on Social Security retirement benefits like the rest of us, and not drawing their "golden parachutes" with their million dollar retirements paid by political contributors.

It was a beautiful day with clear sunny skies for a flight on the first leg to Dallas. Usually Dallas is covered with thunderstorms, and any flyer with any understanding has "white knuckles" in a thunderstorm. If one is on his way to Hell, he or she has to go through Atlanta or Dallas to change planes at these hubs. Anyhow, our Alaskan traveler lands in Dallas, and runs all about the airport trying to find the next flight to Seattle. Certainly anyone who flies a lot knows the frustration at a hub airport finding the next flight. Those video screens, which are supposed to help travelers just aren't as inviting as a live person to give directions and help. Anyhow, with about 10 minutes to spare, our traveler settles down in the next aircraft for the next leg to Seattle. Used to be that one could find an interesting conversation with the people in the adjoining seats, but now everyone is afraid of whomever is next to him or her. Will Rogers should be alive now for he would surely find some people he wouldn't like. Everyone looks and acts like a terrorist or hijacker!

Sen. Fears never dreamed as a youth in Arkansas that he would ever see Alaska. In fact, he probably never knew such a place existed. It is a lot better than "chopping cotton" in Arkansas for a living. Col.. Pete Peterson (who is from Jonesboro but four years younger than Fears) who Lt. Col. Fears ran into at the Officer's Club in England during WWII in the 92nd Bomb Group during combat operations, was quite a hero as a B-17 pilot with the DFC in combat. Col. Peterson stayed in the Air Force, and lived in Ft. Worth. Fears tried to telephone him, but couldn't find his number in the phone book to call from Dallas. Pete's brother, Brooks, like the Senator, was an Engineering Officer in the Army Air Corps and got to be a Major. Pete told Fears that Brooks lived in Memphis, so one time Fears flew out to Memphis in a Naval Aircraft called a C-9 in space "A" privileges and tried to locate Brooks, but couldn't find a number for him either. Guess neither of them is now alive.

As an added interest, the young defense lawyer in the Norfolk deposition was the successful image of a newly hired associate with an established law firm. He was white, Anglo-Saxon, with perfectly formed features (eyes, mouth and ears). His hair was trimmed just right and he had the egotistical air of a "Dorian Gray." This is the reason the Senator wanted to smack him. Fears' grandson, Matthew, is now a lawyer, and he wishes to practice International Law, but he has a long way to go. Matthew is tall and lanky, lets his hair grow long (to Sen. Fears' dismay) and like his father's mother, has a large "Gallic" nose. So he will have to shape up and be better groomed before he can succeed in an old conservative law firm like White & Case. Unfortunately, good features and good grooming are the first requisites for opening the

---

door to an old established law firm, unless one wants to be a hero like Bill Kunstler, Esq. Sen. Fears learned this lesson early when he was seeking a job as a lawyer.

The Alaskan Cruise started with two days rest in a small airport motel in Seattle, in a dark and dreary (but inexpensive) room, followed by a very tiring, bumpy bus ride to Vancouver to board the boat. Anyhow, it is now 4:30 PM and the "queue" has been long since 2:00 PM. Sen. Fears refuses to stand in this line for hours, after his experiences in the "chow lines" in the Army; so he found a Greek restaurant, and has stuffed himself with a "pita" and a bottle of Canadian beer. The Greek owner was quite friendly after Sen. Fears said *fairisto* (thank you) in Greek. He also told the Greek he was a member of the AHEPA, a Greek organization that assists Greek immigrants on entering the U.S. and Canada. After the line had dissipated Fears completed all the paper work and boarded the "Regent Star," and was directed down into the bowels of the ship to his "cheapie" cabin. It was unbelievable, with no porthole, and wasn't larger than a clothes closet. It had a double-decker bunk and a small curtained shower with no sides, only a drain hole in the bottom. The air conditioner couldn't be regulated so the room was freezing, and the toilet wouldn't flush. What a mess! Everyone below decks complained, as if complaining might help.

This is the "geriatric Noah's Ark," and no one is under the age of 70 it appears. After a day of freezing to death in his cabin, Fears got someone to cut off the air conditioner entirely, and unplug the toilet. Then, being next to the engine room, all the Senator could smell were diesel fumes. Anyhow, here we were on our way to Alaska, and everyone made the best of it. The shower was a long "snakelike" hose hung on a bracket, and when the Senator turned on the shower the showerhead flew around the shower and almost beat him to death. He had bruises all over his body after this, and had a terrible time explaining this to Dr. Belle, his wife, when he got home.

The "Regent Star" must have installed the original Edison tungsten filament light bulbs, because it takes a seeing eye dog to get about the ship, and everyone is "bitching" about the defective equipment, and the accommodations. It is learned that this was an old cargo ship that was refurbished as a passenger ship by some Greek financial backers. Just after this voyage, it is learned that the "Regency Lines" went out of business for financial reasons. At least the Senator didn't lose his voyage advance payment.

The first docking was in Ketchican. It was overcast, raining, foggy, and chilly. Four of the male guests (including the Senator) signed up for a salmon fishing trip to try to break the boredom. All four fishermen gathered at the dock, met each other, and boarded the boat. It was a forty-foot twin-engined fishing boat, and well equipped for salmon fishing. The weather was rough, blowing hard, and pouring rain, but it didn't dampen the fishermen's enthusiasm. The Captain was an old skinny guy with a beard, and the mate was a young college student following his father's footsteps as a pharmacist. He attended college in Seattle. He knew his fishermen's "stuff," for he baited the fishermen's hooks with fresh herring and each fished with a hand-held reel. Another line was submerged by some kind of gadget which trolled the bait about fifteen feet deep. The fishing was good, and each fisherman caught a twenty-pound salmon, and it was as much fun as anticipated. The other three fishermen had theirs dressed and packed at $5.00 per can at a processing plant right at the dock, but Sen. Fears brought his aboard the cruise ship where the chef agreed to prepare baked fresh salmon, and serve it to the six people seated each night at Sen. Fears' table, where they were served at the second seating at 8:30 PM every evening. After eating at this hour, Sen. Fears went to bed feeling literally like a "stuffed salmon." In New York City this meal would have cost at least $100 each. By now Sen. Fears really wished he was home in his comfortable bed instead of the "bunk bed torture rack" in which he was trying to sleep with a full stomach every night. This trip is not what was pictured in the colorful brochures, but it is something reasonable for this "geriatric crowd" that's different from their routine life at home. This is a first and last experience in Alaska for William Earl, and he certainly has no intention of retiring to Alaska to put up with all these wonderful hardships. Everyone living in Alaska loves the place, but Sen. Fears would rather be living on the "Costa del Sol" in a nice condominium, and dining on *paella*.

On the next leg of the Alaskan cruise, the ship went outside the inside passage, and the water got rough, with plenty of icebergs. Everyone kept thinking of the *Titanic*, but then we had all gone through the lifeboat drill several times. We did see a whale flap its tail, and saw several dolphins playing about. The next day we docked at Steward, and from there took a bus to Anchorage over rough roads, stopping to observe many road repairs along the three-hour trip. The Alaskans describe the seasons as the "ice/snow season," or the "construction/repair season." We drove through one place that had been wiped out by the earthquake back in the '60s. This place was surrounded by muck, and if one walked on the muck it would draw one under like quicksand. No one was interested in trying this walk. Arriving in Anchorage, we found a thriving metropolitan area with lots of industry and plenty of retail establishments. Then we boarded Alaska Airlines and took off for Seattle. The flight was uneventful, but it was instruments all the way. Sen. Fears spent the night in the same motel in Seattle, and left the Seattle Airport via American Airlines the next day.

They didn't land in Norfolk until dusk. It was "raining cats and dogs," and the Senator had forgotten that the roadway to Accomac was under repair. Visibility was terrible, and with no white lines here to follow. It was one of these black shiny nights, with heavy traffic when one takes his life in his hands. When the Senator reached home, his wife called him an idiot for not staying in Norfolk in a motel until morning, but there is nothing like two big belts of scotch to tranquilize an unnerved one at home. The trip was interesting, and so were some of the people. The service was outstanding and the nightly shows were great. There was a vibraphone player who was unequaled by anyone, including Lionel Hampton, and his performances were outstanding. Sen. Fears has a vibraphone which he "hunts and pecks" on while his wife plays the piano some – shades of President Clinton and Lamar Alexander. Now, after this trip, Sen. Fears was ready to return to the daily grind in his country law practice, and walk around the house taking a look at the yard work.

Several of the cruise guests, including Sen. Fears, took a tour by bus, to see the Governor's mansion which is really a modest house, and the State Capitol is unimpressive without the usual Capitol dome. They visited a place called the Red Dog Saloon, which was built in the gold rush days. It still has a dirt floor, with sawdust thereon so the "tobacco chewers," of whom there are many, can still spit on the floor without "gagging" everyone else. A beer costs $3.00 a glass, and next door at a restaurant with the sandwich shop one can buy a plain ham sandwich for $8, and then there is the tip! Being a real tightwad, William Earl returned to the ship where he had already paid for the food, and it was good and plentiful. On the ship, there were also "Specialty of the Day Cocktails" for $2.50.

The boat next docked in Skagway where only 700 hearty souls live in the Wintertime and in the Summer 2,000 people make some kind of living off the many cruise ship passengers. Took the old "White Mountain" narrow gauge railroad about twenty miles up White Mountain Pass, and listened to a lecture about the 1898 gold rush stampede to the Yukon. Sen. Fears thought the gold fields were in the U.S., but learned they were actually in Canada. All these gold rush stampeders, and the ones who built the railroad, had to be crazy. The railroad workers were fairly well educated people who needed a "stake" to enter the gold fields, so they worked on the railroad construction for $30 per day doing extremely dangerous work. This impossible feat – to reach the top of the pass with the railroad – was finished in twenty-six months, and then it was relatively easy going down the mountain to the Yukon River and the gold fields. The scenery on both sides of the train was really beautiful. Literally thousands of people looking for a better life had made this trek by then.

Many visitors don't feel sorry for the stampeders, but the SPCA should have been around in those days because those "gold-crazy" people were really cruel to animals, and some Alaskans still are to their "dog teams" in some of their competitions. Along this trail of death during the gold rush is a place called "Dead Horse Gulch" where 500 starving horses trying to pull the overloads up this mountain fell into crevices, and fell down the mountainside, tearing off legs, and breaking necks only to perish in the end. These crazy stampeders didn't even have the human decency to shoot them in their misery. These old time stampeders were real "bastards" and not great Americans or great pioneers. All their activities were simply motivated by greed and cruelty. Sen. Fears feels like they were "gold rush crazy," selfish and mean to each other and the animals.

An Indian fisherman with Fears saw the fish weren't biting on the salmon trip, so he looked to the East and started some "mumbo jumbo" chant which the rest of us couldn't understand, and immediately there-after those on the boat caught four salmon as fast as they could be reeled in. Whatever his Indian prayer was it was very powerful medicine. The Indian was invited to each of the other's habitats in the lower forty-eight to say the prayer for a good fishing trip. The Indian tried to teach the prayer to Sen. Fears, but it was harder to learn than the Greek alphabet.

So today starts the rainy week on the cruise, and it rains all week. William Earl wishes some of this rain would fall in Virginia where there is a drought, and all the crops are dying on the vine. They surely need the Indian in Virginia, but then one can't fool "Mother Nature" probably. My lesser-educated friends, who work on the water and on the farms in Virginia, believe the bad weather of late is the result of the space exploration, and especially the moon shots by NASA. They feel that the atmosphere was so disturbed that this has caused all the bad weather. They are as bad as many educated scientists who are blaming all the bad weather on global warming, and this may well be, but Sen. Fears feels the earth is simply shifting on its axis, and the U.S. probably shifts either closer to the sun, or further away depending on the axis changes of the earth. All these weather changes probably stirred up the "Hitleristic" groups in Yugoslavia to kill each other. Sen. Fears was a soldier, and to him all Yugoslavs look alike. He can't understand how they know whom to shoot. They must wear different colored armbands to differentiate each clan from the other.

The Indian claims he loves to hunt and fish, and that he has hunted Kodiak bears in Alaska. He says they are eighteen feet tall and weigh a couple of tons, and that they are carnivorous. He claims one cannot outrun a bear and the best thing to do is to face the bear and look docile. Then if the bear keeps coming, get on one's knees and put one's head between one's knees. The guy from Memphis wants to know what good this will do, and the Indian replies, "So you can kiss your ass goodbye."

All docked the next day at Juneau, the capitol of Alaska – known as the most dangerous city in the world because of the frequent avalanches; yet people continue to build on the sides of the mountains. We visited "Mendenhall Glacier" and everyone is awestruck with the magnificence of nature, for these millions of years the huge glaciers have existed. Why doesn't "global warming" melt these ice monsters?

A large brown bear entered a store on his own in Juneau, looking for something to eat – smelled the food in the local supermarket and entered through the electronically operated doors – as the customers and employees vacated the store quickly from the other exit doors. The bear discovered some loosely packaged food, and sat down and helped himself (or herself). Finally, the wildlife agents came, tranquilized the bear, and carted him off by airplane to the high country were bears are supposed to reside, and far enough away so the bear couldn't find its way back to Juneau.

Sen. Fears' salmon was baked to perfection, and served at his table. The group consisted of an elderly lady with her mother (the mother was 82 years old – can't even guess the daughter's age); an elderly gentlemen who had been a submariner during WWII and had lately retired from the Beech Aircraft Corporation (think he was some kind of aircraft line assemblyman); anyhow, he said nothing at the table except that the salmon was good, and a young, hefty, dyed red-haired lady with a "Buster Keaton" haircut talked all the time. She was an artist of some sort, but at least kept the conversation "bubbling" with her very interesting experiences in life. She was from California and, of course, wouldn't want to live elsewhere.

We wouldn't have caught that salmon, for we fished for a long time without a nibble, but one of the four guys claimed to be a Cherokee Indian from North Carolina. He had all kinds of trinkets about his neck and a genuine Indian belt with some "doo-dads" attached. This guy had a bad limp, and we all learned that he had been an electrical inspector working on high-rise building contracts. Somehow he had fallen three floors down a shaft, and was broken up badly, especially his back and legs. He was lucky to be alive, but is now totally disabled and has retired on a successful lawsuit recovery against the main contractor for negligence in not complying with OSHA regulations.

Chapter 16

How to Outlive One's Enemies

Sen. Fears, because he has been so active and doesn't just roll with the punches, and kiss everyone's "backside," did make and has made enemies, but that goes with the territory of being a lawyer, and a public office holder. In 1979, when Fears was trying to get lottery legislation, and ethanol legislation passed, he went to dinner one evening at a Chinese restaurant and then went back to his hotel room after dinner (after a couple of "stingers"). About midnight, he woke up with a terrible pain in his stomach. The pain would not subside with a couple of Tylenols and with a hot bath. He thought it was the Chinese food. He went to the session that day with the pain and got Dr. Buchanan, an M.D. and a fellow senator, to give him a prescription for Paregoric, hoping a little opium would make the pain go away, but it didn't help! The next morning he checked into the emergency room at the Medical College of Virginia for examination.

A Gastroenterologist checked him out with x-ray, palpation, and all that and thought he had an impacted bowel, so the staff gave Sen. Fears an enema, which was the worst thing they could do. Fears actually had a "retrocecal appendix," which the doctor didn't diagnose. (In all fairness to the doctor, he did want to check him into the hospital for further tests, but Fears had important legislation pending and wanted to continue working in the legislature.) The pain continued for a couple of days and then subsided, but William Earl then just felt very sick. William Earl couldn't tolerate feeling so bad, so he drove home and went to bed. Dr. Belle Fears, his wife, immediately drove him to the local hospital, and Dr. Bill Burton, an internal medical genius, immediately diagnosed the problem as a ruptured appendix. Dr. Milton Kellam, now deceased, another great doctor and surgeon, immediately operated on Fears and found a large abscess. It took Fears ten days of being very sick to recover enough to return to work.

The first day back in his law office in Accomac, an IRS agent was waiting to audit his 1979 tax returns. Fears took him to another office in private and showed the agent his gauze-covered incision with the drain. Fears said to the agent, "Fellow, your timing is atrocious." The agent said he would return another time, but Fears simply handed him all his books of accounts, and his checkbooks, gave the agent his back office with a calculator and told the agent: "Go ahead and do your thing, but just don't bother me unless you need me."

The agent worked most of the day without bothering Sen. Fears and took his work back to his Norfolk office. He required Sen. Fears to file an optional form for certain deductions which the Senator had taken on his Schedule C form, which Sen. Fears did himself. However, the Sen. reviewed his and his wife's charitable deductions and added every nickel and dime for which he could find a receipt to the A and B Schedules. The outcome was that the IRS sent Sen. Fears a refund check for $700, and they haven't bothered to audit him since.

The other members of the General Assembly of Virginia felt sorry for their colleague, William Earl, who almost died from the ruptured appendix and helped push forward the lottery legislation, and the ethanol legislation. Ironically, had the Senator been present, he would have had to fight to get the legislation through. Sen. Fears had other operations that were not life threatening, but were painful. The operation, which saved him from very early retirement, was one to remove an eye cataract by replacing it with an implant and this worked well. Then, fifteen years later, he had to have the other eye operated on for another implant to get a total lifestyle change. Sen. Fears can still pass his motor vehicle operator's license examination, but had to give up his love, which is piloting aircraft. He also sold his big Harley Davidson motorcycle when he reached the age of 70 because of his eyesight. He felt that if he had an accident the broken bones wouldn't heal well either at his age; but he was still more active than most men at that age.

Please understand that a single Circuit Judge in a rural area has all the despotic power in the world. Judge Jeff. F. Walter's enemies knew him for what he really was, a "smiling back-slapping politician" who told everyone what they wanted to hear. Judge Walter ran the county with an "iron hand" and was in the background the titular head of the local "Byrd Organization," as it was known then. Now it is hoped things have changed for the better.

As soon as Sen. Fears won his election to the Senate, he wasn't long in signing on as the patron of the bill establishing the "Judicial Review Commission" which is an arm of government acting as the watchdog over the malfeasances of the Virginia Judiciary. In the past few years, several recalcitrant judges have been removed from the bench, or haven't been reelected. Also now if a Judge takes indecent liberties with minors, as the one County Court Judge was accused of doing in Accomack County, the complaint is made to the Department of Social Services and they investigate the offense and then prosecute it if necessary. Thanks to people like Sen. Fears the laws have been changed to help protect the public interests, which takes the political pressure off the elected County Persecutor trying to do his or her job as it should be done.

Before continuing this exposition about one's enemies, and so that the reader doesn't get the impression that William Earl is paranoid and doesn't like anyone, he wants to name a few great personalities whom he respects and would help in any way he could. While at Yale, he met and befriended one Edward Benjamin, Esq., who graduated from Tulane Law School and is a senior partner in a very reputable law firm in New Orleans. This guy grew up with tremendous inherited wealth from his father. He had a new car at Yale and carried William Earl where he wanted to go. He was a down to earth sort of person and was a fine person to have as a friend. William Earl took his wife to New

Orleans in the '90s to the Sugar Bowl to a football game. While visiting there, he telephoned Ed and they had lunch together for which Ed picked up the tab. Jack Selby, an engineering graduate and for years a soil conservation engineer in Virginia, is a fine person, and so is his wife Lee. Jack is one of the most honest men William Earl has ever known and has supported William Earl in all (or at least most of) his endeavors in the State Senate. Then there are Pete Wray, Gary Agar, Esq., and Nick Heil, Esq. Although Hon. Elmon Gray inherited about $30 million from his father, he is not pompous as many rich people are, and has always been supportive of William Earl and his projects.

William Earl's favorite needy child was being raised by her grandmother, and attended Walsingham Academy, but without financial help she would have had to drop out of the Academy, even though she was a top student. William Earl helped her as much as he could, and when he called on Elmon, Elmon gave Walsingham Academy $2,000 to help this child. Elmon has written William Earl and told him he is one of the people he misses most in the General Assembly. Elmon quit the Senate about the same time William Earl was defeated. There are many other great friends, but anyone remembers one's enemies indelibly.

William Earl can't recall the person's name, but there is a quotation that "one can count true friends on one hand." This is really an understatement for most people have more close trustworthy friends than this, but all of us have enemies whom we will never forget. The three great enemies remembered most by William Earl are : Judge Jefferson F. Walter, a Circuit Judge who tormented William Earl for many years until the Judge finally died; E. Almer Ames, Esq., the State Senator defeated by Sen. Fears who always damaged Fears as much as he could (but William Earl understands this); and the Hon. Charles M. Lankford of Northampton County who was a big "Byrd Machine" supporter and politician.

E. Almer Ames was the President of First National Bank, which was bought by First Virginia Bank Shares (a Virginia national bank), but old Almer continued as chairman, and made certain his son, Edward A.

Ames, Esq., got to be Chairman after Almer's death. One of Fears' friends, by the name of Garland Evans, was a member of this board and allegedly made a motion to elect William Earl to this board, but E. Almer Ames, Esq., would have no part of this, and made a 30-minute tirade against Fears. Anyhow, Fears was finally elected to the Signet Bank Board of another local bank by request of the bank chairman, a great Harvard graduate and a brilliant banker by the name of Frederick Deane. Deane died relatively young of a heart attack and William Earl lost another great friend.

Hon. Charles M. Lankford got to be the most politically powerful man in the Eastern Shore of Virginia, and was well known throughout Virginia. He was so politically popular he could have gotten the Democratic nomination for Congress supported by the Masons, for he was once the Grand Master of Virginia Masons which is no small honor. "Charlie," as his friends called him, was highly respected by all but didn't want the upstart "come-here" Fears to get elected. He hurt Fears some, but Fears got elected. Charlie was so powerful and so close to Gov. Mills Godwin that he got the Circuit Judgeship for a while even though he was over 70. Then he retired from the bench four months before the General Assembly met and used his influence on Gov. Mills Godwin to get his friend Wescott Jacob, Esq., appointed in the interim as the Circuit Judge by the Governor.

One of the closest and best friends William Earl claims was one James N. Belote. Jimmy was the Battery Commander of an Army National Guard Battery in Onancock, Virginia. William Earl was a First Lieutenant in the new U.S. Air Force, but there was no place to join an air force unit in the Eastern Shore of Virginia. Capt. Belote encouraged William Earl to join this battery, which he did as a platoon commander. This involved lots of work and study of artillery and related subjects. William Earl performed in this unit for eleven years, and got to be a Captain. He and Capt. Jim became fast friends. They made trips together and worked well together. William Earl owned a one-third interest in a Cessna aircraft, and Jim and William Earl used to take a break and fly around the country to various places. In 1958, before Castro ruined Cuba, they flew the aircraft to Veradero, Cuba, landed at a Cuban air base, and had a week's wonderful time on the lovely beach there. Unfortunately, Jim died suddenly at the age of 65; so another good friend is gone.

Now that some of William Earl's best friends are dead – and his most ardent enemies as well – we can proceed with our story. When William Earl was a younger lawyer, and had just lost the reelection as County Prosecutor (because of bad publicity supplied by Judge Walter, Ames, Ayres and Lankford) he was quite irritated at them all. One day on his way to the Battalion in Portsmouth he was riding the ferry, which was the link to the mainland, and in his Captain's uniform he came upon one Harold Parks from Exmore, but Fears didn't know that Parks would "kill for Lankford." Parks asked Fears how he liked Lankford. William Earl, still stinging from Charley's efforts to defeat him for reelection, replied to Parks, "As far as I am concerned, I can't stand the old son-of-a-bitch." Parks told Lankford about Fears' comment and this came back to haunt Fears later. There is an organization on the Eastern Shore called "The Eastern Shore Shrine Club." Since Fears is a Shriner, a friend of William Earl's came to his office and wanted Fears to file an application for membership in the Club, which Fears did. One can be "blackballed" by three members of the club to stop one from entering. The friend returned to Fears' office and told him he would be rejected because Harold Parks had gotten two of his friends to vote with him against Fears' initiation into the club. Not to be publicly humiliated, William Earl withdrew his application. Harold Parks told Charlie about this and Charlie told Harold not to do it. Charlie was big enough to tell Parks that "politics is politics," but that one Shriner wouldn't do this to another unless there was truly a moral issue involved. Charlie was big enough to do this and immediately gained some lost respect from William Earl. The club finally allowed Fears to join.

Years later, William Earl was called upon to repay this debt, which he did. William Earl had reached senior status in the State Senate, and had some influence. Harold Parks approached Fears and wanted a bill introduced naming the Ocean Highway after Charles M. Lankford. Fears wanted to name the highway after Charles Russell, the one who had really developed the Ocean Highway, but pressure from Harold Parks and Lankford's friends influenced Fears to introduce the bill. Fears really didn't think the bill would pass because he thought Russell's family and friends would defeat it. But the bill became law, and the arterial highway (which is U.S. Route 13) is now named the "Charles M. Lankford Highway" and a dozen signs mark the road, all as a vivid reminder to Sen. Fears. The old adage of "politics makes strange bedfellows" is certainly true. Oh well! William Earl would rather have it called "Charles Russell Highway." The Russells, a large family, probably held this against Fears and probably didn't support him for the last reelection, even though they probably don't know what really happened.

William Earl would lead the reader to believe that he has more enemies than friends, but that isn't the case. In many elections, he has received over 70% of the votes on both sides of the Chesapeake Bay, and really his enemies are few compared to supporters, but the enemies are in positions in which they can greatly harm him, and impede his life's progress. As we had written, most of the old ones are dead, but some new ones are now on the scene.

William Earl, like other people who have lived many years, has had his share of health problems. He had a ruptured appendix; a complete nose resection because of nose polyps; two eye cataract operations; polyps removed from his intestinal tract by colonoscope; and a spondylolythesis of his spine which bothers him when physically irritated; along with the usual run of illnesses. William Earl takes pills for high blood pressure, pills for his enlarged prostate, and pills to keep up his vitamin levels. Other than the above, he is in fairly good health.

While William Earl was at Yale in his senior year, everyone had to take some form of physical training. This was mandated so that all would be good "gun fodder" for the great war effort. He decided running up and down stairs in the Payne Whitney gymnasium wasn't for him, so he enrolled in the Red Cross swimming program. There he earned his Red Cross Instructor's Badge, which paid off in the future, for at one time before entering the armed services he was hired as a lifeguard at a community pool. Then in the service in the Aviation Cadets they woke everyone up at 5:00 AM and ran them for five miles, and then hustled them through strenuous physical training exercises. He was taught hand-to-hand combat, such as "Jiu jitsu" and "Karate," which came in handy later in probably saving his life from an assailant with a gun. William Earl, as an Aviation Cadet, and later as a Second Lieutenant in the Army Air Corps, was in top physical condition, weighing 130 pounds with no excess fat and could run five miles without losing his breath. He did smoke cigars, and chew tobacco in the service when overseas, and continued to smoke cigars and a pipe for about twenty years of his life. He finally concluded that he should give up smoking, which he did. He drinks about two ounces of alcohol nightly, for one of the medical journals stated that this was good for one's health by somehow reducing the bad cholesterol in the bloodstream.

For years, William Earl has jogged two miles per day, lifted weights and ridden an "Exercycle" in inclement weather. He punches a heavy punching bag, and "pulls and hauls" on all kinds of exercise devices daily. William Earl bought a small building, placed it on his residential property, installed an air conditioner for hot weather, and electric heater for cold weather and uses it for exercises. He has now placed all his exercise equipment in this building, and has named it the "pout house." He has bought running shoes, and has various sweatshirts and trousers in which to exercise. This all works out very well for William Earl is now 81 years old, rides his bicycle to and from Accomac, and exercises every day. His blood pressure is under control, but not his weight – for he loves to eat good food, which is his main and only sin. He can see well enough to pass his motor vehicle driver's test and his motorcycle operator's test. This "brass ring" is that he has outlived his enemies, practiced law full-time (which includes extensive trial practice), is studying advanced Spanish and French conversation, and is attending the Community College for computer courses. He has outlived his old enemies, and this is the way to do it; then one can lay back and tell lies about one's accomplishments. *"Estupendo!"*

Chapter 17

ENGLAND REVISITED

William Earl was stationed in England in the 8th Air Force during and at the conclusion of WWII on a base near Northampton, England, with the 92nd Bomb Group, first as an Aerial Gunnery Officer and later as an Engineering Officer. He did fly with crews on a B-17 G on several combat missions over Germany until the war ended in May of 1945. The actual location was at a place called Podington, England, which is just a small village; not really on the tourist map.

During the war in England, William Earl, then Lt. Fears, met a lovely lady in London on leave. She was married to a British Naval Officer who had been stationed in the CBI Theater in India for four years without leave. The lovely lady had a six-year-old girl who was quite attractive and intelligent. With much uncertainly with the bombs falling on London, and with the Lieutenant on a combat status the lady and the Lieutenant formed a rather close friendship. When he could, Lt. Fears went on leave to London, met the lady, and tried to forget the war.

After the War, the lady divorced the Naval officer and married a fine gentleman who had been a prisoner of war in a German prison camp for four years. This new marriage was a good one and another little girl was born. Edward, the new husband, was manager of a manufacturing plant in London and commuted daily from Essex to London. The family owned a cottage in Essex where Rosemary, the first child, and Melanie, the second child, were raised. Lt. Fears continued corresponding with Lady Winifred after the war and each followed the other's careers through yearly correspondence. Dr. Belle Fears was gracious enough to accept the relationship, and Lady Winifred and Dr. Belle exchanged correspondence and Christmas presents over the many years. Twenty-five years after the war, William Earl and his friend Capt. Jim Belote bought TWA tickets on a tour package price and had intended to visit Normandy, France, for the D-Day celebration. First, however, they landed in London for a short stay. Lt. Fears telephoned Lady Winifred and told her they were in London. She insisted on them visiting Essex for a day or so and they took a train from London to Essex and checked in to an antique hotel in Saffron Walden with a room for two. A call was made to Lady Winifred and she and Edward, her new husband, came out in their automobile, picked the travelers up and carried them to the couple's cottage for tea and a visit to this beautiful countryside.

Edward and Winifred drove Lt. Fears and Capt. Belote around Essex for a couple of days and Lt. Fears and Capt. Belote treated the pair to a delightful dinner at the "Rose and Crown" dining hall in the hotel where the happy soldiers were staying. On a trip to the men's room, Edward quietly told Fears, "I had misgivings about your visiting us, old boy, but you are really a regular fellow." Rosemary, who is now married, even told her mother, "I think it is objectionable for Lt. Fears to come out here to visit you now that you are a newly-married woman."

Anyhow, all went well and the Lieutenant and the Captain left, promising to have the teenaged daughter, Melanie, as a guest in each officer's home in Virginia. Melanie did come to Virginia, stayed a week at the Fears' residence and a week at the Belotes' residence. Lt. Fears had his son, Brad (who was then 20 years old and home for the Summer) helped in entertaining Melanie. Capt. Belote also had a teenaged son named Patrick to entertain Melanie at his home. It was a pretty good visit without too many tantrums on anyone's part. Melanie has since married a Public Accountant and has three children of her own, and both Lt. Fears and Capt. Belote are very happy that none of the children resemble Brad or Patrick. Brad is now a medical doctor and Patrick is an engineer working for NASA.

Now as a sequel, Rosemary's daughter, Emma, and Rosemary's husband, Trevor, came to the U.S. about thirteen years ago with Emma's friend, Claire. Trevor visited a couple of conventions as necessitated by his fire director's position in England, and the girls traveled by air and bus all over the U.S. All spent a couple of days at the Fears' residence and new friendships were made. Later, Lt. Fears learned that the hotel in Saffron-Walden had burned and eleven people, guests of the hotel, lost their lives. It's ironic but the room occupied in the '70s by Lt. Fears and Capt. Belote was on the top floor, and had it burned then both would probably have lost their lives.

Edward, Winifred's second husband, died about ten years ago and Winifred has moved to a place in the north of England into a condominium which she owns. She sold the cottage in Essex after Edward's death and she now lives alone. She is 85 years old (or more), Lt. Fears is 81 years old, and his friend, Capt. Belote, is now deceased and his wife has since remarried. Everything has changed and everyone is getting on with his or her life.

Dr. Belle had always expressed the desire to visit England so Lawyer Fears arranged to take a week's course in International Law and the History of English Law at Cambridge University. He booked a charter flight, reserved a room in the Holiday Inn in Cambridge, England, for the both of them, and set off for a three-week visit to merry old England. Belle had arranged to visit Trevor, Rosemary, and Winifred in Dorset at Trevor's home. They arranged to have Emma and her new baby, Kate (who was born out of wedlock), there for the travelers' visit, too.

In Cambridge, England. it was "wall-to-wall" people and, in fact, so crowded one could not walk the streets comfortably. The place was packed with automobiles and, because the students could only have bicycles, the place was crowded with bikes. A U.S. Circuit Judge named Miller was killed by an automobile while in Cambridge. The cars operate on the left and he looked right instead of left and stepped out in front of a car. The streets also have bicycle paths along the road and the bicycles can be operated in both directions. Several times

William Earl thought he would be killed by a bicycle, for while he looked left for an automobile a bicycle would be coming from the opposite direction and almost run him down.

Cambridge Professors were British and because of their accents William Earl had a difficult time understanding them. What he got from the courses would be that "ole England" will never agree to a uniform currency with the other members of the European Market, and the Common Market was formed for one reason alone, which is to "screw" the United States in commerce. Unlike Japan, though, the Ford Escort is a popular car in England, perhaps because it is built there. William Earl learned that Pillsbury Baking Company and Stauffer Chemical Company are now owned by the British, and an upstart entrepreneur now operates an airline called "Virgin Airways," and owns the Coca Cola franchise and many other businesses. Wonder if he pays his taxes to support the crown? He probably resides in the Cayman Islands, and has a Swiss bank account.

While in Cambridge talking to the British, William Earl learned that this great country has the same development problems as the U.S. They have the same labor movement problems, and the "Underground," similar to the New York Subway transportation system. Employees were on strike so the cabs were prospering. It costs about $7.50 to go any short distance in London by cab. The British mail carriers and other employees were on strike, and the usual student protestors were in the streets, but William Earl couldn't figure out what they were really protesting.

William Earl finished his courses in Cambridge, and he and Dr. Belle thoroughly enjoyed the great English breakfasts for they were paid for with the room charge. Neither wanted their cholesterol counts checked after all the eggs, ham, sausages, rolls, butter, fruits, kippered herring, milk, and preserves and both gained too much weight on the trip. They attended a student presentation of Hamlet in one of the colleges, probably Emmanuel College. The performers were very professional and all remembered their lines perfectly, but the play was too long for William Earl so he went out for air and remained outside at intermission.

On a Friday, the travelers took a bus to Northampton for a couple of days, and then a cab to Podington, and the air base where William Earl had served with the 92nd bomb Group of B-17s. The base is now a farm, and some clever entrepreneur had bought the old runway and some of the Nissen huts, and has resurfaced the long runway and turned the place into a "drag strip" which is now quite famous. The place is named "Santa Pod." No one seems to know why it is named that. The management allowed the travelers to enter the place and the owner came over for a chat with this 92nd Group ex-servicemen. William Earl told his great war stories and the owner listened with what appeared to be rapture, but perhaps he was just being polite. The ex-Lieutenant visited the runway, and Dr. Belle took pictures with him giving the victory sign. Then they went to an old church in Podington and there found a memorial with the emblem of the 92nd, reading "To Fame's Favored Few – to the Gallant Airmen of the 92nd Bomb Group." At least the British remembered the "boys over there." More than once William Earl heard the Brits comment that, "The damned Yanks were over here – over-paid, and over-sexed." Oh well! It's all in life's game.

From Northampton, England, our travelers journeyed to Bath, England. This is where the medieval Londoners showed off their frills and tried to emulate the Romans. They even have a monument to "Beau Brummel" who claimed to be the King of Bath. During his time, he closed the town down after 11:00 PM and prohibited dancing. It is said that Princess Anne told him she was a Princess and she could dance as long as she wished. Beau Brummell told her he was the King of Bath and if she didn't obey his commands she could return to London. The old Roman Baths, for which the town was named, are still there and it cost $6.00 each just to look and listen to recordings describing the history of this place. One needs a seeing eye dog though to get through the exhibits.

Back in London, the travelers didn't stay at a very expensive hotel, and deferred high meal costs by staying at the Victory Club right in the center of the city. Of course, the Lieutenant and now Lieutenant Colonel had to join, which cost $20.00 and the room was about $45.00 per night. They had to use bathrooms down the hall, but they were adequate if one didn't have "old-age bladder" trouble, which William Earl did. He solved this problem by using an ice bucket for his frequent "pees." The place had a cafeteria-style dining room but where one could order a la carte, and the place even had a dining room for good evening meals.

The Fears' saw many sights during their four-day stay. They took the tour bus around the landmarks of London first, and then took other buses to visit Buckingham Palace and the Gardens, and some museums and churches. The Palace was opened the first day for visitors and cost £7.00 each for admission, the fee supposedly used to repair the fire damage to Windsor Castle. The line "snaked" all over the gardens for the tickets, and the line to enter the palace exceeded about a thousand people. William Earl and Dr. Belle weren't willing to suffer this much so walked through the beautiful gardens and saw the changing of the guard, that is, what they could see of the guard. William Earl looked at old Queen Victoria's statue sitting on top of her monument and realized that she had "fleeced" all the colonies around the world during her reign to accumulate this tremendous wealth for the royal family. The royal family is so wealthy William Earl can't write the number of British pounds they are worth. What nerve to expect the public to pay the cost of repairs to Windsor Castle! All their holdings are so many and so extravagant that it costs a fortune for all the dress uniforms for the guards, the gardeners, and the many household and other servants. William Earl simply cannot understand why the poor people of England put up with all these costs and extravagances. It's something called the "Monarchy." What a waste, and now all the scandal in the royal household?

William Earl envies wealthy families who inherit so much in the U.S. without earning it, but he is completely shocked at the waste of wealth on the spoiled Monarchy in England, with all the homeless people sleeping and existing in the subways and the underground tunnels. Also, many people are actually going hungry in England, as they do in the U.S. It's ludicrous for the average Briton to tolerate this situation. No wonder the IRA is blowing up parts of England to try to prove their plight in Ireland, not that William Earl believes in the indiscriminate killing of innocent victims. He doesn't believe in Communism or Socialism, although these same conditions caused the rise of Hitler in Germany, and caused the French Revolution. There is no rich Monarchy now in Germany, nor in France – for in these countries the leaders are elected as they are in the U.S. President Clinton will leave office bankrupt after he pays his legal costs for all his problems.

England has the same social and economic problems and conflicts as the United States; however, I'll wager the English really regret placing the "tea tax" on these colonies when the United States was governed by England. In a way, England reminds William Earl of the United States and especially Mexico in its capitalistic structure. In Mexico, about 35 families control all the wealth in the country, and they are "Castellanos" or "Spanish Creole" families. The poor Indian descendants are a minority race as far as money and opportunities, and the wealthy families control all the economy. The remainder of the citizens are mere "peons."

In the U.S., about 5% of the population controls most of the wealth and industry; 20% of the population just doesn't have a chance of success and advancement. The very rich in all countries have all the advantages. One example is the Kennedy family. All the Kennedy children, with all that money, simply settle in a state and run for U.S. Congress and win. There were two Kennedys in the younger generation in Congress recently – one in New York and the other in Rhode Island. Certainly, if they hadn't the name, and the money, they wouldn't have been elected. In England, the Royal Family, the Grovesnor Family, Freddie Laker, and about 35 other families control all of the wealth and the industry. What William Earl can't understand is how they pay their taxes legally and still maintain all this wealth.

William Earl was born in a very poor family in Arkansas, and he tries to pay his taxes as he should. There is no way to compete with those who inherited their wealth before the tax system started to take the "big bite" out of everyone. William Earl is also doubtful that when Joe Kennedy and some others made all that money there wasn't a lot of "hanky panky" in the moneymaking deals.

William Earl doesn't have any derogatory thoughts about people like Bill Gates and Ross Perot, for they added much to this country's prosperity and scientific development. But people like Steve Forbes, the Kennedys, the Vanderbilts, and the Rockefellers add little to the good of the country. People like the late Doris Duke and the Kennedys invest all their money in tax-free bonds and other "freebie" investments and, being on the inside, simply make more money on "hot tips."

William Earl was impressed that in the Hyde Park area of London there are thousands of foreigners. They own businesses and most of the professional places such as pharmacies, etc. These immigrants come from Saudi Arabia, Morocco, Iran, Iraq, Turkey, and other far-flung places. These people came to England with their oil wealth, and have made a great impact on the social structure of England. William Earl and Dr. Belle entered a Turkish restaurant thinking it was a Greek restaurant, and William Earl, in his naiveté, ordered a Greek salad. They were lucky to get out of the restaurant alive.

England, like the U.S., has many racial conflicts. Blacks from Jamaica, "mulattos" from black soldiers in WWII, as well as black immigrants from Africa, feel as though they are being discriminated against – and perhaps some are – but they are so much better off than they were in their countries of origin. The crime rate is higher now, and the drug violations are rather pronounced. The white native Briton blames most of the drug and crime problems on the blacks, just as the average white American feels about crime and drug use in the U.S. The English call the blacks "nig nogs." Teen pregnancy in England is rampant, and also resented by the older generation. In England they have free medical care, and they have aid to dependent children also. The sales tax in England is 17% and gasoline costs more than $4.00 per gallon to pay the expenses for all this government help to the people allegedly in need. The teenagers smoke cigarettes as addicts, and most of the smokers are dying of lung cancer in the government-supported hospitals before age 50. England is crowded with people, cars, bicycles and motorcycles – unlike it was when William Earl was there during WWII.

There are just too many people in the world now and William Earl and Dr. Belle are glad they will not be around to witness the economic downfall of the U.S., but it's coming again just as it did in 1929. England is no longer a world power, nor will the U.S. be in the future. William Earl is convinced that China, the new Germany, and Mexico will be the coming new economic and political world powers. To William Earl's shock and surprise he has just learned that the largest balance of trade deficit is with China. The trip to England has been enlightening. The Irish situation is the final thorn in England's side. The IRA is still killing innocent people in England, and William Earl and Dr. Belle were very happy that there were no explosions on the buses on trains on which they were passengers.

At the Victory Club, where our travelers stayed, William Earl talked to a porter from Ireland. He was a Catholic. William Earl expressed his concern about the dangers in London and the Irishman responded, "Well, you are here and alive, aren't you?" William Earl asked the Irishman to explain what this was all about in Ireland. The Irishman said, "You'll never understand. We just like to fight."

William Earl has decided that all the strife in Ireland and Yugoslavia will never be solved because of the conflicting economics and long-standing ethnic and religious hatreds. Perhaps the U.S. should stay out of these worldwide conflicts for they will never end – we have needy people in this country who deserve our financial assistance and we owe our enemies overseas nothing. They don't care for us anyway.

England is such a pleasant country to visit, and if a citizen of the U.S. could earn a living there by being welcomed into the professions I'm sure that more North Americans would like to live there. If it weren't so expensive to retire there, William Earl would like to do just that. With Belle with him he also learned that she liked England, too. In their travels by train, bus, and taxi they found the average

Englishman or Englishwoman more than courteous. To enter a busy place in England everyone "queues up" in an orderly and courteous manner for service. Our travelers were most impressed with the conduct in the Underground (or subway), unlike in New York City where it is a real battle to get on or off the subway. In London, to use the Underground when crowded, as it usually is, the British "queue up" and there is no pushing or shoving. Also the British have a great sense of humor. William Earl and wife Belle visited Duxford, England, and toured the Air Museum, where there is a collection of WWII aircraft and they are all being restored to flyable service. While there, on the outside, our travelers observed a beautiful Spitfire taking off from the grass, and performing aerobatics with probably a British pilot at the controls. A British gentleman was standing near William Earl. This gentleman commented that he was an ex-Spitfire pilot, but stated he hadn't served in WWII. He claims to have served in the RAF in the '50s. Mind you this visit was about 1994. Fears said he had served in the 8th Air Force in WWII, and (teasing the Englishman) he claimed to appear as young as the Englishman, whereupon the Englishman retorted by saying, "I say, ole chap, you obviously haven't looked in a mirror lately." Our travelers also visited the Cambridge WWII cemetery where many U.S. Army Air Corps personnel, who were killed in that war, are buried. Those who survived that war and others realize that any war is a waste of men and materials for naught. Anyway someone had to stop the German "juggernaut" started by Hitler or we all might have met the fate of the Jewish people in Hitler's final solution.

Chapter 18

ONWARD TO SPAIN

Retired Master Sergeant William P. Bell came by the Senator's office and convinced William Earl that they should go to Spain on a gigantic U.S. Air Force C-5 cargo plane leaving Norfolk Naval Air Station. Now this airplane is a monster with a huge body and four jet engines. One can stand up in an engine intake and not touch the inner engine ring. It has eight massive landing wheels in groups of four on two struts and two nose wheels on one strut. The cockpit of this giant looks like a "penny arcade" with all the lights, buttons and dails. This airplane does occasionally carry passengers with the cargo, seating about 70. The seats are on the upper deck and each passenger must climb a 40-foot ladder to enter the seating compartment. Each passenger sits in a comfortable seat which faces backwards for added safety reasons. One can't see out like commercial passengers, and has absolutely no control of the airplane or the crew.

William Earl is a retired LTC and Bell is a retired M/Sgt. Bell and has been retired after 33 years of service. His father was an early Army Air Corps aviator trained at Randolph Field, Texas, and was an instructor pilot. After the downsizing following WWI, Lt. Bell, Sr., returned home and was killed in an aircraft accident in an old seaplane flying passengers for fun. Sgt. Bell was three years old when he lost his father, and his twenty-year-old mother had to go to work to help support them. He was raised by a step-grandmother, and really came up the hard way.

During WWII Bell, through a tortuous route, ended up in the Army Air Corps in Italy during combat. LTC Fears ended up in England in combat. Fears was released in 1946 and returned to law school. Bell reenlisted a couple of times and finally ended up as the aerial engineer on plush U.S. Embassy passenger aircraft as part of the crew, flying political "big shots" such as Generals or Admirals all over the world. Bell jokes that he used a "wet gunnysac" as the fire control on ground starts for Gen. Billy Mitchell, and as the aerial engineer on Air Force Two flying Vice President Alvin Barkley here and there. LTC Fears stayed in the active reserves and got his 28 years in the service. Both men had retirement rights, and the right to fly in military aircraft as Space A passengers (that is, if seats are available).

People joke about this and complain that if a prospective Space A passenger has loads of time and patience he or she can fly Space A. For the taxpayer's benefit, it doesn't cost them any more because the aircraft is going there anyway. Fears and Bell checked into operations at the Norfolk Naval Air Station on March 3, 1996, and luckily got the evening flight in pretty rough air across the Atlantic. It was rough enough for the pilot to throttle back to a reduced speed to take the load off the wings. The flight takes about nine hours and it's noisy and uncomfortable. In fact, one must wear earplugs to protect his or her hearing for the inside is so noisy. They landed in Roda, Spain, about 9:00 AM local time, with five hours of jet lag, and found quarters in the Navy Lodge (for $52 per night, in case the taxpayers think retirees get rooms for nothing).

The Spanish government runs everything on base under a "status of forces agreement." The retirees can't shop at the Base Exchange or in the liquor store. They had breakfast the next morning at the terminal, got some Spanish money, and rented a small 5-shift SEAT auto to drive to the Costa del Sol. They talked to the pilot who was a Captain from the U.S. Air Force Academy, and had trained to fly four-engine heavies. The pilot had been flying about five years and knew her business. The pilot was an attractive 26-year-old woman. Isn't this most interesting?

The fellow travelers, M/Sgt. Bell and LTC Fears shared a nice room at the base Navy Lodge, but each snored so loudly that neither could get any sleep. The room was quite comfortable with a private bath and a kitchenette. The next morning with the small Spanish SEAT, our travelers headed for Torromolinos, Spain, which is the busiest resort town on the Costa del Sol. M/Sgt. Bell wanted to drive, claiming to know where he was going from prior experiences. After four hours of driving, Bell missed the exit to Torromolinos and there are no exits along this express roadway until one reaches the city of Malaga, a crowded industrial place with a port and the railroad terminal. By now it was getting dark and our travelers got lost in the city of Malaga.

Fears insisted that Bell stop at a service station so Fears could try out his newly learned Spanish to get directions back to Torromolinos before dark, but Fears lost his $200 pair of prescription dark glasses, and there was no way to turn back. Bell missed the exit again and they ended up on another express highway to Seville, Spain. Now the men's friendship was really tested. Fears wanted to drive but Bell insisted on driving. Somehow our travelers got on the correct road back to Torromolinos, found an exit, and entered the town; now a city.

Now that our retired military travelers had finally found their prearranged apartment, called the "Bajondilla," and checked into a small comfortable room with two small beds with a private bath and small kitchenette, they learned early that one doesn't dine in the hotel restaurant associated with the "Bajondilla." The restaurant's menu is suited for Malcolm Forbes, Jr., based on its prices. The bar does make the most palatable Margaritas for about four bucks, American money.

The next morning our "Marco Polos" scouted the lobby and the programs. On entering the lobby a voice called out, "Is that you, Bill Fears?" It was a guy from York County who never once voted for Fears. He had owned an insurance business in Yorktown, and vacationed in this place every Winter to enjoy the climate, the food, and the older ladies on the loose. With him was an 84-year-old man from York County who also knew Fears; he lived in Torromolinos in the Winter, also. Can't remember his name but he had retired from NASA as a GS17, with plenty of the taxpayer's money for the good times. He had a replacement hip and knee, and would you believe he played tennis every morning with a different lady friend. The second day our travelers saw our old guy moping about, lovesick, because his wealthy 50-year-old Austrian widow had returned to her home in Austria. He must have had something on the ball because the attractive lady was planning to buy a place in Florida (where our elderly friend now lives to escape Virginia income taxes, which Florida does not have). Anyhow, with his "love" gone our friend waited until the next day to find a new tennis partner, and whatever else he could find. There was quite a selection of wealthy, elderly widows from all over the world, including several French Canadians from Montreal.

Our travelers then started to find some excitement in the beautiful city of Torromolinos, and there were many interesting nationalities present: Japanese, French Canadians, Danes, Swedes, French, Italians, Germans, and more. The largest groups on tours were from Canada, Denmark, Germany, and England. All but one Danish man was friendly. Sgt. Bell asked the Danish lady where she was from, and her jealous husband walked over to Bell and in an angry voice said, "We don't ask people where they are from." Sgt. Bell and the lady involved both apologized. LTC Fears talked with several French Canadians about the Quebec separatist movement. Fears suggested to each that they were hurting themselves economically and politically, and that they were hurting the United States economically, but each one suggested that the British government in Toronto was treating the French people unfairly and it was a matter of pride. Each then reminded Fears of the Revolutionary War, and the Civil War, and this Fears understood.

The first night Bell and Fears visited a famous restaurant called the "Casita something-or-other." If one orders the *Especialtie del dia*, it's a set reasonable price that includes soup, an entree, and dessert. But if one orders *a la Carte* the price doubles. Fears ordered lamb chops and Bell did the same. Bell also ordered dessert, a flan of some sort. Of course the bill was double the price as compared with the *El Menu* meal. Bell got mad and reluctantly paid his half, but informed Fears that damned if he was going to listen or follow Fears' advice again for dinner. After that, the friends parted company and each went his own way. Hunter Fletcher, the guy from Yorktown, introduced Bell to a wealthy, fat, middle-aged lady from upstate New York, and it is suspected that from then on she paid his and her way. He is quite a charmer, so the ladies say!

After the day of discord over the expensive dinner, the men didn't see each other until bedtime. And since they shared the room they did exchange greetings. Also, M/Sgt. Bell and his rich widow companion had a party in her apartment, and invited all the widow's friends and Bell's newfound friends. Fears was invited too, but he couldn't remember the lady's name or apartment number so he missed the party, which he heard later was quite a good one.

Fears did a lot of exploring. He found a public elevator that would take one to the top of a hill from the waterfront to the main part of the city for a cost of 25 *pesetas*. He discovered the bus station where (with his newly practiced Spanish conversation) he bought a cheap ticket and went to Mijas up in the mountains for the day, and visited this beautiful little town overlooking the City of Fueringillo on the Mediterranean. It was a picturesque sight. In Mijas Fears had a lunch of seafood soup and a bottle of locally produced Spanish beer. He started a friendly conversation which some nice folks from Wales. They had a house in Fueringillo and drove up into the mountainside that day just for lunch. When Fears told them he had served in the 8th Air Force in England in WWII the "Brits" became even friendlier.

The next day was cold and rainy, but Fears didn't let this dampen his spirits. In addition, the Margaritas at the apartment hotel bar were the best in the world and could lift the spirits of even a "chronic depressive." Fears caught the train from Torremolinos to the big industrial city of Malaga, and then the bus to another coastal town called Nerja, which had the reputation of having many Brits living there and many "Brit-run" restaurants. At one of these establishments Fears ate some kind of beef dish and when he returned to the States he wondered about the now-discovered "Mad Cow Disease." Since he was 75 years old then he guessed it wouldn't kill him before his time! Why add more worry to life? The beef was well prepared in the British way. Had Fears bought the tours to these places it would have cost about $60 each trip and he would have had to tolerate the slowness and regimentation.

LTC Fears walked a lot on the beachside promenade called the *Calle Maritino*. Every day he lunched at different restaurants there and found the Spanish meals delicious. His favorite at *Almuerzo* was *sopa mariscos*. It was a seasoned soup made of prawns or shrimp, small clams, small mussels, maybe some lobster, and squid. Thank Heavens it was well cooked for no one wants hepatitis. The Mediterranean Sea is a large cesspool from which are taken all kinds of contaminated seafood. Fears wouldn't dare eat raw or steamed shellfish from the Mediterranean. People in Italy have caught cholera and many people in sea resorts have died from various forms of hepatitis. The French, Italian, and Portuguese still "slurp" raw oysters and mussels at open oyster bars with gusto. It is a way of life with them and "to hell with the risks." Many women bathe on the beaches topless, and one gets used to it in a short while, although Fears feels like an "ant at a picnic" at times. For dinner, or *cena*, Fears tried to dine at a different restaurant each night. The menu in each was about the same. It seems that all the chefs must have attended the same culinary school. For a change Fears dined one evening at a Spanish-speaking Chinese restaurant, and another night at a French restaurant. It was all tasty but some were better than others. In each restaurant Fears talked to the people at adjoining tables and usually found them receptive and friendly. The Spanish people outside Madrid are extremely helpful with everything one attempts, including conversation. It's a great country and many North Americans enjoy living on the Costa del Sol. It is much more friendly than New York City, and a lot less expensive.

After a week in Torromolinos our travelers checked out, paid their "habitation" bill in *pesetas*, told everyone goodbye, and headed for the

SEAT five-speed car for return. In front of the lobby was a suntanned lady about as tall as Fears. She was packed and ready to return to her home in Denmark. Fears started a conversation in Spanish and learned she was fluent in English. He asked her where she had been all week, and she replied, "Around." Fears said, "I wish I had met you earlier," and she agreed. It's a good thing they didn't meet earlier or it might have led to big trouble!

Bell and Fears headed for Roda. Fears wanted to drive this time but Bell insisted on driving and on the way to the express highway they got lost again. After losing an hour they got back on the right road heading in the right direction, but the two travelers were hardly speaking to each other by now. After about a four-hour drive, they entered the Air Base at Roda and checked in at the expensive Navy Lodge, since the BOQ and BEQ were already full. Fears tried to get some sunglasses, but the Base Exchange wouldn't allow him to shop there and it was frustrating to see all the kinds of sunglasses on racks right at the entrance. Fears found a "merchant mariner" with PX privileges to purchase a cheap pair of sunglasses for him. Fears gave him $20 in cash and waited a long time outside with Bell, trying to decide if the unknown mariner would return with the glasses or the MPs. The honest man returned with the glasses, and the change and Fears gave him $3.00 for his honesty. They then wanted some dinner, but the Officer's Club was closed from lack of business; so they entered the Enlisted Men's Club and found a "zoo" and a den of noise, full of cacophony, and all other kinds of annoyances, but they did get a couple of "tube steaks" (generally known as hot dogs) which was better than nothing.

After the first night in Roda our travelers had breakfast at the terminal, checked in the SEAT and signed in at operations for a possible flight to the States on any aircraft going there. While eating breakfast, a voice from the next aisle said, "Aren't you Bill Fears?" And Fears replied that it was he. The white-haired, pudgy guy identified himself as Col. Riley from Washington, DC. Fears barely recognized him but Riley stated he had served in the same reserve unit with

Fears, and had worked in the same department for the FAA as Fears, and had resigned from the FAA about the same time as Fears did in 1962. Fears ended up as Claims Manager and House Counsel for the Avemco Insurance Co., in Silver Spring, Maryland. Riley had found a job as litigation attorney with the National Transportation Board in DC, and later as an Administrative Law Judge with them. Fears remembered trying an aviation accident case for Avemco in the '60s in Howard County, Maryland, against a lawyer named Paul Connally, Esq. Connally was tall, blond, and dressed in a $500 suit, and was good at his trade. Fears learned that Connally was a partner with Edward Bennett Williams, doing business as Williams & Connally. He also taught law in the graduate law school at Georgetown University Law School. Fears cleared the pilot, but a jury verdict for $100,000 was rendered against the flying club, so Avemco had to pay under the policy anyway and both Avemco and Fears were quite unhappy. Riley was there at the trial on behalf of the NTB (National Transportation Board), and had observed the trial and made Fears feel good by telling him he thought he had done an excellent job of defending the case. Anyhow, Riley had found his "brass ring" and was retired on at least $100,000 per year, counting his civil service and military retirements. Fears lost his "brass ring" by not getting the Accomack County Circuit Judgeship, which pays $115,000 per year. This is proof of the old adage about "how the cookie crumbles."

Fears is convinced there is a higher power controlling each person's life. Fears, in resuming his law practice, found he is the popular poor person's lawyer in his rural area, and much of his work is "pro bono." He is starting to enjoy helping other people who can't really afford a private lawyer. He lets his young partner make money with all the real estate closings and the like. Now Fears is retired.

After breakfast on the third day, our travelers waited again until about 6:00 PM and boarded the same old C-5 from Travis Air Force Base in California. Finally all took off into the "wild gray yonder" in a bad cross wind. They flew for three hours, intending to land in the

Azores to unload some cargo, refuel, and then head for the States, but the wind was so fierce the pilot aborted and all returned to Roda after six hours in the air. This reminded Fears of the old story about the pilot announcing his navigation system was inactive but there was good news, and that was they were making good time. The aircraft landed in Roda in the rain and heavy winds. Although all had been warned not to wear hats on the apron, Fears forgot to remove his cap and when he stuck his head out the door off whisked his hat! The airport employees are Spanish and a nice employee offered to help Fears find his *sombrero*. Fears thanked him and remarked that, "That cap is now in orbit over Paris."

What was even more aggravating was that they landed at 1:00 AM in Roda and Bell and Fears had no quarters. No one would answer the phone anyplace, so a cab was called and for $5.00 the travelers were carried about a block over to the BEQ billeting office. A patronizing Navy Chief at the desk gave them a room with two beds in an enlisted barracks, a long distance away. It was dark as a cavern outside and Bell, who can see at night better than Fears, headed off for the barracks. Fears called and said he couldn't see well at night, and Bell replied, "Then feel!"

Anyhow, after reaching the barracks the stairwell to the second floor was hard to find. The travelers went to the end of the building, opened the door to the end stairs, but this and the other door were fire doors, and closed behind them, locking them out. Bell, who had had a liver shunt operation, fell on the steps carrying two large bags. He had bought some dinner plates for his lady friend in the States, and a couple of bottles of Irish Bristol crème for his distant relative Mary Rose Lewis, who is the only divorced virgin in Accomac. Bell scared Fears because he was actually unconscious, and the backs of his ears were even white. Fears told Bell to lie right there and he would find the entrance, the stairs, and the room and come back for Bell and the bags. After the task had been accomplished, Fears went to the fire door and called to Bell. There was no answer, so Fears went out the fire door – which promptly locked behind him – and found no Sgt. Bell. Being very hardheaded,

Bell had recovered, carried the bags around to the front of the barracks, climbed the stairs and somehow had found the room, and was impatiently waiting there for Fears with the key. They entered the room, which was extremely dark. Fears reached around the door to find the light switch but couldn't find it. Bell stormed into the room in the dark and Fears heard a thump and then, "Son of a bitch!"

Bell had found the coffee table in the room with his shin. Fears remarked that it was better that Bell had found the table than he, and they didn't speak to each other again after that for a while. The latrine was down the hall and both men had "old-age bladders" and had to go to the bathroom four or five times per night. Fears, for the first "pee," put on his stockings, walked down the hall and into the latrine, and stepped into a wet area, which he hoped was water. After that an ice bucket was found for the remainder of the night. The Sergeant caught on and he too used the same means with another ice bucket. Anyhow, with the light of morning both felt better and Fears was extremely happy that he hadn't had to arrange transportation for Bell's body back to the States. The next morning, after two flights had been aborted, our travelers checked into operation at the terminal and around 8:00 PM all passengers boarded the same C-5 for the third attempt to get home. After 30 minutes in flight, the Air Force steward announced the aircraft had mechanical troubles. The pilot aborted again and all landed at Roda. The trouble was that a well door wouldn't close. All disembarked and Bell and Fears tried to get rooms at the BOQ and BEQ, but everything was full. So the "grumpy old men" checked into the Navy Lodge again, which was expensive. They had an argument over something, and Sgt. Bell checked out in a huff and sat up all night in the terminal. That night Fears was sleeping soundly when the phone rang at 5:00 AM. It was operations telling him that the same C-5 was taking off at 8:00 AM. Fears checked out, got a cab, and entered the terminal to find Sgt. Bell. Bell had tried to catch another plane to the States but there was none. He had told a couple of other "old coots" about the hat, and when LTC Fears walked by them they were saying something about a cap being hung up in the wheel well causing the mechanical failure of the landing gear. The joke was great, but Fears didn't bite. When all passengers got aboard, the pilot took off and they were on their way to the States. A good landing was made in the Azores and the cargo was successfully off-loaded and the aircraft refueled. After about four hours, the pilot took off but not until LTC Fears had told the crew that he had hired an artist to paint the name "CHRISTINE" on the nose of the aircraft. Everyone on the crew enjoyed the joke, and the male pilot, a very young Captain and an Air Force Academy graduate, complained that they had handed him this "piece of junk" at Travis Air Force Base in Los Angeles, and that he had been flying this wreck away from home in Europe and the Middle East for more than a month. He would be delighted to deliver it back to Travis for all the necessary repairs.

Knowing the condition of the airplane, a couple of passengers decided they would wait for another flight. But LTC Fears and M/Sgt. Bell, having been through rougher times on other events, decided that the pilot didn't want to kill himself so they stayed with the aircraft.

The flight was uneventful and all landed at Dover Air Base in Delaware, but Fears' car was parked at the Naval Air Station in Norfolk, Virginia. Fortunately, a Lieutenant in the Navy, who was a weapon's officer flying F-14s, and his young friend, an Ensign who had just been accepted into the naval flight program, had a car at Dover and all drove together to Accomac after dark.

Fears paid for the gas to fill up the car at Dover and bought dinner for all in Pocomoke, Maryland, on the way home at the "Upper Deck," which is noted for its variety of seafood. Sgt. Bell got mad about a discussion back in Dover regarding which gate to exit and "stomped out" of the restaurant leaving his luscious crab cakes on the bar. Fears asked the waitress to pack the dinner and asked the Navy Lieutenant to take the dinner to Bell. Bell "swelled up" all the way to Accomac and wouldn't talk to Fears.

The driver of the car let Bell and Fears off at Fears' law office. There Fears tried to call his wife Belle to come immediately to take Bell home.

Bell was anxious to call his lady friend, Ann, in Annapolis before 9:00 PM. Fears suggested he use the office phone, but Bell said he didn't know how the name was listed. Dr. Belle continued to "filibuster" as she usually did on the phone so Bell called Donald Sawyer, his other traveling companion, to come and get them. Sawyer wasn't at home so his wife Jane drove out to take Bell home first. It was a foggy night and the windshield was all clouded. Jane said she hated to drive at night, but Bell didn't care – just so he got home before 9:00 PM to telephone Ann, which aggravated Fears and Jane Sawyer.

Jane then dropped Fears off at his home. In a couple of days, Belle drove her husband to Norfolk to get his car. On the way back Fears stopped at Office Max and bought a Packard Bell computer which he had been wanting. Bell is still "swelled up" but he now speaks to Fears at the Elks Club. He hasn't cooled off enough to drop by his fellow traveler's office to make up though. LTC Fears and his wife Belle went to the movies to see "Grumpier Old Men," and invited Sgt. Bell to go along, but he declined.

Incidentally, M/sgt. William P. Bell has recently died while a patient in the "Old Soldiers' Home" in DC. We did hold a memorial service for him here in Accomac, Virginia. LTC Fears presented the eulogy.

Chapter 19

POLITICS

Incidentally, the old political boss, Judge Jeff Walter, was elected Judge by the Virginia General Assembly while he was in his second year of a four-year term as a State Senator. This election was illegal for the Virginia Constitution prohibits a member of the General Assembly from being elected a Judge during his or her term of office, but then – who would have the nerve to object? Fears tried to remove him from office, but that's another story. He was elected to office when the old "Byrd Machine" ran this state, and their Lieutenants influenced each county. At this time, there was a poll tax to prevent the blacks and the "poor folks" from voting. The poll tax was $1.50 per year, and one had to pay back taxes for four years. With the average poor person only earning $1 per day working for the landed gentry, they simply didn't vote. I recall B. Drummond Ayres, Esq., one of the "Byrd Machine" powers, stating that "everyone shouldn't have the right to vote." He was the epitome of the old pompous "landed gentry" of the times. The first thing Sen. Fears did after his resented election to the State Senate in 1967 was to sign on to a great bill which was passed to repeal the Virginia poll tax. A second bill, which also passed, created a Judicial Review Commission so that complaints could be filed by the public, and especially practicing lawyers, against bad Judges, and it works!

All the old conservative families in Virginia believed that U.S. Sen. Harry Flood Byrd was the "Virginia Messiah," but Fears felt that the Byrd "pay-as-you-go plan" set Virginia's infrastructure back several years. When Virginia did decide to issue bonds for infrastructures, it cost five or six times more than it would have cost had bonds been approved in the '30s and '40s. When Fears reached the State Senate in 1968 much was changed. Virginia issued bonds for highway and bridge construction, and bonds for educational buildings. Fears practically single-handedly pushed through the lottery, which provides Virginia with about 500 million dollars for the general fund each budget biennium. Also, Fears voted for mixed beverages instead of the hypocrisy of the "brown bag carriers." From 1966 onward, Virginia came into the 21st century, and at least Virginia is competitive with other states, and has a "AAA" bond rating.

After ex-State Senator Ames blocked Fears' appointment to the local First Virginia Bank Board, and got his son appointed as the Vice Chairman of the Board, Fears got the chance to return the favor. Ames represented the Virginia Highway Department in the Eastern Shore of Virginia Counties as its lawyer. He made about $50,000 per year from this in retainers. Anyhow, this position was a political appointment by the Virginia Attorney General. Ames, who always claimed to be a loyal Democrat, displayed a "Lane for Attorney General" bumper sticker on the right side, and a "Dalton for Governor" on the left side of his bumper. Dalton was a Republican, and Lane was a Democrat. Fears took a photograph of the Ames bumper with the Lane sticker and mailed it to the Republican candidate for Attorney General, Marshall Coleman, Esq., and suggested that if Coleman were elected he dismiss Ames. Lane lost, for the blacks voted against Lane who had, as a Democratic Delegate, supported massive resistance to early school integration. Dalton won the Governorship as a Republican and Coleman won the Attorney General's Office as a Republican. Coleman promptly dismissed Ames, and appointed a Republican friend of Fears.

One day Fears told Ames they were now "even" over the bank appointment, but of course the feud didn't end there. The poetic justice will get more interesting. Sen. Ames has a son named E.A. Ames, III, Esq. He was brought in as a partner in law practice with his father. Fears formed a law partnership with another local person who had returned home. This partnership was formed in 1961 and about 1966 Wescott B. Northam, Esq. (Fears' partner), was elected County Prosecutor. E.A. Ames, III, Esq. (nicknamed "Pooh" by his mother, for some reason), had imbibed too much with a local wealthy stockbroker friend and, while on his way driving home, an African-American man backed out with his car in front of Pooh and an accident occurred. Ames "raised cane" with the black driver, and a crowd of African-Americans gathered. A State Trooper was called. If Ames had apologized to the other driver and hadn't been so arrogant he could have settled the matter on the spot. The Trooper arrived, gave the black driver a ticket for "failing to yield the right of way" and Ames a warrant for "driving under the influence of alcohol." Fears noticed Sen. E. Almer Ames afterwards exiting from Northam's office, across from Fears' office. The Senator's lip was "poked out," which it was known to do when he didn't get his way. Fears learned that Ames had tried to get Northam, the then-County Prosecutor, and Fears' partner, to reduce the "drunk driving" charge against his son to "reckless driving," but Northam refused to do this. Sen. Ames quietly got his son to plead guilty before his friend, the then County Court Judge Ben Gunter, and had his license suspended for six months. Pooh Ames had to hire a chauffeur, an elderly retired member of the political elite, who had to drive E.A. Ames II, Esq., around for Ames to practice law. It didn't hurt Ames' practice though for all the "drunk driving clients" showed up in the Ames' law office after that.

In the late '80s Earl Jr. was invited to Ft. Monroe, Virginia, as a dinner guest of the "TRADOC" Commanding General Maxwell Thurmond, probably because Earl Jr. was one of the senior State Senators in Virginia, and by then a retired Lieutenant Colonel from the Army Reserves. It was a small group, one of the guests being the managing editor of the peninsula newspaper, The Daily Press. Fears also represented York County and part of Newport News, contiguous areas to Ft. Monroe. Anyhow, the General asked Sen. Fears what his plan was to take care of the drug problem, and being displeased with the

Senator's answer he opined that drug violators should be summarily executed as they are in Singapore, and that was that! Gen. Thurmond was designated as the Southern Commander to invade Panama and arrest Gen. Noriega. Thurmond's troops captured Noriega, but no one now seems interested in him. He is being fed, housed, and apparently treated well at U.S. taxpayers' expense. Sen. Fears wrote to Gen. Thurmond and asked him why he hadn't simply executed Noriega after a summary Courts Martial but, of course, the General didn't answer the letter. After the Panama success Fears learned that Gen. Thurmond had died of leukemia. Fears suspected this was the result of "Agent Orange" in Vietnam, for Gen. Thurmond had been a battalion commander there. At the dinner party, Gen. Thurmond told Sen. Fears he was a graduate of Kansas State, and not the USMA.

Another General at the dinner was a VMI graduate. Fears asked Gen. Thurmond how the non-West Pointers got to be General Officers. Gen. Thurmond replied that the West Pointers were young, and just wanted a free education, and that the non-West Pointers knew early on that they wanted a career in the military. Also the West Pointers were not assigned to the war in Vietnam, but were assigned to the Pentagon. Earl Jr. would have given his "horse and dog" to have graduated from West Point, and would have made the military service a career. Anyhow, Providence saved Sen. Fears' life. Had Earl Jr. graduated from West Point in the Class of '43, he would have probably been killed in combat along the way before reaching the age of 81.

Sen. Fears believes he is a politician who will "tell it as it is" and tells the frank truth. Politicians will tell the public what they want to hear. Bradley, Buchanan, and Perot did tell the "blunt" truth, but see what happened!

After Sen. Fears didn't get the "brass ring" as the Circuit Judge he returned to his office in Accomac with a new law partner by the name of Robert G. Turner, Esq., and handled a more leisurely practice before retirement. By now Fears is a "triple dipper." He is drawing retirements from the U.S. Army as a retired Lieutenant Colonel from the USAR;

benefits from the Virginia State Retirement Program for 24 years service as a State Senator; and Social Security Benefits. He is now part of the new "elite" living off the young taxpayers, which they have a right to resent. The U.S. Congress has established a huge retirement package for themselves, which they avoid explaining to the voters. Congress could balance the budget if they stopped promoting all the Admirals, Generals, Colonels, and Navy Captains and giving them high retirement benefits. Sen. Fears, as a First Lieutenant in the Army Air Corps with flight and combat pay, was paid the grand total of $404 per month. Now a First Lieutenant gets over $30,000 per year, and Admirals and Generals get about $100,000 per year with benefits. Fears can remember just before WWII, Gen. "Jimmy" Doolittle was a reserve First Lieutenant, "barnstorming" about the country to make a living. Sen. Fears remembers before WWII there were only five Generals, and five Admirals, and only two of these had four stars. Sen. Fears feels that the Defense Department has gotten too expensive, and this will destroy the U.S. economy as it did Russia's. The Defense Budget could be cut if everyone didn't get to be an Admiral or a General, or a GS17. This new elite spends their Summers in Maine in their Summer homes, and their Winters in the Bahamas or Arizona in their Winter homes. They shop at the Commissaries and dine at the Officers' Clubs. The "ring knockers" have a way of perpetuating their speedy promotions.

The news media can be very unkind to a politician, and they can make one or break one. Also, the public can be very unappreciative of a public servant. Gerald Ford was an all-American football player, but a terrible golfer. He should never have played golf for he hit a couple of bystanders in the crowds watching him. Anyhow, the press exaggerated this and branded Ford as a "stumble bum." This is all President Jimmy Carter's supporters needed to claim Ford had been kicked in the head too many times in football. Sen. Fears feels that Gerald Ford was a highly intelligent person. He was a Phi Beta Kappa key holder, and graduated in the top of his law school class from Yale. The news media literally destroyed Ford in his reelection campaign. Sen. Fears had "an apple from this bag" too, for the newspapers finally helped defeat Fears for reelection in 1991.

The Daily Press and a little "jerkwater" weekly newspaper called the Virginia Gazette in the Virginia peninsula destroyed Fears in his sixth election bid. One simply can't tell the truth or make any colorful statements as a politician anymore. Probably redistricting defeated Fears too, for in 1991 Congressman "Bobby" Scott, an African-American Senator, and Sen. Hunter B. Andrews gave Fears 10,000 more people to his 150,000-person district instead the usual 150,000 as Scott and Andrews retained. This gave Fears 120,000 constituents in the peninsula, many from the upper part of Newport News, and the lower part of Gloucester County, leaving 120,000 people in the peninsula, and 40,000 in the Eastern Shore Counties of Accomack and Northampton. Fears won 64% of the votes in the Eastern Shore Counties, and lost with 40% in the "Peninsula Counties and Cities." Also, Sen. Hunter B. Andrews didn't want all these Republicans in his district in the redistricting division in 1991. Scott got his "black district," and is now a U.S. Congressman, and ironically Andrews lost his reelection the following election year – which is some "poetic justice" for Fears.

In Fears' reelection, he was endorsed by the big Virginia newspapers (The Virginian Pilot, and The Richmond Times Dispatch) as a statesman. The local papers in the Peninsula (such as The Daily Press and the weekly Virginia Gazette) really did him in with articles and especially bad editorials. Part of this philosophy was simple: provincialism and supporting the local person who lived in the "Peninsula." Fears also takes much of the blame, for the MADD group was pushing legislation to lower the blood alcohol content to 0.08% for a drunk driving conviction. Fears debated this floor amendment before the world, and he thought he made a great humorous speech for 30 minutes. The Amendment was defeated in the House; Scott had put the floor amendment in and got elected to Congress – which was probably his motive – and Fears helped defeat himself. During Fears' address he made the statement that he had voted to lower the blood alcohol content from 0.15% to 0.10% and that was low enough. He pointed out that every Catholic Priest would be arrested for finishing the wine chalice after every "high mass" and every wedding. He also said that if we continue "we will take all the sport out of drinking – and driving." Politically, this was deadly – the news media had a "field day," and so did the MADD people in supporting Fears' opponent.

The other rich kid who helped build the luxurious law office on Lankford Highway (named by the rest of the struggling lawyers as the "Taj Mahal" or the "vacuum cleaner") got his wealth from his father who inherited his "nest egg" from his father. When this man graduated from law school, the father bought him the biggest mansion in town for a graduation present. The father made his money in selling his Holly Farms stock to Tyson's Foods. No wonder the "poor boy" from Arkansas resents the "rich boys" who compete with the "poor boys." The rich have no idea what long suffering and unfair advantage can do to one's self esteem and ego.

Anyhow, Dr. Belle retired as director of the Health Departments in the Eastern Shore of Virginia, and Bill was finally defeated as State Senator of Virginia after 24 years of service. Both Bill and Belle draw retirement incomes from the Commonwealth of Virginia. Bill remained in the U.S. Army Reserves and draws retirement income from that too. Bill did retire as a Lieutenant Colonel from the USAR. None of this retirement was really planned; it just happened. Bill was paid $1,800 per year when first elected to the Senate, and was told he might get to be a Major in the National Guard, and receive $100 per month retirement; which really turned into $1,000 per month from the Senate and $800 per month from the Defense Department, respectively.

Both Bill and Belle are also receiving Social Security benefits as they are over 80 years old each. Somehow the couple have survived the hardships, raised two children, and now have some financial security, but it has been "rough going" and an American "fairy tale." It is difficult to overcome financial disadvantages, to get educated, and to find an occupation in life that isn't simply drudgery. The rural county law office, and the "G.I.-built home" are both paid for now, and everyone believes the Fearses are wealthy.

If one is endowed with good intelligence, good looks, and good judgment (and some other selected attributes) there is some kind of a career in the U.S. for a college graduate. President Clinton, graduating from Georgetown, Yale, and Oxford, is a prime example of a "poor Arkansas boy" making it on hard work, good looks, and "good luck." Fears will always wonder who Clinton's mentor really was, but that hasn't been disclosed yet. He guesses it must have been Arkansas' Sen. Fulbright, a wealthy Arkansas man who made it through Harvard and created the Fulbright scholarship.

Chapter 20

THE MAKING OF JUDGES

Accomack and Northampton Counties in Virginia now have three Judges: a Circuit Court Judge, a District Court Judge, and a Judge for the new Juvenile and Domestic Relations Court. These Judges are elected by both Houses of the General Assembly, and not by the voters in Virginia.

When Earl Jr. brought his wife Belle and his children to Accomac in 1950 in an old LaSalle Sedan with a baby crib tied on top a new era was started. He rented a house for $50 per month, and began to work for an older lawyer by the name of Ernest Ruediger, Esq., for $35 per week. Fears didn't know it but Ruediger had another older lawyer in a "cubbyhole" sharing the office, and Fears ended up as the research "lackey" for Ruediger. The other lawyer had the nickname of "Turkey" Mason, and this is how he was known. He did look like a turkey, for he had a heavy "comb" hanging from his chin. Ruediger had led Fears to believe he would soon be a partner, as he had led Mason to believe the same thing years before.

Anyhow, Fears thereafter left Ruediger, opened a one-room office (after about six months with Ruediger) over a Medical Doctor's office near the courthouse area. Fears hired a handicapped secretary who typed with one hand, for the other was deformed from birth. He paid her $15 per week, and made about the same himself. This lady could type very fast with one hand, and was a very loyal employee.

Belle's father first built Belle a small office from which she practiced family medicine, and she was loved by the community, as was her father, Dr. DeCormis, who was in his 80s and still practicing medicine. He had been a member of the Board of Supervisors; Jailhouse Physician; County Nursing Home Physician; and Mayor of the Town of Accomac. After his death in 1966, a bronze plaque was placed in the new county office building honoring him for public service.

Earl Jr. established a reputation as a "fair and fearless" trial lawyer. There were about six established lawyers in the county at that time, but they were all "homegrown." Their fathers, grandfathers, uncles, and brothers had the practice of law "sewed up." The good old hometown boys got the "gravy;" and the "come heres" got those clients with sparse funds who wanted an honest hard fighting lawyer. All of the local banks were controlled by local lawyers, either as Presidents of the banks or as controlling board members. The real estate and bank practices belonged to a "closed shop." Now all the local banks have been merged with holding companies of national origin. Earl Jr. threatened all local banks in the area at that time ethically through antitrust laws, and now each has approved Fears and others for real estate closings, if the borrower requests Fears as his or her lawyer. The insiders still have the advantage, for if the customer has no lawyer the bank simply refers the client to its own lawyer. Anyhow, because things have improved so much, young lawyers from everywhere have flocked to the counties here and opened practices. There must now be 40 lawyers in the area, but the population of the county remains the same. In fact, there are too many lawyers everywhere in the U.S. It's no longer a top-rated profession, but a business. Lawyers seem by reputation below "used car salesmen" in the ladder of respect by the public.

The late Sen. E. Almer Ames was President of the local First National Bank, and at that time was also County Prosecutor, having been appointed to this position when a very kind and considerate lawyer by the name of C. Lester Drummond, Esq., was called to the Navy for service. Lt. Drummond had two years left of his elective term. The Circuit Judge at that time, by the name of Hon. Jeff Walter, appointed Ames (his buddy) to Drummond's unexpired term because he was in the "royal clique." When Lester Drummond, Esq., returned from WWII, Ames wouldn't give Drummond back his job, so Ames kept the job for several years. Fears, the "come-here" upstart, announced himself as a candidate for the position. Ames then ran for the State Senate against a delegate by the name of Hon. Wrendo Godwin. The "Courtyard Clique" was not going to give Fears a "free ride;" so they ran one of their relatives, whose grandfather had been a very "crusty" Circuit Judge, for the position. His name is Hon N. Wescott Jacob. But then two other hometown boys from old-line families jumped into the race. The "courtyard clique" thought Jacob would win, but Fears got more votes than the next two highest vote getters together, and because the Democratic Primary was the only contest in those days, Fears was elected County Prosecutor. He was hungry and really needed the position, and the $5,000 per year salary. The Circuit Judge at that time (1955) got only $6,000 per year. Now Judge Jacob's salary started at $14,000 per year, and the County Prosecutor now receives $80,000 per year. Some inflation since then!

At that time, the average busy country lawyer made about $8,000 per year net profit. At this time, the old lawyer's club managed to control the ethics rules. Fears couldn't advertise for business, and couldn't even hand out a card; so his wife Belle, at the breakfast table during the political campaign, said, "You don't really think you can win this election against the hometown boys, do you?" Fears replied, "Of course not, but legally I can advertise that I am a lawyer, and I can get to know everyone in the county." Anyhow, Fears worked his butt off and he doesn't know who was more surprised at his winning – his wife, the other candidates, the Circuit Judge who was the local political boss, or Fears' mother-in-law. The Circuit Judge, Walter, let Fears know in no uncertain terms that he was displeased and gave Fears no courtesies during Fears' four year term of office.

In 1959, the "good ole boys" of the local political machine picked one R. Norris Bloxom, Esq., an established lawyer from an old established family, to run against Fears. He had run second to Fears in the

1955 campaign, and was picked to oppose Fears on a one-on-one basis in 1959. Bloxom defeated Fears by 600 votes, for many reasons, one being the heavy rains on Election Day. Fears' supporters didn't vote – and Bloxom's friends, and/or Fears' enemies, did vote. This defeat was orchestrated by the "political machine" at that time, and the "poll tax" was an impediment to a large voter turnout, especially African-Americans who were then friendly to Fears.

L. Brooks Smith, Esq., a lawyer with a speech impediment who was the son of Judge Walter's client and friend when Judge Walter practiced law, was appointed by Judge Walter as the local part-time County Court Judge. This was a part-time judgeship that handled traffic cases, preliminary hearings, and juvenile offender cases. The local people called this court the "low court" and the Circuit Court the "high court." All County Courts at this time were part-time courts, so Judge Walter also appointed Smith as Commissioner in Chancery, and as Assistant Commissioner of Accounts, so Smith could make a living. It is somewhat known in the community that Judge Walter appointed Smith to these lessor paying positions because the Judge claims to have lost money in investments for Smith's father. You can believe it or not, but because of Judge Smith's appearance and personality he would have been unable to earn a living as an attorney if Judge Walter hadn't appointed him to these paying political jobs.

Anyhow, when Fears started practicing law in Accomac, he immediately "tangled" with Judge Smith, brought Smith up before the Circuit Court on a *writ of mandamus* and tried to avoid Smith's court. About this time Judge Smith was diagnosed with consumption and reported to a sanatorium in the Blue Ridge Mountains. What a relief it was to Fears to have a very fine lawyer named Ben Gunter, Esq., appointed as substitute Judge. This new Judge was able, intelligent, and did his job well according to the community. Things went well for Fears for a while. Smith's diagnosis was in error and he returned to the bench.

Another episode created new problems for Fears. Under Virginia law, if a child didn't reach its 6-year birthday before September 30th, the child couldn't enter school. Fears' daughter, Barbara, wouldn't reach her 6th birthday until November 15, so would have to wait a year to enter the 1st grade. There were no kindergartens at this time. Another lawyer had the same problem with his child. Fears talked with then Sen. Ames to try to change the law, but Ames would do nothing. Del. Wrendo Godwin did introduce a bill to establish the cutoff date in January. Fears went to the then Superintendent of Schools, a 76-year-old bachelor, who could care less about the students. Superintendent Henry A. Wise, who had this job since "Moses' time," sucked on his pipe and told the upstart Fears that, "I like the law the way it is." Anyhow, Attorneys Fears and George Walter Mapp, Jr., Esq., who had the same problem, appeared before the Education Committee in the State Senate and, after argument, lost this battle to change the law.

Fears felt that Superintendent Wise acted so much as if he owned the position, and wouldn't respond to him, or the public, that Fears searched the statue books, and discovered that since the Superintendent was 76 years old he was holding office illegally. The statute required mandatory retirement at age 70. Fears filed a *writ of mandamus* before the Circuit Court, Judge Walter for Wise' removal. Judge Walter called Fears to his office and asked: "What are you trying to do to my dear old friend, Henry A. Wise?" Fears told the Judge that the law required Wise' retirement, and that was that. The Judge was furious and threatened Fears again. Fears then filed a motion that Judge Walter disqualify himself. In about two weeks Wise voluntarily retired, and the school board, also controlled by Judge Walter appointed another of Walter's friends as Superintendent. This man was Royce Chesser, and he did a very fine job as the Superintendent in responding to the public. Fears and his wife taught his daughter, Barbara, at home. On her entry into the first grade she was given a test, after waiting two months, and advanced to the 2nd grade, as did George Walter Mapp's child, who was taught at home by her well-educated mother. Anyhow, this ended another era for Fears, but put him even deeper into *kimchee* with His Honor, Judge Jefferson F. Walter.

Judge Walter told his cronies, "Fears was the most dangerous man in the county." To Fears this was a great compliment, and all the other good citizens just smiled. Anyhow, when Fears ran against Ames for the State Senate Fears won by a landslide. The majority either approved of the "come here" Fears, or disapproved of Judge Walter, Ames, and their cronies. Fears would like to think that everything improved for the majority of the citizens of the Eastern Shore of Virginia by his service.

After Fears had served 3-1/2 years as County Prosecutor, Dr. J.L. DeCormis (Fears' father-in-law), and George Hope (the Sheriff of Accomack County) came to Fears and complained that Judge Smith was taking the youthful male juvenile offenders to his office, closing and locking the door, and doing other things. One of these boys was the son of one Brown, who was the IRS agent in the area. This boy was about 16 years old, and his offense was "blowing up mail boxes with cherry bombs." At that time juvenile offenders could be locked in the local jail until the case could be disposed of. Fears interviewed the young man on the Sheriff's suggestion. The lad was crying and told Fears he was afraid of the Judge; that the Judge took him into his office and tried to fondle his private parts. The IRS agent learned of this and wanted the Judge prosecuted. Smith had a wife and two children, and Fears wasn't certain that the lad was telling the truth. He asked the Sheriff to look up the names and addresses of all male juvenile offenders for the previous two years, interview each, and if anything was amiss to contact Fears. The Sheriff brought Fears the names, addresses, and telephone numbers of several boys who told the same story of molestation. The different boys didn't know each other.

During this time there were few laws to protect juveniles – had this happened in the '90s all Fears would have had to do was to refer these cases to the Department of Social Services, and they would have handled this. All Fears could do was take the affidavits of about 10 of these boys, who incidentally were spread throughout the county. Fears walked the floor for a month worrying about what to do. He went to the President of the local Bar Association, but he wouldn't touch this. He then had an interview with Judge Walter, the appointing authority for Judge Smith. He told Fears he wouldn't read the affidavits and these were a "pack of lies," and he would do nothing. He did tell Fears, the then-prosecuting attorney of the county, that he "would cut off Fears' head if he pursued this." The people in office around the courtyard began to talk about this, and Dr. DeCormis and IRS Agent Brown were insistent that something be done. Judge Walter got two of his cronies to investigate. They were senior members of the Bar – B. Drummond Ayres, Esq., and L. Brooks Mapp, Esq. They called Fears to Ayres' office and wanted to interview witnesses. Fears, in a couple of days, brought forth the Brown lad. Ayres and Mapp asked Fears to leave the room, but Fears refused for he felt he had the right to attend the interview. Ayres and Mapp harassed the witness badly and "promised to put him under the jail if he was telling anything wrong." Fears stopped the interview and advised Ayres and Mapp that the next time he would see them would be in a proper Court.

About a week went by while Fears prepared a complaint for removal from office for malfeasance of Judge Smith. This would be filed directly with the Virginia Supreme Court under the writ sections of the code. Another week went by and Judge Smith appeared in Fears' office and stated that "my friends must believe me that I'm innocent in these accusations." Fears handed Smith the affidavits for him to read. He read one or two and turned rather pale. Another week passed, and the weekly newspaper carried one paragraph buried in the middle of a back page that Judge Smith had resigned for personal reasons. Judge Charles M. Lankford who was a powerful politician in the Byrd Machine, along with the great political boss Judge Walter, got Smith a job driving the library mobile bus around the Eastern Shore, and when mumbling occurred among the parents of children entering the bus for books, they then got him a job in the state liquor store as a clerk. He retired from this with some pension, but he was still a Commissioner in Chancery and Assistant Commissioner of Accounts after all these years. This allowed Smith to make a little money to supplement his retirement income, and no one felt he could do any mischief in these positions. Judge Smith recently has expired.

Wise' removal and Judge Smith's resignation helped defeat Fears by 600 votes for his reelection bid as Commonwealth's attorney, for Smith's friends spread it around that Fears had framed him because he didn't like him anyway. Fears certainly didn't care for Smith, but he denies framing him.

Fears built a new office and joined Judge Wescott B. Northam in a new law partnership, but Fears finally had to leave the county where he found a job in Silver Spring, Maryland, as a Claims Manager and House Counsel with an aviation insurance company named Avemco, Inc. The Directors of the company elected Fears as a Vice president after a year. He later built a nice home in Maryland, but his wife didn't want to move to the DC metropolitan area so he sold the new house a week after he bought it. He worked four years in the Washington area. After Judge Walter's demise he returned to Accomac, built a law practice with Northam, and tried to reorganize his life again.

After Judge Smith resigned, Judge Walter appointed a substitute Judge, named Benjamin T. Gunter, Esq., whose father had been a Circuit Judge, Judge Gunter had the qualities of a Judge, and it was a pleasure for Fears and all the other lawyers to practice before his court.

Fears returned to Accomac and started to rebuild a law practice after Judge Walter's demise with his partner Wescott B. Northam, Esq. This was about 1967. Northam had already run against R. Norris Bloxom, Esq., and had defeated Bloxom for the office of Prosecuting Attorney. In Virginia it's called Commonwealth's Attorney, probably because Virginia is still a Commonwealth. At this time, Fears wanted to change a few more things in the Commonwealth; so he ran against State Senator Ames, a great "Byrd Machine loyal supporter," and by much luck and hard campaigning defeated Ames for the office in the Democratic Primary. There was no Republican opponent. Ames had held the seat for three four-year terms, and was ripe for defeat. In this race Fears, in winning, didn't know whether Ames or Fears was more surprised. By this time the community began to believe that Fears really hadn't framed Judge Smith; so Fears was elected by a margin of about 3,000 votes. Ames was highly respected by his cronies in the legislature, but had lost his support in Accomack, Northampton, York, Gloucester, and Mathews Counties, which comprised the Third Senatorial District.

Sen. Fears in his first session of the General Assembly ran into the Byrd Machine supporters of Ames, who Fears had just defeated for office, and the Senate members were "mad as hell" that Fears had defeated Ames. The old members of the Senate referred to Ames in endearing terms as "the Senate lawyer." The Senate leaders and the Clerk of the Senate placed Fears in the last seat in the right corner of the Senate Chamber. The first day in the session, a friend of Ames, Sen. Bill Stone, came over to Fears in the "coffin corner" and told Fears he had beaten his friend Ames and to "sit over here and keep your mouth shut."

Sen. Bill Stone was a man of integrity, however, and before he died of leukemia in the '80s he and Sen. Fears were the best of friends. When the Virginia Education Association was promoting tenure for teachers, Stone was the main spokesman against the bill. He stated that "good teachers don't need tenure and bad teachers don't deserve it," and Fears voted with Stone for he was absolutely right. Needless to say, the VEA rarely endorsed Fears in an election.

After many years and several elections Fears gradually moved to the center of the chamber, got to be the chairman of the Commerce and Labor Committee, and finally was placed on the Finance Committee. Fears was the desk mate of Majority Leader Hon. Hunter B. Andrews, the most powerful Senator in the Senate during his last ten years. Fears got to be "Number Two" in the Senate in seniority, and had many contributions from the "big money people" in the many campaigns for which he kept his seat for 24 years, because of his newly found "clout" as a chairman of that committee.

In 1991 Fears was defeated for reelection, mainly due to redistricting so that an African-American, Sen. Bobby Scott, could have a "black district" in order to get elected to the U.S. Congress, and Hon. Hunter B. Andrews could get re-elected. Scott is now a Congressman, and Fears and Andrews are out of the State Senate.

After Judge Walter died in 1967, the General Assembly elected one Hon. Charles M. Lankford as Circuit Judge, and Fears had to support him in the Senate nomination because Fears was a freshman Senator without any influence. The Senate was still full of the old Byrd Machine cronies. Lankford had been Grand Master of Virginia Masons, had been the Commissioner of Fisheries for years, and had support from all over Virginia. The local Bar Association members were so fearful of Lankford that no meeting was held, and everyone was afraid to run against Lankford, for he wasn't only politically powerful in Northampton County but throughout Virginia. The Governor, who was at the time the Hon. Mills E. Godwin, would have "bowed" before Charlie Lankford. Lankford never opened a law book while on the bench, and he came in at 10:00 AM and went home at 4:00 PM. His decisions were made "from the hip." First he ruled with his favorite lawyer; then he ruled with the favorite client, if a friend; then came the facts; and finally the law. Oh! but he smiled at everyone and patted all his constituents on the back.

Fears tried two heavy civil cases before his court by jury, and got big verdicts in each case. Lankford threatened to reduce the second verdict, and put Fears on terms to reduce it. Fears said, "Go ahead, and if the Supreme Court rules with me I'll collect 9% interest on the judgment." Lankford was about 68 years old when he went on the bench, and there was a statue mandating that all Judges retire at 70, but Lankford sat on the bench until well after he was 70 years old. Anyhow, the "Byrd Machine Boys" outsmarted Fears, for while Fears was still a freshman Senator, Lankford retired near the end of Lankford's term, before the General Assembly met and the great Governor Godwin gave N. Westcott Jacob, Esq., the interim appointment.

When the General Assembly did meet in January, Judge Jacob had been on the bench for four months. Fears wanted to nominate Wescott

B. Northam, Esq., and elect him to the seat. Sen. Garland "Peck" Gray, just before the Democratic Caucus met (and Gray was the caucus chairman), came over to Fears' seat with Jacob's name on a piece of paper and said, "Are you going to nominate this man, or am I?" Fears wanted to nominate Northam, but the Governor had already passed the word to his "Byrd Machine buddies" so the effort would have been futile, and Jacob would be elected anyhow. Jacob received one vote at the called local Bar Association meeting, Northam received one, and William King Mapp, Esq., received 22 votes for the Judgeship. At that time Lankford and Sen. Ames were "wired in" with the Governor, and although Godwin told Fears at a personal meeting with him that "I haven't made up my mind," Jacob had already arranged for other employment for his secretary. Godwin, the great Governor, had already made up his mind before Fears' visit. The Mapp supporters had met with the Governor, but these machinations are how the system worked in all areas at the time. The old saying "the name of the game" is how it works.

Fears wasn't supportive of Judge Jacob from the beginning for the Circuit Court nomination, but after Jacob assumed his duties on the bench he developed into a very fine Judge — by studying the law and preparing for each case before it was heard. He stayed on the bench for 25 years, and retired in 1991 on a full pension. Judges get three-and-a-half years credit for every year served on the bench in retirement credits; so Jacob probably receives more than $75,000 per year in retirement benefits, which is a rather high income in a rural area. When Fears entered the State Senate in 1968, the Circuit Judges received $14,000 per year, and the lower Court Judges were only part-time Judges. At first the areas with a higher cost of living supplemented their Judges' salaries, and the rural Judges made about as much net income as the best lawyers in each rural area. Over the years, Sen. Hunter B. Andrews, Chairman of the Finance Committee, with the help of the judicial patronizers, got the salaries of all Circuit Judges raised to about $95,000 per year, and passed a bill for full-time District Court Judges, and

Juvenile and Domestic Relations Court Judges, paying about $90,000 per year, with great retirement benefits.

Fears opposed these changes each year, claiming that the rural Judges shouldn't receive these yearly raises unless the other state employees got the same percentage increases. Fears finally learned that the General Assembly was filled with lawyers, and that the "Judicial Lobby" was the most powerful lobby in Virginia. In one floor speech, Fears said, "Our Judges are the best golfers in the U.S., and it isn't difficult to fill these positions," for there were many applicants for each of these choice positions. In fact, Sen. Peter K. Babalas was sincere when he offered to serve in Judicial office *gratis,* but the Senate didn't take him seriously. In 1979, Judge Jacob visited Fears' office and informed him that he was not going to reappoint Judge Gunter to the position of District Court Judge but was going to appoint one George Willis, Esq., the part-time Judge in Northampton County in the interim as the full-time District Court Judge. Before the General Assembly met in January, Fears asked Judge Jacob not to do this, and the Judge told Fears, "I owe this to Willis. I know Willis is an 'ass' but he has served a long time and I have to do this." The old machine was at it again, for they knew Fears wanted to nominate his law partner, Wescott B. Northam, Esq., and this Willis interim appointment was made four months before the General Assembly met. The "good ole boys club" thought they could outsmart Fears again, but they didn't get the "brass ring" this time.

In the contest between Northam and Willis, the local Bar Association didn't meet to vote because secretly most lawyers didn't support Willis, who was by then the sitting Judge, but they were afraid he would win and then be vindictive – and he would have been! Willis – even though he was a sitting Judge and this appeared highly irregular – went to every lawyer's office and tried to get each to sign a petition supporting him. Some, who had the "guts," wouldn't sign, but the weak ones signed. This petition hurt Willis before the House Courts of Justice Committee, for they felt that this was undue influence for a sitting Judge to put this kind of pressure on lawyers practicing before him. They didn't know the politics in the Eastern Shore of Virginia!

MAKING OF JUDGES (CONTINUED)

The Virginia Senate Democratic Caucus met first, and Ames had gotten his old cronies in the Senate to support Willis. Willis had driven all the way to Lynchburg to persuade Sen. Elliot Schewel that Fears was doing Willis wrong; so Senators Willey, Parkinson, Fred Gray, and Schewel walked out of the caucus, and didn't vote. The other 28 Democrats voted with Fears for Northam. Northam didn't try to persuade anyone; he left all the work to Fears, and this seemed to work for Northam. When the Senate voted on the floor, a turncoat Senator by the name of Herbert Bateman (who had been elected a Democrat and switched to the Republican Party) made a stinging floor speech against Fears for unseating a sitting Judge without sufficient evidence of misconduct, to prevent Fears from electing his law partner to the bench. Fears arose and reminded Bateman that he had put his brother-in-law, Judge Jacoby of Newport News, on the bench when Bateman was a Democrat in the Senate. The body went into laughter, and so did the gallery, but the press editorially criticized Fears, claiming a conflict of interest. An opponent from Northamptom County ran against Fears on this issue as a Republican, but Fears won the race handily. Northam was elected by the Senate and the House with overwhelming majorities, and Northam served for 10 years before retiring. No one in either body even nominated Willis.

No one ever complained about Northam's career, and in fact there were many compliments on his demeanor and ability as a Judge. Finally, Fears had a good, fair, and reasonable Judge before whom to argue cases. In fact, the Judge bent over backwards in Fears' cases to rule fairly. He many times ruled against Fears if there was any doubt, to impress the public that he wasn't biased. Fears was probably glad when Northam retired about 1990.

Fears asked Judge Jacob to hold off announcing the District Court appointment until Fears could talk with Willis. Fears went to Eastville to Willis' office, and suggested that he wasn't going to nominate Willis in the General Assembly session, but was going to nominate Northam. He suggested that this would be embarrassing to Willis and to Fears. Willis, in his anticipated pompous arrogant fashion, told Fears that "I have more friends here and in Richmond than you do, and I'll beat you in the General Assembly." Ex-Senator Ames orchestrated Willis' attempt to get him elected General District Judge, and Ames loaded about 50 of Ames' cronies in several automobiles and showed up for Willis' Courts of Justice interview in the Senate. Fears couldn't get witnesses to oppose Willis, except for a couple of ineffective constituents whom Willis had supposedly wronged. Anyhow, three lawyers, one being Daniel Hartnett, Esq., an "English import" who had married B. Drummond Ayres' daughter. Ayers had put Hartnett through University of Virginia Law School, and immediately made him a partner in his firm of Ayres and Hartnett. Hartnett appeared for Willis in the Senate Judiciary Committee. Hartnett's sign, after Ayres' death now reads, "Attorney at Law and Barrister." A year before Hartnett had urged Fears not to elect Willis as the Judge, and then when the "chips were down," he appeared before the committee as Willis' chief spokesman before 50 or more of Willis' supporters, and the Senate Courts of Justice Committee members. Two other local lawyers from Northampton County also asked Fears not to nominate Willis, one named C.A. Turner, Jr., Esq., and the other named Benjamin Mears, Jr., Esq. Both of these appeared before the Committee supporting Willis. Mears is dead for he shot himself, but when Fears reminded Turner and Hartnett what they had said to him before the nomination, Hartnett denied having said anything, but Turner was honest, and said he had had to support Willis because they both lived in Northampton County, and he was afraid not to support Willis because he thought he would win. Not to be outsmarted, Fears called Richard F. Hall, Jr., Esq., and advised Hall that if he didn't want Willis as Judge he had better gather all the lawyers he could to come to Richmond to appear before the House of Delegates Courts of Justice Committee when Willis was interviewed. The present District Court Judge, Hon. Robert Phillips, along with one L. Franklin Davis, Esq., Hall and Fears all appeared before the House Committee in executive session and they testified against Willis. The Committee almost didn't certify Willis' name as qualified to the Democratic Caucus. Finally, the Chairman of that committee stated that they had never disqualified anyone before.

In the buffet line of a charitable dinner party at the local country club, Willis smiled and spoke to someone behind Fears, and Fears thought Willis was addressing him. Sen. Fears thought he was speaking to him and responded favorably. This was a mistake for Willis "swelled up" and ignored Fears.

These Accomack County lawyers who came to Richmond to appear before the House Courts of Justice Committee didn't "pull any punches," for they openly testified that Willis was inept as a Judge, was opinionated, arrogant, and didn't know the law. The House Courts Committee almost rejected Willis as unqualified. Anyhow, after a "battle royal," Northam got the position. The news media, however, criticized Fears in all the editorials by accusing him of a conflict of interest in nominating his law partner to the bench. The Republican Delegates also yelled "foul play" for the "unseating" of a sitting Judge, but in spite of all this Fears prevailed and was reelected that year (1979) in spite of the criticism.

Northam was a very fine Judge, and after 10 years, with his additional credit of 12 years as County Prosecutor, probably retired with an income of approximately $75,000 per year. Northam's wife, a doctor's daughter, also inherited some money. Now Northam is in the "elite social class," had a couple of boats and a BMW sedan, and has put two sons through VMI on paid scholarships. One son is a medical doctor, and the other a lawyer. Judge Northam, now retired, does speak to his mentor, Sen. Fears, once in a while, but he is now elevated to a new "social status," and only mixes with the "high social elite." Sen. Fears is still struggling to survive. Northam's mentor is now all but forgotten after his defeat.

All citizens and lawyers indicated that they thought Northam was the best Judge that the area ever had. Anyhow, Judge Willis' death really triggered the trip to Alaska. Sen. Fears couldn't help but being depressed because of this, and the attitude of his protégé, Judge Wescott B. Northam. Fears got an ulcer after single-handedly noiminating Northam for the bench. Northam had now reached Judge Willis' level of aloofness, and has lost all the good qualities which he had, and which all judges seem to lose once they get on the bench. Fears feels sorry for Judge Willis' family, for they are all very fine people, and depressed at Judge Northam's attitude toward him; so it's off to the beautiful land of Alaska to try to sort it all out. Fears can't help but feel that if he had to do it all over again he might cooperate with the Northampton County lawyers, and some of them might have supported him when he tried to get the Circuit Judgeship in 1991.

After Northam was elected Judge Gray and Schewel came to Fears and wanted Fears to support one of the judicial nominations in each's district. Remembering that these two walked out of the caucus on Northam's nomination against Willis Fears told both gentlemen that they had short memories, and that "what goes around, comes around," and it was a pleasure for him to vote with the opposing nominations. Later, Sen. Ed Willey died, Gray suffered a terrible automobile accident that broke his neck, after which he retired, and finally another "walk-outer," Parkinson, got defeated by a Republican.

Fears ran every four years thereafter, and had opponents in the Democratic Primary, and in the General Elections. In other words, Fears had a "double header" in each election year because of the makeup of his district. The Third District was comprised of 40,000 constituents in the Eastern Shore Counties where he lived, and 110,000 in the "Peninsula." Then in 1991, the district was redistricted, and a "black district" was created by Sen. Andrews and Scott so Scott could have a black district, and Andrews could keep his seat. Fears picked up a new territory in Newport News and Gloucester Counties which added 10,000 new Republican voters to his District, which helped defeat Fears in 1991 for that reelection. Scott got elected to Congress, and Andrews, the great Senate leader, got defeated in 1994 by a Republican.

In the 1979 election, after defeating one Judy Fried (a Democrat in the Primary Election), and a Republican named Bill Bowditch from York County in the General Election. Fears won again. Bowditch's wife, Marion, was on the school board for York County; one brother-in-law was the Mayor of Williamsburg; another was on City Council for Newport News. Bowditch, in one year, had first announced as a Democrat, then an Independent; then was nominated in a "telephone booth convention" as a Republican by that party. Fears accused him of being a "Dr. Pepper – at ten o'clock, a Democrat; at two, an Independent; and at three, a Republican." With the influential family backing, and with plenty of money, it appeared Bowditch was like a Kennedy in Fears' judgment: Bowditch was bound to win! Fears estimates Bowditch spent $100,000, and Fears spent about $25,000. Finally, when the votes were counted, Fears received 72% of the total vote. After the election, Fears asked people in the Peninsula (where Bowditch owned Bowditch Ford Co., and where he lived in York County) why Bowditch hadn't won. The reply was, "We're not voting for any used car dealer." The public has many reasons for voting against a person, and this was a good enough reason; in spite of the fact that the old "drum beat" was used by Fears' opponent: "There are too many lawyers in the legislature."

After Judge Wescott B. Northam retired, substitute Judge Robert Phillips wanted the position. A couple of lawyers didn't want Phillips on the bench, for they thought him too opinionated; so Fears got Phillips to request a Bar Association meeting so that Fears would not be criticized again. The meeting was called, and no one else had the nerve to offer his or her name, so Phillips got the unanimous vote of the local Bar Association, there being no other candidate. Fears had no problem in electing Phillips. Phillips is still a District Court Judge, and does a better job than most District Court Judges. Fears was defeated for reelection in 1991, and that same year the Circuit Judge named N. Wescott Jacob informed Fears he was going to retire. During Fears' Senate campaign one Glen A. Tyler, Esq., went on the radio to publicly support Fears for Senator. Fears had told Tyler that when Jacob retired he would support Tyler for Judge if Fears was still in the Senate. Anyhow, Sen. Fears felt that this would be his last chance to grab the "brass ring" as the Circuit Judge, and offered his candidacy for election by the legislature.

A lawyer named Nick Klein, Esq., a "come here" from Tennessee who had married a local girl, and had somehow gotten into the old law firm of Mapp and Mapp in Keller, Virginia, was President of the Accomack Bar Association. He had been the Republican Committee Chairman of the County and "got into the act" immediately, for he was an ardent political enemy of Fears. Klein, as President of the Bar Association, "stirred up the press," and the "MADD crowd," who were already mad at Fears for opposing the 0.08% driving drunk law, and orchestrated early opposition to Fears. Then Klein called a Bar Association meeting for a vote. Judge Phillips, one Jon Poulson, Esq., who had defeated Judge Northam once for Prosecuting Attorney, Glen A. Tyler, Esq., whom Klein supported, and one Bob Oliver, Esq., who had been County Prosecutor for Northampton County, all "threw their hats into the ring" and were voted on. On each vote, the low man would withdraw. In the early voting, Fears had 16 votes to Tyler's 13. Oliver got one vote, his! Poulson got about six votes, and Phillips also got about six votes. Then Klein pulled out two signed proxy votes and voted them for Tyler, and the vote count was 20 for Tyler and 19 for Fears. A motion was made and passed that the association not endorse either candidate, and simply send copies of the minutes to the Virginia Legislature showing the close vote, and requesting the Legislature to select whom they desired.

After Sen. Fears' defeat in the State Senate reelection in 1991, Judge N. Wescott Jacob stopped by Fears' office and informed Fears that he was retiring as a Circuit Judge, and asked Fears who he wanted to take

Jacob's place. Fears replied, "I want this judgeship myself to finish my career of public service." Jacob reacted as if someone had "struck him in the face with a wet mackerel," and told Fears, "These many new young lawyers will worry you to death." So it was obvious to Fears that Jacob didn't want him to have the position. Klein wrote a letter to all members of the General Assembly on Bar Association stationery as its president that the Bar had unanimously elected Tyler, which wasn't so, but before Fears learned of this Klein had already done the damage. The Northampton County lawyers, all six of them, did their damage too. They were irritated at Fears because he had removed their neighbor, Willis, as District Court Judge, and had elected Fears' partner Northam to the District Court position. Now they could get even and they did!

The lawyers practicing in Northampton County had no organized Bar Association, but they are all relatives or close friends. It's a very "closed shop," similar to the Inns of Court in England. They make it difficult to come here to practice law in this small county of about 17,000 people. Several "come heres" have tried it, but have "thrown in the towel" and moved on to more friendly pastures.

The key to getting elected a Judge in the Eastern Shore Counties, and for that matter in any area of Virginia, is to get the support of the members of the General Assembly in that Judicial Circuit. In 1991, those members of the Fears district – Dr. Clancy Holland in the Senate, and Hon. Robert Bloxom (a Republican) and Glen Croshow (a Democrat) in the House of Delegates – all represent the Judicial Circuit supported Tyler. Bloxom, from Accomack County (a Republican), claimed to be neutral, and he in fact did introduce both Fears and his opponent Tyler to the Courts of Justice Committees of both houses, and didn't seem to support either candidate. But Fears suspects he did support Tyler. Holland and Croshow live in Virginia Beach, and this is all part of the same Judicial Circuit. Probably something transpired in some smoke-filled room somewhere. The six members of the Northampton County Bar went to Holland and Croshow early in the campaign, and convinced them to support Tyler, which they did. One Hon. William Robinson from Norfolk, and chairman of the black caucus, told Fears he would nominate him in the House if Croshow didn't. But Robinson didn't, for he allegedly made a deal with Croshow that he would back off Fears' nomination if Croshow would support the black candidates running for "Judicial Positions" in Norfolk and Virginia Beach; so Robinson did not nominate Fears, and the two black aspirants got elected by the General Assembly. Had Robinson told Fears he had changed his mind, Fears would have tried to get another House member to nominate him in the House Democratic Caucus in the House of Delegates. The Senate Caucus gave Fears a majority vote two times on called votes, and finally Hon. Hunter B. Andrews, as the Majority Leader, got a couple of Senators to change their votes. Andrews had just reintroduced a bill to make it mandatory for all Judges to retire at 70 years of age, and Fears was 71. Finally, both houses elected Tyler, who was 51 years old then. Had Fears won in the Senate, and lost in the House, the appointment would have gone to Governor Wilder. Who knows what he might have done!

Wilder and Fears were close friends, but Fears feels that Wilder would not have appointed him because the MADD people were putting political pressure on everyone to keep Fears off the bench, and Governor Wilder had aspirations for the U.S. Senate against Sen. Robb in the Democratic Primary. Wilder threw his hat in the ring for U.S. Senator, and the public threw it right back. Fears would have supported Wilder for U.S. Senate, but Wilder got "cold feet" and withdrew to everyone's surprise. In fact, before Wilder withdrew, he spent the weekend at Fears' home with his aide discussing the election. Fears still feels that Wilder would not have appointed Fears for the Judgeship, for Wilder is a "political animal" and would have protected his own backside. Anyhow, it is all over; Northam was elected to the District Court, Milbourne was elected to the new Juvenile and Domestic Relations Court; then Robert Phillips takes Northam's place on the District Court when Northam retired; Fears did practice law with friendly Judges for a short while, but he didn't get the "big brass ring" for himself on the Circuit Court. This was his last chance because of his age and other reasons.

There is always some "poetic justice" in politics, for Sen. Hunter B. Andrews of Hampton, the Majority Leader of the State Senate, and the one man influential in costing Fears the Senate vote in 1991, has been defeated by a Republican in 1995. Had he been in Fears' district, Fears would have voted for him, for Andrews was the most knowledgeable one in the Senate, and a great leader. However, Fears had the pleasure of writing him to congratulate him on joining the ranks of unemployed politicians. Also, Sen. Clancy Holland, whom Fears thought was a very good friend, got defeated for reelection by another Republican, and Croshow has also been defeated by a Republican.

This was Fears' last chance to get elected as Circuit Court Judge because of his age, and the 70-year mandatory retirement age statute which passed. Times have surely changed, for now Justices Cardoza and Holmes couldn't get elected to a Circuit Court in Virginia because of their ages. To Sen. Fears it was worth the chance to try to get the position, for the retirement benefits amount now to approxiamately $100,000 per year. Politics is a very interesting and exciting game, but the news media can make or break a candidate. Most politicians call the news media "the fourth estate," and a book was written with this title. Early in Fears' career, the news media told the truth and printed or broadcast the facts, but since the "Sullivan vs. Times case" Supreme Court decision the media can tell untruths about a public figure, and are free from a libel suit unless the wronged party can prove actual malice. In other words, when it comes to a public figure, editorial writers and reporters can practically report anything they want, even if it is a lie. All reporters now want to establish themselves as great investigative reporters. Fears wants to be reincarnated as a news media editor, for he can do anything he wants (practically) with legal immunity, and be a pundit about every topic!

Most political candidates would appreciate it if the news media would stay out of the process, but of course they will not. When Sen. Fears first ran for the office of County Prosecutor he spent about $800; when he ran the last time for State Senate he spent about $80,000. It was very interesting to see whether Forbes could buy the Presidency. Fears feels that only the very wealthy now can run for national political office, and that only the wealthy can run for statewide office. Sen. Fears feels that the entrance of television has affected all campaigns. One has to be photogenic, and be an outstandingly handsome charismatic person, to get elected. All of the media together, with enough money, can probably elect any candidate they support. Fears feels that the media has interfered and "skewed" the electoral process, and that it is doing the public a disservice. The great actor and communicator President Reagan slept through most of his last term, but he came across on the TV as a great leader. No one wants to give him responsibility for the five trillion dollar debt he created with his "trickle down" economics, which simply didn't work. Rich people, and big corporations, invest in tax-exempt securities, and they don't start new businesses. They are for themselves, not for the country as a whole – take Ross Perot: his millions are being spent to satisfy an expanded ego, all suspect.

All of us want to take the "drunks off the road," but all the 0.08% alcohol content does is get all the nice people, who visit friends or have a couple of drinks at a club, in trouble with the law. Sen. Fears, at one time, visited the Elks Club after work for a couple of drinks with other members, but no more. All a Police Officer has to do is wait patiently outside the club, and make his or her arrest quota for the day. The MADD people have done some good, but now they are overdoing it. Fears has jokingly threatened to form an organization with red, white, and blue bumper stickers reading DAMM, which stands for "Dads Against Mad Mothers." There was some irony in all this, for one of the MADD officials was arrested for driving under the influence with more than 0.08% blood alcohol content, and Sen. Norment (who replaced Fears) was even arrested for the same.

Now as to Sen. Hunter B. Andrews, Fears told the news media that he felt that Andrews should have been Governor, that Andrews knew more about Virginia Government than anyone; and that he had rendered a great service to Virginia as Senate Majority Leader, and as Chairman of the Finance Committee. He told the press that had Andrews been in Fears' district, Fears would have worked for him, and would have voted for him – but personally, Andrews was pompous, arrogant, conceited, and self-centered. Andrews accused everyone in the Senate of being stupid, except himself. Also Fears feels that Andrews cost Fears the election in the Senate Caucus for the Circuit Judgeship.

Probably Judge Jacob's feelings go back to 1955 when Fears ran for election as County Prosecutor, and when Fears defeated Judge Jacob for the position. Also, when Fears was a freshman Senator he told Judge Jacob that he was going to nominate his law partner, Wescott Northam, Esq., to the Circuit Court. Later Fears did nominate Northam to the District Court, and after a bitter fight with the political powers in Accomack and Northampton Counties did elect Northam to the District Court Bench. Anyhow, two times the Senate Democratic Caucus nominated Fears in 1991 for the Circuit Court, but Sen. Hunter B. Andrews, who was the Majority Leader, finally got the Senate Caucus to vote for the other candidate on the third vote.

For a time, with Judge Jacob on the Circuit Court Bench and Judge Robert Phillips on the District Court Bench, all lawyers, and especially Sen. Fears, were treated fairly and law practice for Fears was enjoyable for the first time. Both these judges knew and studied the law, and applied facts well in trials which came before them.

Virginia had already permanently allowed both a District Court (which handles civil trials, traffic cases, and preliminary hearings in felony matters) and a Juvenile and Domestic Relations Court in each judicial jurisdiction, but the Eastern Shore area didn't have a full-time Juvenile and Domestic Relations Court. This Juvenile Court hears cases against minors, decides cases concerning child and spousal support, and commitments. Sen. Fears tried for years to get the legislature to authorize a Juvenile Court for the Eastern Shore Counties, but they continued to use the excuse that there wasn't a heavy enough case load to support it.

However, in 1994 the General Assembly authorized a new, full-time Juvenile and Domestic Relations Court for Accomack and Northampton Counties, so several lawyers in the area sought the position. A staunch Republican by the name of John Westcoat, Esq., who served on the Republican Committee from Northampton County, was the leading contender, for most of the local white lawyers "born and bred" in this area were related to Westcoat, or were close friends in some way and supported him, but Westcoat had worked against Sen. Fears' reelection each time, and Fears didn't want Lawyer Westcoat to get the position. An African-American named Bryan Bernard Milbourne, Esq., was Fears' choice.

Milbourne was an African-American, born of a farm family in Accomack County, and had been the first black to enroll in the first integrated high school. He received his law degree from William and Mary College Law School. He returned to Accomack County and wanted to practice law. Fears already had two partners in his office or he would have brought Milbourne in with him. However, Fears had the authority from an estate owner to sell an office building on Front Street near the courthouse. He talked to his client, an elderly woman in a nursing home, to get her permission to sell the office to a black lawyer. She agreed and Sen. Fears put up the funds for the down payment. Milbourne paid Fears back in six months, and after a while was accepted by all the citizens as a very fine lawyer. Fears, while still in the Senate, got Milbourne appointed the Escheat Lawyer for the State in Accomack County, and had an easy job doing this because Gov. Douglas Wilder was black and had been Fears' desk mate in the Senate. Fears had openly campaigned to get the Governor elected Lieutenant Governor, and later Governor. Milbourne was married to a lovely wife, and had two wonderful children. He was a deacon in an all-white congregational church called the Rock Church. Milbourne and wife had dinner with Sen. Fears and his wife, and Fears offered the

Milbournes an alcoholic drink, which he declined. Milbourne asked instead for a glass of orange juice. Milbourne is religious, uses no profanity, doesn't approve of off-color jokes, doesn't womanize, and in fact is quite free of all sins. He was an ideal candidate for the Juvenile Court, except that he was black in a prejudiced community.

Sen. Fears got busy contacting members of the General Assembly to support Milbourne. The local Bar Association met and voted 21 votes for John Westcoat, Esq., and, believe it or not, 16 votes for Milbourne, who was the only black lawyer, and two votes for a female lawyer named Terry Bliss, Esq. Bliss thought because she was a cousin of Judge Lester Lamm of Virginia Beach Circuit Court (now deaceased), which is in the same Circuit, it would help give her "clout" with the General Assembly, but it didn't work. Fears wrote every member of the Legislature; went with Milbourne before the Courts of Justice Committees of both bodies; and got the black caucus to support Milbourne. Neither Bliss nor Westcoat received a vote in either the House of Delegates or in the Senate, and Milbourne was handily elected. The "good ole boys" with the local insidious power lost this time. It was unusual for Milbourne to receive 16 votes in an all-white Bar Association meeting, but he did out of respect for him.

The main street citizens of Front Street were mad at Fears for locating a black lawyer in an office on Front Street for this was a first, too. Milbourne has proven that he is a very good Judge, and Fears helped give Milbourne the "brass ring." Also, Fears supported an African-American for the elected office of Clerk of Circuit Court, which he won in an election. This Clerk, named Hon. Sam Cooper, has done such a good job that he had the support of all lawyers in this past election and in fact had no opposition. Electing a black clerk from a racially prejudiced community was a first too.

As of now in Accomack County, all the lawyers and citizens have good conscientious Judges for the Judges study their cases and render good decisions, it is believed, and they each follow the law as it is, and apply the facts in evidence before rendering judgment on any case.

Accomack County has a Bar Association with dues and a membership of about 35 lawyers. The Northampton lawyers have no association, and there is only one "come here" lawyer from Boston, Massachusetts, married to a black doctor whose ancestors came from Northampton County. She learned her law allegedly studying and clerking in another woman lawyer's office. (Probably Virginia is the only state allowing one to take the Bar Examination without law school education.) Anyhow, Marsha Carter, Esq., didn't graduate from law school but was certified as qualified to take the Examination by her mentor, Denice Bland, Esq., who thereafter quit practicing law and got a professor's job teaching law in the William and Mary Law School.

The "favored boys' network" coaxed Circuit Judge Tyler, who defeated Fears for the Circuit Judgeship, to appoint Jack Westcoat, Esq., as substitute Juvenile Judge. He also appointed his ex-law partner as substitute Judge of the District Court, which doesn't appear proper to the citizens of this district. Anyhow, no one "has the guts" to complain, not even Sen. Fears – for he already is reputed to be controversial. At 81 years old he is trying to get along, and not be a "lightning rod" anymore. Fears feels he has only done good for Virginia and for this community; so he is now trying to relax in retirement.

Oh yes, that judicial aspirant John Westcoat, Esq., inherited about five million dollars equity from his father, and this is another reason Fears didn't support him for an additional $90,000 per year position. Sen. Fears resents the inherited rich, for the old adage about "the rich get richer, and the poor get poorer" seems true. Fears didn't believe the public offices should be bought, but now he believes they can be.

Count the millionaires in Congress, and the State Legislators, for it appears the millionaire candidates are now in the Virginia General Assembly, and in the U.S. Congress!

Chapter 21
LIFE'S GREATEST
DISAPPOINTMENT

Sen. Fears, while was serving in the Virginia Senate from 1968 through 1991, was finally defeated by a very well qualified lawyer from James City County. Sen. Fears represented one of the larger towns in his district, a town called Chincoteague, Virginia. The town has a population of about 5,000 people year round. It is now a Summer vacation resort of sorts, and now has a state-built bridge from the island town to a wildlife refuge, and public beach on the Atlantic Ocean. It has a very interesting history of the Spanish galleons sinking off the island's shores in the Atlantic Ocean, and the depositing of Spanish ponies on the barrier islands after a storm wreck around the 18th century. A lone survivor reached the shores. It was an infant strapped to a hatch which floated ashore. The folks on the island adopted the baby then as one of theirs. This child grew into manhood, married a local girl and sired many offspring. The child was called "Johnnie Alone," which later came to be the name of "Lunn." One of lawyer Fears' clients and supporters is named Lunn, and is probably a relative of "J. Alone." The present-day town is famous for its delicious Chincoteague oysters and clams. The sewage is now treated by individual septic tank systems, and the fresh water is supplied by NASA wells from the mainland, and piped to the island over a bridge crossing the Chincoteague Bay. The underlying strata are polluted, and the oyster grounds have also become polluted after a 1962 storm when the island was inundated by salt water. Sen. Fears was an officer in the

National Guard in 1962, and helped the residents establish security on the island during this emergency. Everyone on the island was evacuated during this storm. Caskets floated from the graves, and were actually floating down the streets. Dr. Belle Fears, the Senator's wife, was in private medical practice then and assisted in giving many inoculations for various anticipated diseases, and other medical care.

Politically, Chincoteague is most confusing to any political candidate. When William Earl ran in 1955, a majority of the voters voted for him for County Prosecutor; but in 1959 they voted against him and helped defeat him. In 1967, the majority voted for him for State Senate, and did thereafter give him a majority of the votes until 1991, and then helped defeat him by about 100 votes. Usually about 1,200 votes are cast. Sen. Fears thought he had done much to assist the town, and thought surely the majority would vote for him. However he learned later that a Baptist Minister from a new church there had campaigned against him, because the Sen. had sponsored legislation in support of the lottery, liquor by the drink, paramutual horse racing, and other "sin" legislation. During the Civil War the island residents supported the North, and the remainder of the county supported the South. Now about half the voters on Chincoteague are Republicans, and the remainder are Democrats. A Republican Congressman by the name of Hon. Herbert Baterman (since deceased), had convinced the voters there that he had done much for them, and a State Delegate by the name of Hon. Robert Bloxom has the majority believing he is wonderful. The secret of both men's success is to tell the citizens, with support of the local Republican newspapers that they have all done many good things for Chincoteague. In fact both office holders simply tell the voters what they want to hear. Bateman took all the credit for all that Sen. Fears had done while he was Chairman of the Commerce and Labor Committee, and a member of the Finance Committee. Fears was also the ranking number two man in seniority. Sen. Fears learned of the plight of the polluted seafood-producing grounds in Chincoteague, and talked the U.S. Government Corps of

Engineers into planning a sewage plant for the town. With the help of the then-Democratic Congressman he was able to convince the Corps to build the plant; the U.S. Government to supply 4 million dollars, and the state to provide 1 million dollars matching funds, as joint money. The town couldn't afford the matching funds then so Sen. Fears got the 1 million from the Virginia Legislature. All was ready to go and the Senator, with the engineer from the Corp of Engineers, appeared before the town council with the supposed good news. The Town Council had to adopt the program by voted resolution, but damned if the council didn't vote the project down. This was in the '70s. The reasons were that the "poor widows" on the island couldn't afford the $300 hook-up to the sewer lines, and the local hotel owners didn't want competition. Now much of the shellfish ground has been condemned by the Virginia Shellfish Department and Chincoteague will never have money to build a sewage plant. Sen. Fears still can't believe this happened, and it is the greatest disappointment of his life. Incidentally there is a public park in the town, and the American Legion Chapter wanted to hold a *fiesta* in the park one Memorial Day, and wanted to supply a free keg of beer in the park for the Veterans. The despotic Rev. Broward, who tried to run the island his way, opposed the placing of the keg of beer in the park. Thereafter, the Rev. Broward was deposed from the island – the pressure was so great he had to leave. He is now back in his home state of Florida, and Sen. Fears is retired from practicing law. The newly elected State Senator from James City County has done little for the town. In fact, most of the voters there do not even know his name. His name is Hon. Thomas Norment, and he is a Republican voting for all the tax cuts proposed by Virginia's new Republican Governor, the Hon. James Gilmore, who will probably throw Virginia's budget out of balance with his many tax cuts during the period of prosperity. When the economical climate reverses the great Republican Governor will quickly lose his popularity when the agencies get budget cuts. By statute, Virginia must balance its budget, but Sen. Fears doesn't think Gov. Gilmore has read this law.

While on the subject of disappointments, there is another small town by the name of Tangier, located in Accomack County in the Chesapeake Bay, which is in Sen. Fears' district. Sen. Fears helped them get an electric plant to supply electricity to the residents through funds from the REA (Rural Electrification Administration) in the early '50s. He also was responsible for getting an airport, a recreation and community center, and a crab packing plant all built with the help of Sen. Fears, but Congressman Bateman took credit for all these, even though he wasn't even a member of Congress when these were built. In fact he was a Democrat in the State Senate at the time. Sen. Fears lost the majority of the votes on this island in 1991 because of the anti-Fears position. The minister was a despotic man who also tried to run this island his way. Sen. Fears met him in 1991 while having lunch at a family-styled restaurant known as Hilda Crockett's restaurant. It is run by her daughters, now that she is deceased, and they are friends and clients of Sen. Fears. The preacher would not support Sen. Fears probably for the same reason Chincoteague didn't support him; that is because Sen. Fears was for all the "sin" legislation. There is one large Methodist Church on the island run by the minister; so out of the 400 votes on Tangier Fears lost by 100 votes on election day in 1991. Mind you, alcoholic beverages are "taboo" on the island, and none are sold, but many of the residents are "closet drinkers." Anyhow, one of Fears' clients from Tangier while in Fears' law office in Accomac told the Senator that the preacher disappointed the constituents and was requested to leave the island and the church. The reason was that the preacher "got too close." (The rest of this statement by the Tangier client can't be printed for it may be gossip!) The island is still run by a part-time preacher, and schoolteacher, who is now the mayor of Tangier, and is a great Republican. This man is no friend of the Senator's either. A film was to be produced on Tangier, and the actor protagonist was to be Paul Newman. It was a film called "Message in a Bottle." The production of this great film would have been a financial and publicity "bonanza" for Tangier and Accomack County, as well as the Commonwealth, but this preacher/schoolteacher/mayor Crockett, and some of his followers on the town council, did not agree to the filming. The production company went elsewhere, where they were welcomed. The reason given by the Mayor was that the bad language was not appropriate for the "young ears" of Tangier. Sen. Fears saw advertisements of the picture, and it seems tame compared to most productions.

Chapter 22

HISPANICS

Sen. Fears is now 81 years old, and has been trying to practice law with Robert G. Turner, Esq. But there are so many hometown lawyers who have returned home to practice in the area that it is difficult to simply pay office expenses; so the Senator has to find other ways to supplement his income.

In the past few years, the migrant African-Americans have been vacating the agricultural jobs requiring "stoop labor," and now prefer to carry briefcases. Hispanics from Puerto Rico, Mexico, and Central America are delighted to fill the gap. They are willing to work in the fields, and in the labor-intensive chicken processing plants in Accomack County, but most of them only speak Spanish. Perdue Industries, operating a large chicken processing plant, advertises on the local TV station in Spanish welcoming applicants of Spanish origin. The Hispanics are hard workers, loyal to their employers, family-oriented, mostly law abiding citizens, and generally sober and serious workers. They are polite and courteous to William Earl and his office personnel. It is surmised that it is better to earn $6.00 per hour in a hard job here in the U.S. than 50¢ an hour in a job in Mexico. Of course with NAFTA, and the U.S. industries moving to Mexico, it won't be long until the Mexicans will stay in Mexico where Spanish is spoken.

Many migrant Mexicans were born in the U.S., or in Puerto Rico (which is now a protectorate of this country). People ask the Senator, "Why are there so many Mexicans in the western part of the U.S.?" And he replies, "The western states were part of Mexico at one time, and these citizens were born and raised in California, Arizona, New Mexico, Texas, and the like." If the Mexicans had never accepted Santa Anna as president of Mexico they would still own the western states. The United States Army defeated Santa Anna in *Matamoras,* and was going to execute him so Santa Anna gave the western states to the U.S., except Arizona (and he sold that state to the U.S. for 10 million dollars), returned to Mexico and gambled the money away on "cock fight betting!" It's ironic that Mexico lost California about a year before gold was discovered there.

William Earl has been studying Spanish for about four years through the computer, audio and videocassettes, and of course grammar books, and practicing Spanish with Spanish-speaking people. He can now relate to the Hispanics with his newly found language. For the past two years he joined an "Elderhostel" group of language students in Guadalajara, Mexico, and the group has spent six hours per day with Mexican instructors who speak little English for two-week periods, learning more Spanish conversation. A person over 55 years of age can purchase four airline coupons from Continental Airlines for a little more than $600, and can fly from Norfolk, Virginia, to Guadalajara and return for about $300 – then use the other two coupons within a year. The hotel accommodations in the package, provided by an Arizona travel agency for a very reasonable price, are excellent with three meals per day and housekeeping. Because the tap water may be contaminated the management furnishes a 5-gallon bottle of purified water with the room. The water supplied to Guadalajara is probably not contaminated, but the old conduit pipes allow seepage from drain run-off and the like. The tour guides provide side trips to museums and cathedrals for the guests, where one can view and study the Mexican art and their very interesting murals. After two two-week periods of intense study in Mexico, William Earl has become more proficient in Spanish conversation, and was even summoned to the District Court in Accomack County to act as an interpreter in a small traffic matter.

Guadalajara is a beautiful city with an ideal climate. The temperature averages about 75° all year round. It rains at night and the sun shines during the day. Mexican food is delicious, and the citizens are very friendly. If William Earl could convince his wife to do so he would retire in this area of Mexico immediately, as many U.S. citizen retirees have already done. William Earl became interested in Mexican history, and realizes why there has been so much unrest, and so many revolutions in Mexico. About 1914, when Emeliano Zapata and Pancho Villa tried to overthrow the national government, President Wilson dispatched Gen. John J. Pershing with an expeditionary force to Mexico to try to capture Villa and to suppress that revolution. William Earl's uncle Frederick E. Humphreys, a 1906 graduate of West Point, was a First Lieutenant in that force. Aunt Myrtle joined him there and lived in a tent with him until the force returned to the U.S. It is alledged that Gen. Pershing told the U.S. President that we were supporting the wrong side.

If one studies the history of Mexico, it can be understood that the problem with all the unrest began when Hernan Cortez when his "brigands" invaded Mexico through Vera Cruz, with the support of the Spanish government and the Catholic church to find gold and jewels in the old Aztec city, which is now Mexico City. Cortez destroyed the city by burning it, but the church rebuilt it. The native Indians were simply slaughtered, and Mexico became "New Spain." The Spanish took over the country, the "Church Viceroys" ran it, and a few Spaniards practically turned the natives into slaves. During the 16th century in Mexico, after the destruction of the Aztecs and Spain had conquered the country, the Spanish *Castellanos* (native-born Spaniards), and the *Creoles* (Mexican-born Spaniards) controlled the country by owning all the land in large *Haciendas* operated by the *Hacendados* who used the native Indians as peons and serfs to plant and cultivate the crops, and to do the hard labor in the silver mines. Life for the native Mexican Indians was difficult and brutal. It is little wonder there was so much unrest in Mexico. The lot of the populace improved somewhat after a native Indian was elected president of Mexico. His name was Benito Juarez, and he was the only Indian president of Mexico. He tried to return the land ownership to the native Mexican Indians but failed. Mexican Indians have been fighting through many revolutions for centuries. William Earl thinks he knows why there is so much social unrest in Mexico, for it's the universal problem of the "have nots" versus the "haves." The wealth of Mexico is still owned by the *Creoles* or by the old Guggenheim interests who stripped Mexico of its iron ore, oil, and silver in the 19th century when President Perfirio Diaz was in office. It's the same old problem worldwide, and that is that the "have-nots" want what the "haves" possess. The wealth of Mexico is still owned by a few Spanish *Creoles* (those born in Mexico) and the *Castellanos* (those born in Spain), and the peons and serfs (or native Mexican Indians) are still working for pittances from the Spaniards. Mexico is very crowded, and the native Indians can find very well paying jobs to the North, so they are immigrating to the U.S. – attempting to find a piece of the "American Dream." Many are succeeding too, especially in the fields of music and the theater, and some even in the business world. In Mexico the native Indians are still working in agriculture on the great *Haciendas* for the *Hacendados* (or landlords) or in the silver mines for a mere meager existence. It is understandable why so many Mexican Indians are risking life and limb to cross the Rio Grande as illegal immigrants.

The two elderly student groups, most being retirees with living spouses, went on excursions to the art museums to view some of "Orasco's murals." All murals are done in black, white, and brown and are very somber. The murals generally depict scenes from various Mexican revolutions. One particular mural shows many fingers pointing in different directions. One lady stated that it reminded her of a "bunch of politicians not being able to make a decision," whereupon William Earl replied that it "appeared to be a straw vote trying to decide which direction the hot air was blowing."

One of our lady instructors was a *gorda* lady (meaning rather plump) and played the Mexican guitar. She tried to teach members of our group some Mexican songs and dances. William Earl greatly appreciates Latino rhythm, and recalled a beautiful Mexican song re-edited in the U.S. with English lyrics called "Yellow Days." The Spanish lyrics and music were first published in Mexico under the title of *"La Mentira,"* meaning "The Lie." William Earl learned to sing the song in Spanish with this guitarist.

The last evening of the program the instructors threw a *fiesta* for all with great food and a *Mariachi* band. The teacher insisted that William Earl sing *"La Mentira"* with her with the *Mariachi* band accompaniment. The audience stomped and clapped presumably in approval. The next morning at the hotel entrance, in the presence of two male guests, our singer stated that he didn't know whether the applause was for the performance or because he had made a fool of himself. A smart lady nearby said, "A little of both." So our singer decided he had better stick to practicing law.

Chapter 23

ONE CAN'T TEACH AN OLD DOG NEW TRICKS

William Earl had a friend in Accomac who knew the timber and lumber business well, having grown up on the Western Shore of Maryland with a father who was self-educated in the business. Melvin Lewis probably only passed the fifth grade in school, but he must have had a very high IQ. He and his brother Clarence formed a partnership and built a lumber mill here in Accomac right after WWII.

They were both in the armed forces in WWII, and were both in actual dangerous combat. Melvin was a Sergeant in Gen. Patton's tank corps, and was at the Battle of the Bulge operating a tank platoon. He tells some tales of the war which are interesting. Melvin, now deceased, weighed about 250 pounds, but during the war weighed about 160. He has a story of being in bivouac in combat one night. All Americans were in sleeping bags or in pup tents. A German soldier slipped into the area and, while all were asleep, set up a machine gun right in the middle of the bivouac. When the people started to arise, the German "cut loose" with the machine gun. Melvin, on his stomach, hugged the ground. The small caliber bullets went across his back close enough to burn him, but not low enough to wound or kill him. Had he been as fat as he was later he would have been dead. He showed the scars one day at the Elk's Club because no one would believe him. He made a believer of his friends.

Melvin and his brother bought timber land with the timber, because the sellers wanted to get rid of the land off their tax records back in the

'40s and '50s. The brothers ended up being the largest landowners in the area. At one time Melvin came by the Fears' house for Dr. Fears to examine him because she was practicing country medicine then. He was in a sweat and pale as a ghost. Dr. Fears sent him to the hospital immediately for Melvin was having a heart attack. He was confined to the hospital for two weeks. At that time, he was in debt about $10,000, so his long-time lawyer friend, George Walter Mapp, Jr., Esq., the wealthiest man in the county, bailed Melvin out. Melvin was from then on a client for life of George Walter.

Melvin and Clarence continued to buy timber, run the mill, and a bark plant in Delaware. They sold the bark plant for several million dollars, and had already sold the lumber mill for several million. Melvin built a mansion with a large swimming pool, owned several racing horses and enjoyed a good life with his second wife, his adopted children, a boy and a girl, and a whole bunch of grandchildren. The Lewis brothers are still the biggest landowners in Accomack County, second to their lawyer friend, George Walter Mapp, Jr., Esq.

Melvin owned a 42-foot yacht which he operated himself. He taught himself seamanship and complicated navigation with "Loran," compass and charts, and all kinds of telecommunications navigational equipment. He was so smart as a waterman he took his boat to Florida every year through the inland waterway and never ran aground. Sen. Fears is an educated and trained navigator and has flown his own aircraft all about the country but has been lost several times. Fears also owned a 20-foot boat which he has run aground several times.

The Lewis brothers sold the mill to another corporation because they claimed OSHA worried them to death. Melvin claims that he had a band saw protected with a wooden cage cover but OSHA made him cover it with an expanded metal screen. He said that when the saw blade broke with his device made of wood the blade simply jammed in the wood, but the metal shrapnel flew all about the place. He also claimed OSHA made him paint yellow lines about the mill yard so people would know which path to walk, if they didn't already know.

Melvin was a great friend of ex-Gov. Linwood Holten, and the ex-governor went with Melvin fishing on his boat, and they also did a little relaxing with the best Scotch whiskey. Melvin was a great Republican leader, and he mixed with Presidents, Governors, Congressmen and the like. He was a member of the Republican Central Committee, and told Sen. Fears that he attended a "carcass" at the Republican Convention, and he called a bulldozer a "bullnozer," but in spite of the lack of formal education he is brilliant enough to be a millionaire. Fears said to Melvin one day, "If you had gone to college and got a degree in business or finance you would have been a billionaire." And Melvin, who could bring his comments off the wall, simply replied that, "If I had wasted my time in college I would have been a poor man like you." He was absolutely right and Fears was poor and is quite proud of his friend Melvin. "You can't teach an old dog new tricks."

One other story about Melvin is worth telling. He had a horse barn and a practice track, and used to race horses – the pacing and trotting types. He walked behind a colt in the presence of workers in the barn one day and the colt kicked him hard in the stomach. This really knocked the wind out of Melvin and he had to hang onto the stall to catch his breath. His workers had to laugh at the sight. Melvin said, "When I get my breath, I'm going to beat the hell out of you bastards." The workers all left the barn to avoid getting the hell beat out of them, and Melvin recovered. However, he developed a hernia in his stomach wall which continued to haunt him. He had several operations to repair the hernia but, unfortunately, it still persisted.

The last time he was operated on in the local hospital, Fears' son, Dr. Richard B. Fears, who is an Ob-Gyn on the hospital staff, visited Melvin in his room. Melvin claimed that Dr. Fears made him laugh so much he broke some stitches, and he had to be re-operated on. Sen. Fears questioned his son who said that it is almost impossible to pull sutures out of place, and that he doubted the story, but it did make a good tale.

Melvin's case is one of the Horatio Alger types, and the Lewises really did deserve the success they have had. They are very honest and generous people and the Fears family got to repay them for a favor they did for him back in the '50s. Sen. Fears was trying to build a house on his own by hiring carpenters and bricklayers by the hour. Fears thought he knew what he was doing for he was an engineering graduate, and with a borrowed level and transit, he had laid off the house foundation himself. He placed the "batter boards" and had staked off the depth for the footing pour. He called the concrete supplier and had concrete poured while he saw that the footing was wide, deep and level enough. Fears knew the Lassiter Bros., who ran a lumber mill with a kiln dryer near his home, so he visited the mill with a list of lumber for the house framing. Phil Smith, who ran the mill, promised Fears he would have the lumber on site the next Monday. Fears hired the carpenters to start on that day, but no lumber showed up. He met the Lewis brothers at a diner in Tasley and told them his plight. They filled the order and delivered the lumber Tuesday so Fears could keep the paid carpenters on the job. A friend of Fears who worked at the Lassiter mill later told Fears that Phil Smith had gotten a big order and a big price from a buyer in New York and had simply shipped his lumber to New York.

Anyhow, Fears got his house built on the GI Bill with a 3% bank loan on time and never afterwards respected the Lassiters or Phil Smith. Smith died about ten years later with cancer, and although Fears felt sorry for Phil's family, he couldn't sympathize with Phil. Years later Fears and his wife sold a piece of her farmland on the main road in Accomac so that Clarence "Seaboy" Lewis could build his mansion near Fears. Fears figured he could visit Clarence for a little nip now and then, but Clarence's wife was a hard-shelled Methodist and would allow no liquor in her house. All are good friends though and Fears does his imbibing in his home, or at the local Elk's Club.

Incidentally, Fears sold the three acres to Clarence for $5,000. That lot is now worth $50,000 on the market, but Fears has now a good, honest neighbor and returned the Lewis brothers' favor.

A lawyer should never get personally involved with people he represents because he cannot be objective as he or she should. William Earl's father, Arthur Earl, and his mother, Katherine, were raised on sharecropper farms in Arkansas, and William Earl tried to get them interested in learning proper English grammar, and how to appreciate better social things in life. They both had good native intelligence, and each in his or her own way could do things which required natural abilities. Arthur Earl had learned to play violin from his father. Now mind you, this music was not Beethoven or Bach, but country music right out of the lowlands of Arkansas. In the '30s and '40s this music was not popular, but now country music is in and Pappy could have been good enough to play in Nashville. But in spite of William Earl's attempts to get Pappy interested in the English handbook and proper language course Pappy never changed his ways. In typical Arkansas twang, he always said he "eeched" and not "itched" and he knew only one verb tense. It was "I come, I come back, he come back," etc. And that's the way it was. Pappy, in his body and fender shop, could make a crumpled car fender look like new. He was a master at this. Katherine could look at a child's dress in a window and return home and copy it exactly on her old faithful sewing machine with the foot petal. William Earl bought a console sewing machine for his home, but was never able to thread the needle nor insert the proper bobbins. William Earl gave it to a needy friend, and his wife, Belle, continues to use her old portable sewing machine. It is so true that "you can't teach an old dog new tricks."

Pappy did things his way and that is the way it was. Although William Earl was a licensed aircraft pilot, Pappy explained to his son one day he had figured how to get an aircraft back to the airport in case of engine failure. Simply put the nose down and build up speed and then pull back on the stick to aim for the field and keep "roller coasting" until one returned to the airport for a safe landing. Great!

Brother Carl E. lived with Pappy and Katherine all his life and he grew up as Pappy had – with a very hard head. Carl served in the Navy for a spell and was a great sheet metal repairman on aircraft. He thought he wanted to become a dentist so he entered Mississippi State University and lasted one semester. Didn't like it and went to Memphis as a parts manager for White Trucking Co. He thought after 20 years he had accumulated a reasonable retirement fund, but the company went bankrupt and carried retirement money with them into bankruptcy. Now finally Congress is trying to do something about this by legislation. Brother Carl is living on his Social Security, and has recently acquired wealth from Aunt Myrtle's estate which William Earl the lawyer got for him. William Earl has prepared a "capital gains report" on a Schedule D for the gains on the farm property in Maryland from Aunt Myrtle's estate of which the sales profits were divided. Carl E. got 1/6th of the sales profits. He wrote William Earl and informed him that he didn't intend to pay any capital gains taxes on his gain. He claims a CPA in his home area near Moscow, Tennessee, told him there was no gain, for the value should have a value at the time of Pappy's death. William Earl, feeling that he knows the law and tax statutes still feels there is a capital gains tax owed. He has paid his taxes on his gain for 1995, and did so for the next four years just to be on the safe side. Carl E. is hard-headed as Pappy was and William Earl "can't teach an old dog new tricks." That's the way it is in life with people and especially with "know-it-all" relatives.

Brad Fears, M.D., is the grandson of Dr. J.L. DeCormis, and the son of Dr. Belle D. Fears. He had expressed the desire to practice medicine from the time he entered high school. His father, William Earl Fears, stretched his money as far as he could to enter Brad in the Westtown School in Westtown, Pennsylvania, a Quaker boarding school. Brad was an "A" student in grammar school, and William Earl felt he had a promising son for educational success. Brad was also accepted by the

George School in Philadelphia, Pennsylvania, another very fine Quaker school. The George School gave Brad placement examinations and recommended that he commence Russian language and advanced mathematics. The math would have been fine but "Providence" saved Brad and he didn't have to get discouraged with Russian. He entered Westtown and learned French instead.

Gen. George S. Patton and Dr. Einstein were both dyslexic and had difficulty in colleges. No one understood dyslexia at that time and no one knew Brad was somewhat dyslexic. Brad finished Westtown with good grades in mathematics and science, but got a "D" in French for three years. He can read and write French but is handicapped in conversation and essay because of the dyslexia, but no one understood this at that time. Brad could beat the "old fire house guys" in chess and checkers at his grandfather's home in Tennessee when he visited there at ten years of age. He had a game of throwing rubber doughnuts at pegs on a numbered board from a distance and when he was five he could add up the numbers on the board immediately in his head when no one else could, and others didn't understand how he did it!

Brad entered the University of Richmond, and majored in mathematics but he was tired of studying hard and played a lot in college. He did graduate with a major in math, but with a grade point average which wouldn't "set the world afire." After Westtown, he was accepted by the U.S. Naval Academy, and received a telegram to report to duty that Summer, but he came to William Earl and told him he didn't want to go to a military academy. He wanted to study medicine. William Earl wanted Brad to go through the academy and try to become a naval aviator but again "Providence" interfered, for Brad suffered from motion sickness. William Earl flew a Cessna aircraft and would take his young son with him hoping Brad would get interested in aviation, and he wondered why after each flight Brad would become very pale and say he didn't want to fly anymore. William Earl thought Brad had "astrophobia" but he was simply suffering from "mal de mer" so he would have made a rather poor naval aviator.

The first thing Brad did on entering the University of Richmond was to enter the Army ROTC program in the Infantry Branch of the Army. He graduated from undergraduate college with a 2nd Lt.'s Commission, and was immediately sent to the Advanced Officers School in the Infantry at Ft. Benning, Georgia, for the three-month course. What a hell of a swap – a nice clean place in the Navy for the muddy ground in the Infantry! This was the early '70s while the Vietnam conflict was still going on. Again, Providence took care of Brad, for the Vietnam conflict ended while he was in training. Brad was always an industrious young man and had worked each Summer at heavy menial labor in an agricultural grading and packing shed.

William Earl learned early that a parent can't tell a teenager anything in the way of advice, although he tried with both his son and daughter, and with the grandchildren. They are going to do things their own way with perhaps a suggestion along the way. During the Vietnam Era, both children experimented with marijuana, as their peers were doing in college. William Earl learned of this the hard way and knew immediately not to press the issue. While WIlliam Earl was in the State Senate, a Delegate and a lawyer named "Junie" Bradshaw, Esq., came to Fears and asked him if he had a son in the University of Richmond, and Sen. Fears said, "Yes – what's up?"

Delegate Bradshaw told Fears that he had just defended two students for using marijuana and they were on probation, and in trouble with the University. He said, "Your son is a friend of theirs and he 'lucked out' for he had to attend some function with the ROTC the evening his friends were arrested."

Bradshaw later became a Judge of the Virginia State Corporation Commission with Fears' vote in the Senate. Anyhow, Sen. Fears telephoned his son and asked him to come to the Capitol for lunch, which Brad did. During lunch they talked about trivial things mostly, but Sen. Fears gave Delegate Bradshaw's name and office address to Brad. He told Brad that the Delegate wanted to see him. This was all prearranged with Bradshaw, who must have scared the heck out of Brad because

Brad returned to Sen. Fears' office rather quiet and contrite. That's the last time there was any marijuana trouble with his son.

Now Barbara, the daughter, had the use of a small building once used by Dr. Fears as her office, and now converted to a guest cottage. When Barbara was home from school, and the first year she taught in public school, she had the private use of this building. Fortunately, a State Trooper friend of Lawyer Fears told the Senator that a little "marijuana puffing" was taking place in the cottage among friends. So the next evening, while the family was having dinner, Sen. Fears announced that the "puffing" was taking place and he had given the law officers permission to enter the cottage without a search warrant, and had told them if anyone was caught smoking pot there he would help the officers prosecute the cases, since he had once been the County Prosecutor. That ended the smoking of pot in the office cottage. What an era for a parent to go through!

Barbara went to the University of Georgia, and was a real flower girl with a big yellow flower painted on the back of the white Marlin sedan William Earl had given her. She wore large floppy hats and all kinds of long beads, and participated in the marches and complaints about the Vietnam conflict, but she was in good company with President Clinton and his friends, as she has so often reminded William Earl. She graduated on the Dean's List, got her Masters Degree from the University of Virginia, is married to a nuclear technician, and has a son who is now a lawyer.

Now as a grandfather, William Earl visits Barbara's home and just smiles when he hears the tales of the escapades of his grandson, Matthew. Matthew is a fairly good fellow, usually driving the Mustang his grandfather gave him with some care. In fact, he has only wrecked the Mustang twice and has only been arrested once, when he was 20 years old for drinking beer at a "Harborfest." Lawyer Fears got the case dismissed because the officer hadn't kept a sample of the beer nor had the beverage been analyzed by the Virginia Forensic Laboratories. In other words, there was no evidence to convict Matthew of violating this unfortunate Virginia Law. This law makes it a misdemeanor for a person under 21 years of age to even drink one beer at home. Also, the young 20-year-old can lose his or her driver's license, even though not driving a car, when convicted of drinking a beer. This statute was supposedly to decrease auto accidents on the highways allegedly caused by young persons drinking alcoholic beverages. It doesn't cut down on accidents, but simply drives the youngsters to pot smoking or something worse. Sen. Fears voted to give 18-year-olds the privilege of being adults, for he feels that if a person can fight a war at 18 years of age he should have the right to vote, and the right to drink a beer, especially if he is over 18. But that's the way it is now in Virginia! Matthew named his grandfather "Bill the Pill," for getting on his case now and then, but since Grandfather Bill gave him the new Mustang, and proved that he was a good enough lawyer to get Matthew out of trouble, he now calls him "Grandfather Bill" or "Pop Pop Bill," and Bill appreciates this. Matthew is now an Alabama lawyer, but Grandfather Bill wanted him to study medicine. Again, "one can't teach an old dog new tricks," and besides, medicine is too difficult a course to study.

Brad was released from the U.S. Army, returned to Accomac and taught mathematics in a private school for a year. He was reputed to be a fine teacher and was liked by his students. Now it was his turn to have the privacy of the cottage office, and he made good use of it. Once Sen. Fears found a pair of ladies' little red shoes under the bed. Also, Brad got his second conviction for speeding and had his license suspended for 60 days by Judge Benjamin Gunter, Jr. – a wonderful neighbor who kept the secret from Sen. Fears, who probably would have punished his son even more severely. Lawyer Fears wondered why another teacher was driving Brad to teach school each day. Of course there were all kinds of stories about Brad's teaching career. One day a wonderful French lady teacher, who was born and raised in France and had language degrees from a University there, and spoke French, Spanish and English perfectly, privately asked teacher Brad what a "blow job" was, and Brad explained that it was oral sex. The French lady left Brad's presence quickly, red in the face. She had overheard a student use this expression. The same French lady, Mme. Maude Frazer, later taught William Earl French and Spanish for his trips to France, Mexico, and Spain. The private school closed and Mme. Frazer got a full-time position with the Employment Commission to help the French- and Spanish-speaking migrant farm laborers in their travails. Her husband died and she has now retired and is believed to be living in Charlottesville. What a very fine French lady she is!

Brad tried his hand as an apprentice carpenter after marrying a girl from Luray, Virginia. He went to Randolph Macon College for Graduate School after being discharged from the Army, and took difficult graduate courses such as Advanced Calculus and Intermediate Organic Chemistry, and got a solid "B" average. After working that Summer in the hot sun for a minimum wage as an apprentice carpenter, he literally threw his hammer away and was glad to enter Medical School at the University of Virginia, where he was miraculously accepted. It cost the Senator an extra $5,000 for an apartment for Brad and his wife for a year. Brad did well in his sciences and did graduate from Medical School with a degree in medicine.

After graduating from the University of Virginia Medical School, Brad accepted a residency in the Eastern Virginia Medical School in Norfolk, and managed to finish the four-year residency in Obstetrics/Gynecology. He could have gotten a Commission in the Navy and William Earl tried to convince him that he should do this to get the benefit of medical malpractice protection without the high malpractice insurance costs, along with all the other good benefits from the Navy, but, oh no! – "Old Hardheaded Brad" would not take the advice of Sen. Fears and wanted to return to the Eastern Shore of Virginia to practice in the local hospital, then known as Northampton-Accomac Memorial Hospital.

A big and tall medical doctor had come to the area a year before Brad and had started a practice. This physician is a brilliant person, and somehow got through the University of Cincinnati Medical School. He had taken his residency in Norfolk, too, and had practiced there for a time. This new physician visited the office of Sen. Fears about two years before he came to the Eastern Shore and wanted to know how he would fare in the Eastern Shore community. This physician explained that his grandfather was an early native, and had been some sort of Delegate or Congressman as a Republican immediately after the Civil War. Sen. Fears explained that African-American physicians had done well here, and had as many Caucasian patients as African-American patients. Dr. Allen of Eastville was a highly respected physician and was a close friend of Sen. Fears' father-in-law, Dr. J.L. DeCormis. Sen. Fears told the new physician in good conscience that as he was an Obstetrician, Fears doubted that many Caucasian women would seek his services. He did well in practice, and was going to accept Brad in his practice as a fellow practitioner. This physician had a contract prepared and showed it to Dr. Brad who brought it to Lawyer Fears, who would not legally consider the contract for many reasons. Rather than get involved between his son and the new physician, he suggested that Brad get independent advice from a lawyer in Norfolk, which Brad did! The contract appeared so unilaterally unfavorable to Brad that the Norfolk lawyer advised Brad not to agree to it.

Most states have statutes which give complaining physicians on hospital staffs the right to accuse another physician of alleged incompetence with immunity from libel or slander actions. In Virginia this statute is 54.1-2906. The NAM Hospital on the Eastern Shore of Virginia has all kinds of committees, including a "peer reviewed" hospital-controlling medical staff and a civilian board of trustees. Many articles have been written criticizing these statutes, for if a physician doesn't want competition in a hospital, he simply makes a complaint before the applying physician is granted permanent privileges. This is happening elsewhere under the guise of public protection, but this law has been used as simply a "turf protection" means for existing doctors in a hospital and may deter competition.

Many Obstetricians have been in and out of NAM Hospital, but there were none on the staff when the new doctor applied for privileges. A competing physician in another surgical field, on the Credentials Committee, objected to the admission of privileges for the new doctor because he alleged that this doctor had some sort of arrest record. Something allegedly had occurred in another state when the doctor was very young and was allegedly a member of the Black Panthers. Anyhow, it kept this new doctor from getting permanent hospital privileges for a year until he probably somehow threatened the hospital board with a discrimination suit. He finally got his permanent privileges and was the only qualified Obstetrician/ Gynecologist then on staff. He had been practicing in Norfolk, but finally moved to Nassawadox, Virginia, to practice there. There was a lien filed by the Treasury Department for taxes owed (about $135,000) on record in Northampton County Circuit Clerk's Office. No one knew the details but it was marked satisfied just before this new doctor ran for the Northampton County Board of Supervisors and won!

He brought a young doctor named Dr. David Scott on board, and both practiced together for several years. Now the first doctor has sold the practice to Dr. Scott, and is active in handling millions of dollars of grant money to allegedly improve the lot of "poor folks" in Northampton County. He has just returned as a member of the Board of Supervisors; he also has given up practicing medicine. His future will be very interesting for Sen. Fears and the entire community to consider. Later his motives may prove to be generous and benevolent to help the poor citizens of the Eastern Shore of Virginia, or otherwise.

Dr. Brad Fears wanted to come home after his residency and he had intended to practice with this specialist under the terms of the alleged unfavorable written contract. Instead he opened his own practice in an old medical office of one Dr. Joseph Gladstone who had retired and is now deceased. Brad purchased a house near the hospital. William Early tried to persuade his son to go into the Navy, or to settle in an urban area with a group of specialists, but his son did as he pleased as usual and started practicing in Northampton County. Sen. Fears had already heard that certain members of the staff didn't want Brad practicing in their hospital. Brad also didn't realize he would only have temporary privileges for six months while the staff "looked over his shoulder."

Brad immediately developed a large practice and the elite whites among the school teachers and many African-Americans were his patients. His reputation was already established through his grand-father, Dr. DeCormis, and his mother, Dr. Belle Fears, who had been on the hospital staff and on the hospital board of trustees. But Belle had retired from all this and Dr. DeCormis was deceased by now. Brad was doing so well his father was waiting for the axe to fall, and it did!

Brad one day had an obese woman in the hospital for a hysterectomy, and called for surgical backup because of some problems. A general surgeon on call came into the operating room to assist Brad. After the operation was completed, this surgeon filed a complaint under the peer review statute that Brad didn't know his anatomy. Now, mind you, this surgeon had been doing hysterectomies and other gynecological surgical procedures, and he was "suspect" by lawyer Fears. Anyhow, the medical staff denied Brad his permanent privileges; the entire Fears family was devastated and Brad was terribly damaged. William Earl also became very depressed. Sen. Fears and Dr. Belle Fears met with the medical staff at the request of Sen. Fears and tried to resolve the situation. The staff did agree to request an investigation by the members of the American College of Obstetrics and Gynecology and the College agreed to investigate. Two members came down to the hospital and one was an African-American Obstetrician/Gynecologist. In these cases, the College investigators usually "rubber stamp" the staff's actions, but they didn't reckon with lawyer Fears.

After many years of struggle to get through medical school, and a very thorough and difficult residency under the tutelage of Dr. Mason Andrews, a great Obstetrician and a great recent Mayor for the City of Norfolk, Dr. Brad's career was now in shambles because of one complaint from this surgeon, whose motives might be questionable. Again, father William Earl advised his son to leave and try to get started someplace else, but again his "hardheaded" son was going to stay and oppose what he thought was an injustice. So Sen. Fears advised Brad to get the services of a lawyer and Brad chose one Lawyer Nussbaum of Norfolk, Virginia.

With a stroke of luck, Fears came upon a young Obstetrician/ Gynecologist in the Regional Medical Center in Salisbury, Maryland, who asked Fears how "that SOB, Dr. So-and-so" was doing in Nassawadox. Fears, who was seeing a client in that hospital, wanted to know why "the SOB" had entered the conversation. This young doctor's name was "Dr. Gray," and he was practicing with a group in that hospital. He told Sen. Fears that he had graduated from a Virginia Medical School, and wanted to practice in the NAM Hospital. He was allegedly interviewed by the Credentials Committee and the "SOB doctor," a member of the Credentials Committee of NAM Hospital. Dr. Gray told Lawyer Fears that, "Dr. So-and-so told me in no uncertain terms that he was doing gynecological surgery, and I wasn't wanted in that hospital."

Dr. Gray, probably realizing the danger of "Immune Peer Review" and the "Probationary Period Requirement for Privileges," got frightened and went to Regional Medical Center in Salisbury, Maryland, to avoid any trouble with the NAM Hospital. Later, Lawyer Fears got Dr. Gray's permission to disclose this to the investigating physicians from the American College of Obstetrics and Gynecology investigating the complaint against Brad. Bill Fears wrote a long brief explaining the entire situation, and placed it all in a package. He suggested the investigators interview Dr. Gray in Salisbury, which they must have done.

Brad didn't know what his father was doing, but the entire package prepared by Lawyer Fears was delivered in two copies to the investigating physicians who worked for three days in the hospital reviewing medical records of everyone in the surgical field, and they reviewed operating procedures in the hospital. The package of information could have saved Dr. Brad's ass, for after the investigation the investigating physicians didn't simply "rubber stamp" the hospital's action, but gave Dr. Fears the highest recommendation, criticized the hospital staff for not having two surgeons present in the operating room for each serious surgical operation, and finally recommended that the general surgeons not perform gynecological practice, but leave that to the Obstetrician/Gynecologists. They also recommended that the Family Practitioners not do obstetrical work. The staff allowed Brad "permanent" privileges but, as a condition, wanted the other OB/GYN Specialist to observe Brad on each delivery or operation for six months. Brad would not agree to this of course, and Lawyer Nussbaum threatened the staff and hospital with some sort of legal action.

After the NAM staff gave Brad permanent privileges, he has been doing a good job for more than 17 years; has passed the Specialty Examination, and is now a member of the American College of Obstetrics and Gynecology, and has been a Department Head in the NAM Hospital. But Brad has finally left the area and joined another OB/GYN Specialist in New York state.

Dr. Scott now has a new partner. The other OB/GYN Specialist has quit practicing medicine and he was influential on the Northampton County Board of Supervisors for several years. He was smart enough to get several million dollars from government funds and has used that money allegedly in an organization supposedly to improve the lot of the poverty stricken people in Northampton County.

Lawyer Nussbaum charged Brad $5,000 for one letter to the hospital, office consultation and advice, but it was probably worth it. The folks in the hospital wouldn't have changed their old tricks because of Brad's father, but they must have paid some attention to Lawyer Nussbaum. Anyhow, it appears that justice may have been done. Sen. Fears tried to get the peer review statute changed to allow legal action against a complaintant for "bad motives" or a falsity, but he could not get anyone to introduce the bill. He feels it would have been improper for him to do so himself. Still, one must prove "bad faith" or "malicious intent" to win a civil suit on peer review.

Several years later, the Hospital Administrator, Bill Downing, who later operated a restaurant in Nassawadox, Virginia, told Fears, "I couldn't get into that, but one doctor used the Credentials Committee to cause Brad this problem." He also said that, "Since I was the Hospital Administrator I wouldn't get involved."

Incidentally, the surgeon has also retired from medical practice, but Brad has now sold his office and home and moved his family to New York. Although "one can't teach an old dog new tricks," Providence has a way of handling things, with a little help from a caring father. Brad's patients miss Dr. Fears very much, as does his family in Virginia.